Advance Praise for *Finding a Spiritual Home*

"This is an extraordinary book, a clarion call for spiritual leadership in a post-ethnic age—and just right for the times. Synagogue transformation is the "in topic" for the coming decade, and Sid Schwarz knows that topic. He blends a study of synagogues that matter with insight into what makes them so, then synthesizes his findings in an accessible but insightful summary that is bound to help synagogue leaders reevaluate their practices."
—**Rabbi Lawrence A. Hoffman,** Hebrew Union College, New York; co-founder, Synagogue 2000: Institute for the Synagogue of the Twenty-First Century; author, *The Art of Public Prayer*

"With stories both of individuals and synagogues, Sidney Schwarz shows that old religious structures can indeed become alive with new spiritual meaning and sensitive to generational change. His is an encouraging, beautifully written account of congregations in positive transition—at once inspiring and instructive."
—**Dr. Wade Clark Roof,** author, *A Generation of Seekers: The Spiritual Journeys of the Baby Boom Generation* and *Spiritual Marketplace*

"Finding a Spiritual Home *is a thoughtful, insightful treatment of the synagogue, its limits and its real potential to sustain a new generation of Jews. Schwarz, an outstanding community builder and creative figure in American Jewry, skillfully interweaves human interest personal accounts and case studies in effective synagogues in his own incisive analysis. If you care about the future of Jewry, you want to read this book."*
—**Rabbi Irving Greenberg,** president, Jewish Life Network; author, *The Jewish Way*

"Finding a Spiritual Home *is one of the most thoughtful and provocative books I have ever encountered. It chronicles the dramatic changes taking place in the Jewish community today and demonstrates their far-reaching significance. This is the right book at the right time."*
—**Dr. Jonathan Woocher,** executive vice president, Jewish Education Service of North America; author, *Sacred Survival: The Civil Religion of American Jews*

FINDING A SPIRITUAL HOME

FINDING A
SPIRITUAL HOME

*How a New Generation of Jews Can
Transform the American Synagogue*

Sidney Schwarz

JOSSEY-BASS
A Wiley Company
San Francisco

Jossey-Bass books and products are available through most bookstores. To contact Jossey-Bass directly, call (888) 378-2537, fax to (800) 605-2665, or visit our website at www.josseybass.com.

Substantial discounts on bulk quantities of Jossey-Bass books are available to corporations, professional associations, and other organizations. For details and discount information, contact the special sales department at Jossey-Bass.

 Manufactured in the United States of America on Lyons Falls Turin Book. This paper is acid-free and 100 percent totally chlorine-free.

Library of Congress Cataloging-in-Publication Data
   Schwarz, Sidney, date
      Finding a Spiritual Home : how a new generation of Jews can
   transform the American synagogue / Sidney Schwarz.— 1st ed.
         p.   cm.
   Includes bibliographical references (p.) and index.
   ISBN 0-7879-5174-9
      1. Judaism—United States—Customs and practices.
      2. Jewish way of life.   3. Synagogues—United States.   I. Title.
   bm205 .s35   2000
   296.69590973—dc21   99-050449 √

FIRST EDITION

HB Printing   10 9 8 7 6 5 4 3 2

CONTENTS

PART FOUR
Building Community Through Empowerment
in a Reconstructionist Congregation

PART FIVE
Dancing in the Aisles at a Conservative Synagogue

PART SIX
The Spiritual Possibilities of the American Synagogue

ACKNOWLEDGMENTS

IN MANY WAYS, I have been writing this book for the past thirty years, which makes it hard to identify all of the people to whom I am indebted for its completion. The actual writing of this book was made possible only after one of the hardest decisions of my life—to step down as the rabbi of the congregation that I founded in 1987, Adat Shalom Reconstructionist Congregation. This decision was made necessary by the fact that both Adat Shalom and the Washington Institute for Jewish Leadership and Values, which I had founded the same year, were thriving. I could not possibly continue to provide adequate attention to both. I did pledge to myself, however, that any time I would gain as a result of my decision would be devoted to writing this book.

Most of this book was written at ungodly hours, on planes and trains and in airports during my travels around the country. I don't recommend that approach, though it did radically improve my attitude toward travel delays! But I kept at it because it was a labor of love. I also came to feel that by producing this book, I was keeping faith with the hundreds of people who sustained me in my belief about all that is possible to accomplish in a synagogue-community.

I would not have become a rabbi were it not for the Reconstructionist Rabbinical College (RRC). Its philosophy, which saved me for Judaism during my college years, and the institution, which audaciously suggested that there might be a better way to address the needs of Jewish life in America, were ideally suited to my temperament.

The members of Congregation Beth Israel of Media, Pennsylvania, my first pulpit, could not have been more supportive of my interest in experimenting with any new idea that came my way during my eight-year tenure. Beth Israel became a laboratory for me, and I became increasingly encouraged about the possibilities of synagogue life. The late Ira Silverman, as president of the RRC, gave me the confidence to think that I had something to teach other rabbinical students about synagogue life when he invited me to develop and teach a course on alternative synagogue communities at the school.

When I sat with some friends in my backyard to launch what would become Adat Shalom, it was in large measure in the hope of filling what we perceived as a gap in the greater Washington area. We were given important support by the executive director of the Federation of Reconstructionist Congregations and Havurot, Rabbi Mordecai Liebling, and later received significant consultative guidance from the dean of the RRC, Rabbi David Teutsch.

I was blessed to have true soulmates in the launching of Adat Shalom. Neil and Lisa Makstein were our founding co-presidents. Two of my closest lifelong friends, they were indispensable in creating the special environment and community of Adat Shalom. Similarly, their successors as president, Phyllis and Frank Goldstein, Mel Cheslow, Steve Shapiro, and Robert Barkin, worked tirelessly to make Adat Shalom a magical place. They represent hundreds of other volunteers without whom Adat Shalom would never have succeeded. Fred Dobb, who served as my student rabbi for two years and then succeeded me at Adat Shalom, is a spiritual leader of great skill; that he allowed me to mentor him was a particular privilege. He cannot imagine how much I got out of our regular meetings while working on this book. Being able to see the leadership of a synagogue through someone else's eyes provided an important perspective for my thinking.

The rabbis of each of the profiled congregations were most gracious with their time—Rabbis Larry Kushner, Roly Matalon, and Avi Weiss. It was exciting to spend time with them, to learn from them, and to share ideas. They are exemplary spiritual leaders, treasures of the Jewish community, from whom much can be learned. I feel privileged to call them colleagues. Rabbis Harold Schulweis and Ed Feinstein, of Valley Beth Shalom Congregation in Encino, California, were also generous with their time and helped me understand how they accomplished some remarkable things in their congregation. Similarly, Rabbi Jacob Rubenstein of the Young Israel of Scarsdale, New York, was extremely helpful to me in understanding the inner workings of the Orthodox community and in sharing with me some of his own creative approaches to the rabbinate. I also benefited from regular conversations with my very talented brother-in-law, Rabbi Eliott Perlstein of Congregation Ohev Shalom in Richboro, Pennsylvania.

I was fortunate to have angels in each of the synagogues who were patient with my every request to send just one more document or to track down one more phone number: Sandy Hall, at Congregation Beth El, in Sudbury, Massachusetts; Helen Radin and Lisa Schachner at Congregation B'nai Jeshurun in New York City; and Rabbi Aaron Frank and Hillel Jaffe at the Hebrew Institute of Riverdale, Bronx, New York.

Rabbi Ira Eisenstein, David Shneyer, Jack Wertheimer, and Jonathan Woocher were kind enough to read early drafts of this manuscript and provide me with extremely useful feedback. I also am indebted to Leonard Fein, Rabbi Yitz Greenberg, Rabbi Larry Hoffman, Wade Clark Roof, Rabbi Harold Schulweis, Gary Tobin, James Wind, and Ron Wolfson for their review of the manuscript.

Much of the work that I am doing in the Jewish community is as founder and president of the Washington Institute for Jewish Leadership and Values, an educational foundation committed to the renewal of American Jewish life through Judaic study, social justice, and civic activism. My outstanding board of directors, chaired, successively, by Aaron Goldman, Norman Pozez, and Ellen Waghelstein, has been unflagging in its support of my every idea and initiative. To have that kind of encouragement for one's creativity is a blessing.

Cheryl McGowan, Rachelle Solkowitz, and Eric Feder provided me with valuable administrative support at various times.

Gail Ross became a friend at just the right time in my life as I discovered over a breakfast meeting that she was a literary agent. I am in her debt for the enthusiasm she showed for my project and her commitment to find the book a publisher. Sarah Polster, my editor at Jossey-Bass, continually saw things in my manuscript that I did not see. The quality of the end product has much to do with her incredible skill as an editor.

Last but not least, my unending love and gratitude go to my family for their support. I can only hope that my children, Danny, Joel, and Jennifer, will one day read their dad's book and forgive me for taking as much time away from them as such a project must. I pray that each of them finds a path in life that is as rich and fulfilling for them as the rabbinate has been for me. My wife, Sandy, has been at my side through every project and venture that I have taken on. She has sacrificed much to let me pursue my dreams. Her insight into people and situations has helped me in innumerable ways. In the end, it is her support and love that sustains me.

I finished the first draft of this book during the week of my forty-fifth birthday. My generation, when it was younger, was quick to say, "Never trust anyone over thirty." Perhaps that explains why, as I grow older, I become increasingly partial to the wisdom of the Jewish tradition, which tells us that the forties represent the age of discernment and intellectual capacity (Pirkei Avot 5:21). I trust that this book proves me worthy of that estimation.

S. S.

To my mom and dad,
Judy and Allan Schwarz,
Who gave me the gift of an observant
Jewish upbringing
and then had the wisdom to let me
find my own path

PREFACE: MY PATH

I GREW UP as a *shul* (synagogue) kid. Every *shabbat* (sabbath), I found myself in synagogue with my father. I know that I started going long before I could walk or talk. It was simply where my family went to celebrate the sabbath.

As a small, fairly traditional Conservative congregation, those of us who "counted" needed to be there in time to make the *minyan* (quorum of ten adult males required for a religious service). This was always up for grabs. My dad, one of the regulars, made calls during the week to ensure that the requisite ten men would show up, but it didn't always work. Falling short of the ten on *shabbat* morning sometimes required surreptitious phone calls urging members to "come right away." Because use of the phone was prohibited on the sabbath, the men would gather around the non-Jewish custodian and tell him whom to call.

My sisters and mother would come later in the morning. It took me years to realize the many ways in which the synagogue of my childhood told girls and women that they did not count. Jewish law prevented them, at that time, from being included in the *minyan;* social convention signaled that the "sisterhood" (as the women's club was called) was where they belonged. I used to think there was some kind of rule in Judaism that women could attend only the last half-hour of a service.

That I have fond memories of the synagogue of my childhood has more to do with its familiarity than its practices. I came to know each of the handful of men who were the loyal attendees on *shabbat* morning—where they would sit, the jokes they would tell, who gave out the candy, and who would shush the few kids who would show up. I knew that my dad would chant the *psukai de'zimrah,* the early part of the service, which came before we needed the *minyan* and before the cantor revved up for the "big crowd." I sat in awe of Mr. Drexler, a Holocaust survivor who lived behind the candy store, who read the entire Torah portion each week directly from the scroll, without vocalization notes or vowels.

I also cherished the special privileges that came my way because even as a child, I was "one of the men." At first it was spending time with my dad, knowing that I could usually get him to carry me on his back as we walked home from *shul,* since we did not ride in a car on *shabbat.* Later it was getting called up to the *bima* (the raised platform in front of the sanctuary) which was the center of all ritual action. The final coup was getting paid $15 to lead the junior congregation service. To a boy educated in a *yeshiva* (Jewish parochial school), this was like paying a sports fan to watch a ball game.

As a teenager, I thoroughly enjoyed my involvement with USY. United Synagogue Youth was the national youth movement of Conservative Judaism. The conventions, camps, and trips it organized gave Jewish teens the opportunity to take ownership of their own Judaism. I remember most fondly the wonderful spirit that we could create at a USY-sponsored *shabbat.* Ironically, there is an entire generation of Jews of my age (mid-forties) who experienced the richness of *shabbat* through youth movements and camps only to despair of ever being able to rediscover it in synagogues once they came into adulthood.

I learned an important lesson in my teen years, holding several positions of leadership in USY. A large part of the energy for what we did "Jewishly" came from the participants as much as it came from the tradition. Some years later, as I began to struggle with my own philosophy of Jewish life, I would again confront the issue of how much religion came from inherited tradition and how much was generated by the group experience of that religion.

Two events in my last two years of high school provided turning points in my life. Like most teenagers, I had taken much for granted—my Jewish education, my general education, my family. I did OK in school, but not great. I had left *yeshiva* after sixth grade, and I got to know the principal of my public high school through some notoriety that I had acquired as the sports editor of the school paper. I was conducting a one-man campaign to expose all of the "abuses and hypocrisies" of our high school sports programs. This did not endear me to the jocks in my school, who were considerably bigger and tougher than I was. On more than one occasion, I took refuge in the principal's office, fearing that one or more of the linebackers on the football squad would act on the "wanted" posters with my picture on them hanging all around the school.

The relationship served me well. My principal was also the chairman of the youth committee at a small synagogue on Long Island. As he got to know me and became aware of my strong Jewish background, he asked me whether I wanted to work as the director of the USY chapter at his congregation—for money, no less!

There was something oddly precocious about all this. USY was a program for ninth to twelfth graders; I was only in eleventh grade myself. I couldn't even drive yet. But naiveté served me well, and I accepted. Having been assured that most of the kids were on the younger side of age spectrum, I nevertheless inherited a group whose president was older than I was! My sensitivity to the linkages between age and status in high school led me to some creative ruses. Among them was making sure that I arrived an hour early and left an hour after programs, for I lived in fear that a member of the youth group would discover that my mother had to drive me to the synagogue.

Nevertheless, the position gave me a valuable opportunity to assume the responsibility of being a role model for a group of younger Jewish teens. The questions they asked, the struggles they had over their identities, and the ways they challenged what little that they had learned in Hebrew school forced me to crystallize my own thinking about key issues of American Jewish identity.

Their questions were not much different from my own. If I hadn't had that job, I could easily have ignored the issues as most young Jews do, growing into adulthood convinced that the unaddressed doubts about my religion revealed some fatal flaws in a system not worth preserving. Gradually, however, my confidence in addressing such issues grew. The position with USY marked the beginning of a string of jobs through my college years as youth director, teacher, and staffer at two different Jewish summer camps. I found something that I loved doing and was good at.

The second experience was an opportunity to travel behind the Iron Curtain in the summer between my junior and senior years of high school. The year was 1971, and USY had set up an Eastern European pilgrimage program traveling to Romania, the Soviet Union, and Israel. This was the second year of the program, and one of the leaders was a young rabbi named Jonathan Porath, whose passion for the plight of Jews behind the Iron Curtain was contagious.

I was transformed by the experience. The briefings before we left raised our consciousness about the difficulties faced by Jews living under communism. Part of the reason for our visit was to bring to these Jews the hope that we in the West would not rest until they had the right to emigrate or to practice their religion without government interference. The program itself was a response to Elie Wiesel's classic book *The Jews of Silence,* in which he pricked the conscience of the West to mobilize on behalf of Soviet Jewry.

We spent a *shabbat* in London before flying to Moscow, and I recall a meeting that we had with the chief rabbi of Great Britain, Immanuel Jacobovitz. He told us that we should be modest in what we thought we could bring to the Jews of Russia: "You will take away with you far more than you will bring." It was a puzzling statement at the time, but for years after the experience, I marveled at its wisdom.

Meeting with Jews who studied Hebrew surreptitiously, who put themselves at risk by attending worship at the few state-licensed synagogues, and who pointed out the person in the synagogue who was a paid informer for the KGB was an awakening. It felt as if I had entered not an airplane but a time machine that had placed me into circumstances experienced by thousands of my ancestors over the centuries.

I returned with a sense of mission and purpose. I realized how fortunate I was to have received a strong Jewish education. I realized how much I took for granted my ability to practice my Judaism. I realized the incredible privilege of growing up in a democracy. In my senior year of high school, I had numerous opportunities to tell the story of Soviet Jewry to audiences and to mobilize them to action. I felt I had something to give the world.

In retrospect, it seems a lot less surprising that I became a rabbi than it originally seemed to me when I made the decision in my last year of college. In my essay for admission to the Reconstructionist Rabbinical College (RRC), I noted that many of the rabbis I knew chose that path because some rabbinical figure, often their father, had been a positive influence on their lives. Despite the fact that I had been around synagogues all of my life, including several in which I had worked professionally during my undergraduate years, I could point to no such rabbinic role model. Similarly, I was left unimpressed by the synagogues that I had come to know fairly intimately. In fact, it seemed to me at the time that whatever positive impact I might have had on the young people I was working with as a teacher, youth worker, and camp staffer had occurred *in spite of* the fairly negative experiences that these kids had had in their childhood synagogues.

My interest in becoming a rabbi grew out of my experiences working in informal Jewish education. I came to realize that I had a talent for turning kids on to Judaism. I rejected thoughts of several other career options primarily because, given the choice between being a good rabbi, a good lawyer, or a good professor, I believed that being a good rabbi would make more of a long-term difference in the world. I certainly came to believe that it was more important. But at the same time, I was persuaded that synagogues were not the institutions capable of transforming Jewish life.

My plans to use my rabbinical education to work in Jewish camping or informal Jewish education were foiled early on. One of the requirements of the training at the RRC was to have some form of Jewish community placement. There were plenty of Hebrew school teaching jobs available and a handful of jobs working at Jewish communal organizations. By far the most sought-after jobs, however, were student pulpits. Though these positions were usually available only for fourth and fifth year rabbinical students, I was invited to become the part-time rabbi for Congregation Beth Israel of Media, Pennsylvania, in my second year. Based on my having led a *shabbat* service in my first year, the congregation's leadership felt I had the skills to take over from the former student rabbi, who was now graduating and moving on to a full-time pulpit in Montreal.

This was true on-the-job training. On the surface, the job seemed simple—lead services. I had done this at age fourteen in my first paid job as a junior congregation leader. The congregation consisted of about thirty-five families housed in a quaint old sanctuary that seated only one hundred people. For many years, Beth Israel was a Conservative congregation served by a rabbi ordained by the Orthodox-affiliated Yeshiva University. The shrinking of the synagogue's membership and the passing on of its rabbi coincided with the establishment of the RRC in the late 1960s. The invitation to the school to provide student rabbis was less an ideological statement than a financial one: for a few thousand dollars a year, the small congregation could get basic rabbinical services and survive.

I learned early on that leading services and being a rabbi were not the same thing. What would make people come to the synagogue? How could the synagogue get into the homes of its members? What would make the experience of children in our synagogue any different from the experience of the many kids whose negative experiences of synagogue I had struggled to overcome to be an effective youth worker?

I spent eight years at Beth Israel—four as a student and four more after I graduated RRC, as I finished up my Ph.D. in Jewish history. I didn't answer all of the questions that I asked about the possibilities of synagogue life during that time. I felt fortunate, however, for two distinct reasons. The synagogue leadership was totally supportive of my attempts to ask radical questions about what a synagogue was for and how it could be more effective. The synagogue had no investment in any status quo; its willingness to experiment was limited only by my imagination. Second, and equally important, the Reconstructionist Rabbinical College was still in its infancy. There was a spirit of innovation at the institution and a commitment to turn out rabbis who would rethink the nature of the rabbinate and the Jewish community.

During my tenure, the synagogue grew to about 125 households—not an insignificant number given the demographics of the area. More important, the synagogue became a place of great Jewish excitement and commitment. I recall one Friday evening when we were hosting a joint *shabbat* service of local congregations on behalf of the United Jewish Appeal. I was approached by a member of the local Conservative synagogue, a major institution with a membership five times our size, who said, "If I were more serious about my Judaism, I would join your synagogue." I felt a great sense of gratification. That was precisely what I was trying to achieve—synagogue Judaism that did not seek to address the lowest common denominator of what Jews said they wanted but rather an institution that raised the standard of what was Jewishly possible and an ability to get Jews to share that vision.

As the only affiliated Reconstructionist congregation within commuting distance of the RRC, Beth Israel also became a laboratory for many students attending the rabbinical school. Dozens had the opportunity to serve as weekend rabbis or teach in our school. I began to write in Jewish periodicals about my experiments with the congregation. Two years after my graduation from RRC, I was invited to develop and teach a course at the school on "creating alternative synagogues." It was the beginning of a lifelong interest in the challenge of transforming the American synagogue.

I moved to Washington, D.C., in 1984 to become the executive director of the Jewish Community Council of Greater Washington. My interest in social justice issues, activism in the Soviet Jewry movement, and involvement with Israel- and Zionist-related activities made the offer irresistible. It was an opportunity to work on a larger canvas and to make a wider impact on the Jewish community and society in general. During my four-year tenure, I had the chance to work with a broad cross section of the community. I also had a chance to be a congregant. With my growing young family, I attended a variety of synagogues in addition to the one with which we were affiliated. I continued to be fascinated by what made some synagogues "work" and others simply exist.

In 1987, I left my position at the Jewish Community Council. I had two distinct ideas that I wanted to pursue. One was to create an educational foundation that would bring together social activism and Jewish learning. The other was to create a synagogue that worked. Since both were high-risk ventures and I had no financial backing for either project, I decided to pursue both simultaneously. If one succeeded and the other didn't, my career decision would be made for me. If both failed, I could always go out and find a more conventional position. If both succeeded . . .; well, I would cross that bridge if I came to it.

The story of the Washington Institute for Jewish Leadership and Values is best left for another place. Suffice it to say that I started it, it grew, it currently flourishes, and I serve as its founding president. The story of Adat Shalom Reconstructionist Congregation is more relevant.

How Adat Shalom grew and how it created a new paradigm for a synagogue will be outlined in Chapter Eleven. But the way in which I was influenced by what happened in the congregation cannot be overstated. I recognized that a great many people whom we attracted to synagogue life would never otherwise have considered joining a synagogue, ever. I saw a stark contrast in the percentage and intensity of involvement of our members compared with other congregations. I saw a wellspring of Jewish creativity emerge from previously marginal Jews.

What happened was not luck. I had written numerous articles on how to invigorate synagogue life. I had already successfully implemented some of these ideas in Media. Personally, I had acquired some important management and community organizing experience. I had a clear strategy in my mind for what I wanted to accomplish. But the results exceeded my expectations.

If what happened at Adat Shalom was not luck, it also wasn't rocket science. I was convinced that it could be replicated. For more than twenty years, my antennae had been fixed in search of synagogues that worked. I read the articles of rabbis and laypeople that described unconventional approaches to synagogue life. When I heard reports of a synagogue with particularly high energy or a unique program, I would go out of my way to visit. I began to investigate whether there were models from the church world that might be instructive.

Without question, the most powerful motivation for writing this book was the stories of people whose lives were transformed because of their exposure to Adat Shalom. One of our innovations at Adat Shalom was to provide, on occasion, ten minutes during our services for members to use a piece of liturgy as a take-off point for sharing a bit of their own spiritual odyssey. These presentations were often so poignant as to leave me—and many other congregants—breathless.

Not only did this practice bring a given prayer to a new level of understanding among the congregation, but it also brought the sharing of personal stories of people's spiritual journeys into the sacred space of our congregation. It created a strong sense of intimacy among people in the context of our worship experience.

It had become clear to me that although one aspect regarding the spiritual possibilities of the American synagogue had to do with matters of rabbinical leadership, program design, and community organizing, an equally important part is the personal story. So I began to solicit essays from members of my congregation, many of them written versions of presentations made during services. My intention was to produce an interesting volume about Adat Shalom.

But it occurred to me that ours could not be the only congregation in America that was breaking new ground in meeting the spiritual needs of its community. I decided to find at least one synagogue from each of the other major denominations of American Jewish life that was pursuing a similar course. This, it turned out, was easier decided than done. I spoke to many rabbis about their vision of synagogue life. I spoke to scores of Jews who had their own views about what they liked about certain synagogues and what they disliked. Several times, I started to do research for a synagogue profile only to discover that the congregations did not fit the paradigm of the synagogue-community that was taking shape in my mind. I had hoped to present model synagogues all around the United States. But my search led to far fewer model synagogues than I had hoped to find.

I do not presume to suggest that the four synagogues profiled in this book are the best synagogues in America. Nor do I dare suggest that the rabbis of these synagogues are the most outstanding in their field. I suspect that the publication of this book will bring to my attention many outstanding institutions and religious leaders previously unknown to me. The synagogues profiled in this volume were chosen because they manifest approaches to synagogue life that have particular resonance to the baby boom generation of American Jews of which I am a part.

Religion and spirituality, as matters of taste and style, are subjective. In accommodating the tastes and styles of one age cohort of American Jewry, there is the very real risk of alienating the preferences of a previous generation. Yet the religious patterns of the baby boom generation are no less significant than that generation's tastes with regard to dress, culture, and lifestyle—tastes that have shaped American society for more than half a century. It is noteworthy, though, that notwithstanding the influence of boomers on almost every aspect of American society, religious institutions have been remarkably resistant to change. The reasons for this resistance will be examined in Chapter Eighteen. Although the four synagogues profiled in this book have many differences, they share a common responsiveness to the religious inclinations of baby boom Jews. Thus they suggest exciting possibilities for ways in which other congregations might touch the hearts and souls of Jews in the next generation.

About the Book

This book is my attempt to contribute to the reinvigoration of synagogue life in America. To accomplish this purpose, I have woven together three distinct elements—historical analysis, spiritual journeys, and a prescription for transformation. The first part of the book provides a historical analysis of the development of the American synagogue and of the American Jewish community. After an introductory spiritual autobiography that sets the tone for the section (Chapter One), Chapter Two introduces the typology of the "new American Jew" and the eight generational themes that define an age cohort that is now beginning to take its place as the leaders of the American Jewish community. The generational themes help explain why contemporary Jews have had such a hard time connecting with American synagogues. Chapter Three provides a historical overview of how the American synagogue evolved and describes the four characteristics of a new kind of synagogue that I call the "synagogue-community." It is this new paradigm that has the potential to capture the loyalty and passions of the new American Jew.

Chapters Four through Fifteen provide profiles of four congregations, one from each of the major movements in Jewish life, that are actual models of the synagogue-community. The profiles are peppered with vignettes that provide the reader with a feel for what it might be like to be part of these communities. Each profile is preceded and followed by spiritual autobiographies of individuals whose journeys brought them to join the profiled congregations. I call these spiritual autobiographies "paths" because the word conveys both a physical journey to different places as well as a journey of mind and spirit. So many Jews of the boomer generation have taken paths that have led them far away from Judaism and its synagogues. One of the criteria I used for choosing the four synagogues in this section was the ability to attract disaffected Jews back to Judaism. Thus the spiritual autobiographies are mostly "paths of return." Essentially, these spiritual seekers were fortunate enough to find synagogues that met their spiritual needs. Because most synagogues in America were created as a response to the needs and interests of the parents of the boomer generation, the evolution to a new type of synagogue will require listening carefully to the voices of new American Jews who have an entirely different worldview from that of their parents and who are asking very different kinds of questions.

The last section of the book explores how the American synagogue might transform itself to meet the needs of a new generation of American Jews. Chapter Sixteen frames the closing section with the book's final spiritual journey. Chapter Seventeen revisits the eight generational themes presented in Chapter Two, relating them to the personal stories featured in the book. It also looks at similarities and differences between the profiled congregations. And it explores how these congregations implement the four characteristics of the synagogue-community outlined in

Chapter Three. Chapter Eighteen examines obstacles to synagogue transformation and ways in which these obstacles might be overcome. The Epilogue serves both as a summary of the elements that can help transform
American synagogues and as a resource to readers who are inspired to become change agents in their own congregations. A Glossary encapsulates
important and possibly unfamiliar terms found throughout the book. Finally, a Discussion Guide is provided for those groups that want to further explore the themes of the book in a meaningful way.

○

The contemporary American Jewish community is a strange paradox
reflecting both serious danger signs about its future viability and also exciting signs of a Jewish renaissance. This book was born out of a frustration with hundreds of synagogues across America that have yet to
understand the needs of today's Jews. These are Jews who are not so much
rejecting Judaism as they are rejecting institutions that have failed to heed
their voices. These are the Jewish lost souls of our generation, and we suffer from their absence in more ways than we can ever imagine.

Because institutions change gradually, the transition to the synagogue-
community will not happen overnight. Indeed, it is only now in its birth
throes. America's synagogues serve hundreds of thousands of Jews. Many
have outstanding rabbis and educators. More than a few can boast some
exemplary programs. But most are in crisis.

At the same time, a handful of synagogues are responding to the spirit
of the age and the changing needs of a new generation of American Jews.
These synagogues, exemplars of the emerging model of the synagogue-
community, are on the cutting edge. They do not sit comfortably within
the denominations of which they are part. They are criticized and copied.
They are ostracized and emulated.

But in short, they are also places that are magical. To spend time in
these communities is to find places where Judaism seems to matter more
immediately and more powerfully to congregants than in most other
places in the Jewish world. To read the stories of the members whose lives
were transformed because of these synagogues is to glimpse the possibilities of what the Jewish community might look like if it suddenly found
a way to excite the unaffiliated Jews of the baby boom generation about
Judaism.

Taken together, the emerging phenomenon of the synagogue-
community and the Jews who are drawn to them represent the spiritual

possibilities of the American synagogue. It is my belief that our synagogues can address the hunger of tens of thousands of Jews who currently look elsewhere to meet their spiritual needs. I dedicate this book to the hope that American synagogues begin to do precisely that.

December 1999   Sidney Schwarz
Erev Chanukah, 5760

FINDING A SPIRITUAL HOME

PART ONE

CAN A SPIRITUALLY HOMELESS GENERATION REVITALIZE THE AMERICAN SYNAGOGUE?

DEBBIE'S PATH

WHEN I WAS A LITTLE GIRL, my mother taught me to say a nightly prayer. She would remind us: it had to start with "Dear God" and end with "Amen," and we had to be grateful and not ask for too much.

I would lay on my bed, face the ceiling, and clasp my hands with fingers interlaced. My mother warned me not to place my palms and fingers together, flat, Christian-style. I figured that was how God knew which religion you were from.

I developed a formula prayer, which changed little, depending on what I longed for or feared on that given night. First there was a section of thanks. Then blessings. Then requests. Then random observations. Then self-blessing. Then "Amen." A typical night's prayer went something like this:

Dear God,

Thank you for my mommy and daddy, and our nice house and my room and all the food we get to eat. And thank you for the mouse trap game I got for my birthday.

Please bless my mom, my dad, my brother, Mama and Papa [my grandparents], Aunt Homa, Uncle Norman, . . . [this part could get very long].

Please end the Vietnam War. My mom has been crying about Mrs. Elson's son, who died there. And please help find a cure for MS. Please.

Debbie Danielpour Chapel teaches creative writing at Harvard University and at Emerson College. She writes fiction and screenplays and lives in Sudbury, Massachusetts, with her husband and two children.

The lake and the whole area around it at Jonathan Dickinson State Park are really beautiful. We went there on a field trip the other day. I went to that park a long time ago, when my father thought he could still drive. I sat in the back seat and my mother bit her lip and switched places with my father, letting him sit behind the wheel. He drove only a few minutes, swerving dangerously because of his tremor. My mother was scared, almost seemed angry. They switched again. That was the last time I remember him driving. I don't know why I got into that. I just wanted to thank you, I guess, for that beautiful part of the park.

Let myself be a good girl.

Amen.

As I got older, the prayers would leave me crying, tears burning the back of my neck. This went on until college, where my roommate slept in a bed only three feet away from mine and I was too embarrassed to clasp my hands or mutter anything. I started praying silently, but I always fell asleep in the middle of the blessings section. And so, by the age of eighteen, the prayers ended.

Despite the nightly appointments with God, I was not raised as a practicing Jew. My mother wouldn't have any part of it.

Girdled by hardship, my mother found no solace in organized religion. My father was diagnosed with multiple sclerosis when her youngest child was four. My father's family in Tehran refused to dispatch the money he had invested in several business ventures. They disapproved of my mother and assumed she was lying about his disease merely to force the capital out of them. "You're a whore," his family said to her face. "You wear pants and go to work." Ultimately, she gave up on them.

She was going to make a living with her God-given skill, sculpture. Her family said she was nuts. But she took fine care of her husband, raised us admirably, earned enough money, and became an internationally known artist.

Instead of finding peace in religion, my mother turned to tolerance and love. She was a hippie without knowing it. While most Jewish mothers gently advised their daughters, "It's just as easy to fall in love with a Gentile as it is with a Jew, so don't put yourself in the situation where you might fall in love with a Gentile," my mother would say, "It's just as easy to fall in love with a Gentile as it is with a Jew." Period. Having lived in a Muslim country as a child and seen friends and relatives jailed or killed because of differences of religion, she clung to a wish that all people could believe in the same God, a God she believed existed. She worked to forgive her husband's family, she befriended African Americans, gay men, and people of all religions. She identified with diversity, with assimilation —and I did too.

So I grew up knowing no Hebrew. I never read the Torah, sat through only a few services on the High Holydays because we were visiting extended family, and felt the only difference between the Christian religions and Judaism was that we had plain God and they had Jesus-God.

But I kept saying my prayers. And my father, in his quiet, steadfast way, always reminded me that I was a Jew. In North Palm Beach, Florida, my brother and I were the only Jewish kids in the elementary school. Although my parents did not mind us singing "Jingle Bells," eating candy canes, or helping friends decorate their Christmas trees, my father had his limits.

One Yom Kippur when I was eight, my best friend pounded on the door. "Can you play?" I looked beseechingly at my mother. My parents looked at each other. Mother turned and threw me a stern look. "No," I told my friend, "I can't. It's Yom Kippur. It's the Day of Atonement." "Of *what?*" "You're supposed to mope around and think about all the things you've done wrong," I said. And I shut the door. I can still remember standing at that door, shutting it on my very best friend, on a beautiful sunny day, perfect for playing kickball. I remember feeling different, maybe special, but more confused and left out.

In college, I fell in love with a boy from a distance. He was playing soccer, and I didn't know that he was Jewish. Later, when we would talk late into the night about Machiavelli and Mill, when I was already in deep, I learned his family was observant, traditional, very Jewish. He became my first step toward discovering my own religious ancestry—and it was pure luck. But then again, some say there are no coincidences.

This boy, now my husband, was groomed to be a rabbi. And yet he ate a big breakfast on Yom Kippur and took second helpings of ham at the dining hall. This he would never tell his parents. But he *did* tell them that he no longer believed in a Jewish God—or any God for that matter. So started my Jewish learning.

Somehow my boyfriend still identified himself as a Jew and couldn't completely let his parents down. Let his parents down? Wasn't telling them that he didn't believe in God worse than eating on Yom Kippur? According to my mother, God was the center of everything. And religion was supposed to be a spiritual thing. Not just a cultural point of identification. Not an "I eat *matzah*, you eat *matzah*, isn't that great!" sort of affair. Praying was supposed to elicit cascades of meaning, revelation, humility, and graciousness. All those times I came as a visitor, tiptoeing into my friends' massive churches, I searched for people experiencing epiphanies. I was confused.

At my husband's parents' *shul,* I surveyed the faces. Often they were mouthing the words to the songs while nodding to friends across the aisle. "What does that prayer mean?" I would ask, hoping for a translation of the Hebrew. But they didn't know. At Passover, I asked if God could really be so cruel, particularly with the killing-of-the-firstborn bit. Are we really so chosen? What about Mother Teresa? Isn't she chosen? Why do we pray to this God like a "king"? What's this servitude thing? Why can't religious women be considered part of a *minyan?* Why don't women really belong? They didn't have the answers I hoped for.

In the San Francisco Bay Area, many of the Jews we met bought Christmas trees, stuck a piece of *matzah* into their child's lunchbox to show they remembered Passover, and might attend Rosh Hashanah or Yom Kippur services as long as their kid didn't have a soccer game. Identifying oneself as a Jew, in a Jewish community, which was graciously acknowledged by a larger, non-Jewish community was, at best, difficult. And I noticed that. For some reason, I felt a loss.

Then the symptoms started to pile up. It was after ten or so years in California that I started to realize I had no home. We moved several times when I was a child. Three places in New York, two in Florida. After I left for college, my mother moved once more. The small house in Florida, where I lived during high school, had been leveled. An elaborate Spanish thing had been squeezed onto the tiny lot. My mother drove us past this empty memory, barely pausing when we came upon it, and I felt a dark ache in my gut. Soon after, my aunt, who also moved many times, informed me that her beautiful old colonial home in New York, where I had spent many childhood summers playing with my cousins, had also been demolished. During a visit, she invited me to drive by the site with her. "Maybe another time," I said.

I was among the most fortunate, yet I was homeless, spiritually lost, a refugee from my past. In my "homes" and my religion, I didn't belong. I would gaze at the beautiful brown hills of Marin County, across the sparkling bay from San Francisco, and long for something else. As insane as it was, I needed those big deciduous trees, the humidity, the mosquitoes, the low sun, the snow, the politically incorrect lawns. I needed these parts of my past to reconnect, to feel that ecstasy I knew so well at a sniff of a freshly cut grass.

My husband and his siblings would pile into their childhood home for Passover and remark, "Oh, Mom you changed the wallpaper in here!" or "Does Mr. Segal still have that vicious dog?" I would watch them and notice, in the casual way they loped up the familiar stairs or in their automatic knowledge of exactly where to put the *chametzdic* plates (the dishes that observant families put away during the Passover holiday). They remember who they were. I don't know who I am because I can't see who I was.

What had become the most important thing in my early adulthood was not Judaism, as it was in my in-laws' lives. It wasn't security, as it was in much of my extended family. It was choices. It was designing a life that guaranteed as many choices as possible. As long as I could choose to live somewhere else, do something else, try another coffee shop, read another book, change my job, change my mind, I thought I had it made. It was kind of like picking out chocolates. Bite this one—nah, it's got that runny raspberry stuff inside. Maybe that one? No, too sweet. This one? No, pecans. My addiction cornered me into nowhere. And I came to see that it's not such a good thing for life to be like a box of chocolates.

It was no small feat for me to admit that rules did not mean constraint and that commitment to a place did not produce a trap. The first step was in moving to Sudbury, Massachusetts, finally buying a house, telling our friends they could write our address in their books in pen, planting my herbs cultivated from seeds not in containers but in the ground, and joining a congregation. We had never done any of those things.

The congregation was critical. My husband shopped around, visiting all the synagogues within a tolerable radius. I couldn't shop. I didn't know anything. I wouldn't know brisket from pork. "Beth El was different," he said. "They've got a gender-neutral prayer book. Some people wore jeans, some wore a *tallit* [prayer shawl], some *davened* [prayed] in the corner, some cried, you know. They all wrapped their arms around each other at the end. Beth El was interesting." We asked neighbors. "What about Beth El?" "Beth El?" one neighbor shook her head. "It's way too touchy-feely for me. But then again, coming from California, you may like it." *Oy*.

And so I checked out Beth El. I sat silent during the High Holyday services. I didn't know any songs, any prayers, but no one seemed to mind. People seemed content, generous. They had come not because their parents dragged them or because they would feel too guilty if they hadn't. No moping around per se. Kids tripped over each other. Friends held one another's infants. The cantor smiled as she sang. And she was a she. Music was not an accompaniment to "more lofty" activity; it was the vehicle for getting there. The beauty of her melodies and the congregants' communal voice rivaled my best moments listening to a Bach cello suite, but with something very large hovering near it.

The rabbi gave a sermon I still remember. And he was funny. He described scenes from the movie *Groundhog Day* to weave a message about responsibility and everyday presence. None of the rote seriousness that characterized the other services I'd seen. But at the end of his talk, all the congregants were breathing deep, biting their lip, thinking hard about how they would make the next day worth living. Rabbi Kushner stirred my emotions and my intellect. Without pomp or pretension, people listened, learned, and prayed honestly. I may have even noticed some epiphanies.

I saw families, singles, aged, lesbians, gays, and even one African American couple. The congregation seemed to accept anyone who was sincere in his or her spiritual quest. The prayer book hadn't just substituted *God* for all the masculine pronouns referring to God but had also incorporated *midrash* [Talmudic stories] about the silent women of the Torah. Women belonged. They were considered part of a *minyan*, they read from the Torah on *shabbat*. The rabbi, I learned, had performed commitment ceremonies. He regularly participated in a council composed of clergy from other denominations. And he never talked in "we-they" language. My mother might have approved.

The next week, I attended an informal class the rabbi taught on basic Jewish thought. He adjusted his polo shirt and jeans, waited for everyone to sit, and asked, "How many people here believe in God?" Only half the group raised a hand. "What's your conception of the divine?" I had come to the right place. Someone was going to ask my questions.

What is God in the Torah anyway? God's not on the throne. God is out there and in here. At the same time. Forget the patriarchal duality between inside and outside. God can be a he/she force in and around us that elicits the power and love within ourselves. Who actually wrote the Torah? It's all God or it's this author, that author, this author. You decide. You two disagree? It's OK. Prayer block? Let's interpret. The Garden of Eden is a parent-child separation myth. Crossing over to Egypt is part of the "gaining awareness" myth. *Tzedek* [justice] and authentic spirituality are inseparable. *Shabbat* is a "be here now" proposition, not just a time to tape the refrigerator light off.

The kindergarten religious classes had been asked, What is God? "God is parents." "God is fake." "God is the sky." "God is shapes (with pictures)." "God is a man with a white beard." And they put all these answers on the board. All of them. For all to see. All the choices.

At a Friday night service, a friend nudged me, discreetly nodded toward a middle-aged man. "Only one who survived the Czech death camp," she said. Then the congregants started singing "L'cha Dodi." I watched him.

He was very attractive. He wore a hint of a smile, or maybe it was a constant expression of revelation, perhaps appreciation, as he looked around for his wife, listened, and felt the warm comfort of the sanctuary on a cold January night. But he didn't sing. He kept looking, and I realized, he wasn't looking for his wife, or *for* anyone. He was looking at all of us Jews, singing together without the threat of being found, dragged away, tortured, or killed. He was looking, fully aware of how lucky we all were to be together. And he was probably aware like this every *shabbat*. Every *shabbat*. The song returned to the refrain, and the congregants sang joyfully, without restraint, reaching hypnotic intensity. I turned back to the survivor. His eyes were closed, his head down. After a few moments, he slowly rubbed his entire hand over his face, as though wiping a memory. He returned to looking. I started to sing.

I had never done anything regularly. Routine had always tasted like death. But we started to light candles on Friday nights. We made a big dinner with a dessert. And we did it every Friday night. I did it. I was the one who bought the *challah*, made the meal, lit the candles, covered my eyes, sang. It felt odd at first—an add-on, a peripheral, an upgrade, designed to allow meaning. Soon there came to be a difference between routine and ritual. A routine ritual did not have to be routine at all. At first, just marking cycles of time enabled me to connect. To connect with who I was at the last ritual, with what I thought, with what I hoped for. And to remember. Like meter in poetry or structure in a story, I need those rhythms to make sense of the poem, the story. Rhythms define our lives. The narrowing of choices had already brought some meaning, had allowed me more than before.

But why the Jewish rituals? Why not Catholic modes of spirituality, as my brother had embraced, or connecting through the Buddhist way, as one of my dear friends had? Well, for once, this answer was obvious. I already had a place here. Here in Judaism. And a history. It was the only home that hadn't been torn down.

We were back at Saturday morning services at my in-laws'. I watched my husband's mother. What goes through her mind while she recites the *Amidah*? I wondered. At home, she has eight shelves full of Jewish literature, teachings, memoirs, and Holocaust history. She has read all the books. What goes through her mind indeed? If she didn't know what this prayer said, so what? She had found a connection, a guide for living a life of integrity. She felt something I longed for. We each have our own path.

At the next service at Beth El, it was time for the *Sh'ma*. Through so many services I had watched people, many of them now friends, their hands over their faces, singing this powerful prayer, its musical phrases, the sounds of the words. I had watched and listened, not even contemplating the meaning. I had watched, but I didn't pray with them. Finally, I pressed my fingers to my face. And the emotion welled up. I had cautiously avoided even mouthing the words, somehow knowing their power, afraid. But here I was, chanting them aloud. Senselessly, I shielded my face and said the words, the words I did not understand but knew by heart. "*Sh'ma* . . ." They filled me with comfort, intensity, groundedness, joy, connection—for "no good reason" and for many reasons. It had become the same with the *Kaddish,* at my stepfather's funeral. "*yisrael* . . ." And the same with my father's *yahrzeit* [anniversary of death]. And the same with the lighting of the *shabbat* candles. There is a history, a belonging, a feeling of something larger than me. Even though there is much I don't believe, hook, line, and sinker. Maybe I will, when I learn more. Maybe I won't. "*adonai eloheinu,* . . ." But I see the thousands of years of Jewish intelligence, inquiry, and teaching, glinting like a jewel not so far away. "*adonai, echad.*"

The congregants continued to pray, chant, hum. I felt grateful for my healthy children, a loving partner and friend in my husband, and all the people in my life whom I loved and who loved me. Thanks. I marveled at the fact that I could live comfortably and wished that the indigent and war-stricken of the rest of the world would one day know my peace. Blessings. I hoped for comfort for my mother, peace for the Bosnians, and safety and good health for my children. Requests. And then my mind wandered to the pond behind our house, the blueberry bushes wild and heavy with tiny fruit. And I said, "Let myself be a good girl. Amen."

SYNAGOGUES AND THE NEW AMERICAN JEW

DEBBIE CHAPEL'S STORY in Chapter One typifies a generation. Raised with conflicting messages from her parents about her Jewish heritage, she nevertheless longed to find a place where she felt that she could belong. With only a passing and superficial exposure to Judaism, she acquired no religious language with which to frame her deep sense of spirituality. Her encounter with middle-class, suburban Jewish affiliation through her soon-to-be husband increased her confusion. Long on ethnic trappings and short on God and piety, Judaism did not seem to hold the key to her need for spiritual rootedness.

Until, that is, she happened upon a very different kind of synagogue. At Congregation Beth El in Sudbury, Massachusetts, Debbie found a way to connect her spiritual appetite with traditional Jewish words and rituals. The poignancy of her "return" to Judaism, a return that was really a first discovery, is significant because it represents a path that many others would gladly take if only there were synagogues that understood how to meet their needs.

The closing decades of the twentieth century present the student of the American Jewish community with paradoxical trends. On the one hand, there is significant evidence that bonds of attachment to the Jewish community are weakening. On the other hand, there are new stirrings among a generation of Jews that came to maturity after Israel's Six-Day War in 1967.[1] This generation of Jewish baby boomers began to redefine the dimensions of Jewish identity and in so doing began to mark the transition to a new age in the American Jewish community. It would emerge as an age in which Jews took more ownership of their own Judaism and in which the historic division between the religious and secular spheres of American Jewish life would begin to break down. But it was also a period in which the gap between Jews and their synagogues grew ever wider.

In the decades following World War II, the Jewish community set about becoming one of the most highly organized ethnic groups America had ever seen. Motivated by the failure to exert the kind of political influence that might have saved millions of lives in Nazi Europe, American Jewry mobilized. Federations became the central addresses of the Jewish community, raising record sums of money to fund Jewish needs at home and abroad. The Jewish community rallied around the young state of Israel, raising money through the United Jewish Appeal (UJA) and learning how to enlist American political support in Washington. Defense agencies were created to monitor and respond to manifestations of anti-Jewish sentiment. More blatant forms of prejudice and discrimination were met with litigation or meetings with public officials. Endangered Jewish communities around the world, most notably Jews in the Soviet Union, became rallying points for activist Jews.

Jonathan Woocher describes this array of Jewish loyalties and commitments as the "civil religion" of American Jews.[2] Indeed, even synagogues were enlisted in the service of this civil religion. Affiliation with a synagogue became one tangible way to cast one's lot with the Jewish people— no commitment to creed, practice, or belief required. But by the early 1980s, increasing numbers of observers of the Jewish community were noting that American Jewish life could not forever be sustained on the back of this civil religion. Increasing numbers of indicators suggested that younger Jews were far less inclined to be drawn by the themes of Jewish peoplehood, Israel, and support for the structures of the organized Jewish community.[3] The trend was typical of the baby boom generation, and it has dramatic implications, not only for religious institutions but for American society as well.[4] All indications point to the fact that the baby boom generation represents one of the most dramatic cultural shifts in American history. It is for this reason that it is imperative to understand what drives this generation if there is any chance that synagogues can respond appropriately.

The Generation

In 1993, Wade Clark Roof of the University of California at Santa Barbara published a seminal study titled *A Generation of Seekers: The Spiritual Journeys of the Baby Boom Generation*. It represents the most wide-ranging survey and analysis of the generation of Americans born between 1946 and 1964 and their relationship to religion and spirituality.

The findings help us understand the psyche of what I call the "new American Jew" and in turn the kinds of religious institutions that might resonate with Jews in America today.

Boomers came of age during a time of social upheaval and increased cultural choices. The war in Vietnam unleashed a chorus of protest from a generation that was no longer prepared to defer to those in positions of political authority. This alienation made the boomers the least trusting generation of social and political institutions that America had ever seen. Sexual liberation, feminism, and the drug culture challenged the mores and lifestyles of boomers' parents. These phenomena fostered a commitment to egalitarianism and an openness and tolerance to a wide range of lifestyle choices, extending not only to a redefinition of traditional male-female roles in the family and in the workplace but also to greater social acceptance of nontraditional family arrangements (single parenting, surrogate childbearing, same-sex households, etc.). Widespread access to higher education, a vast increase in the number of hours spent in front of the ever-present television, an explosion of musical and cinematic offerings, and the rise of new computer technologies exposed young people to more information than ever before. All of these supplanted the family as the primary transmitter of cultural values and mores, creating a sharper generational change than had ever been experienced.

Finally, and perhaps most tellingly for our story, middle-class boomers were raised in relative affluence and with a high sense of expectations for themselves. They were raised with a permissive ethos, partly shaped and partly typified by the child-rearing approach of Dr. Benjamin Spock. At home and in school, boomers were encouraged to express their individuality and personality. As the generation came into adulthood, its members were as likely to ask, "How will I find personal fulfillment?" as "How will I earn a living?" Members of the previous generation, raised during the Great Depression, never stopped worrying about where their next dollar would come from; members of its successor generation, raised in material plenty, were more likely to downplay, if not ridicule, their parents' hard-earned prosperity. According to Abraham Maslow's "hierarchy of needs," once economic survival is ensured, people tend toward "postmaterialistic" values dealing with questions about the meaning and purpose of life.[5]

The New American Jew

Understanding this cultural context helps frame the characteristics of the "new American Jew." The baby boomers, born after World War II, are significantly different from their parents' generation, which helped build the organized Jewish community as we came to know it during the second half of the twentieth century. First, having had no firsthand experience of the Holocaust or of the birth of the state of Israel, the new American Jew is less inclined to build his or her Jewish identity around either of those epochal events in contemporary Jewish history. Second, raised without significant experiences of antisemitism or barriers to professional and economic success, the new American Jew is far more secure in his or her Jewish identity. This is a double-edged sword because the openness of modern American society makes it easier to walk away from the Jewish community. For those who stay within the Jewish community, the rallying cry "Save the Jews!" is less likely to resonate than "What wisdom is there in the Jewish tradition that can give meaning to my life?"

Third, the new American Jew, raised in relative affluence and prosperity and with a secure sense of self in America, is looking for different things in a synagogue than might have motivated his or her parents. Jewish baby boomers are more inclined to seek out synagogues that meet the needs of their young and growing families or that provide a sense of connectedness and belonging that is lacking in contemporary upper-middle-class American life. All of these characteristics represent a wholesale change in the makeup of the American Jewish community, and they are bringing new demands on institutions that seek to meet the needs of a changing constituency.

Changing Organizational Styles

The generation that gave birth to the baby boomers created a most impressive Jewish community. It was made up of a complex of secular Jewish agencies that raised money and provided for the welfare and safety of Jews at home and around the world. It built synagogue-centers to meet the needs of the Jews who moved to the suburban frontier after World War II. But that community is increasingly at odds with the tastes and temperaments of the new American Jew. The organizational ethos of the postwar Jewish community and its synagogues were reflective of *The Organization Man,* a book by William Whyte that described the conformity and emerging corporate culture of the 1950s. The new American Jew grew up in an era that ditched *The Organization Man* for Robert Pirsig's *Zen and the Art of Motorcycle Maintenance,* a book that celebrated the personal search for meaning and truth.

Organizational structures that develop over the course of a generation do not change overnight. The secular Jewish world, dominated by the federation and UJA structures, is just beginning to deal with the challenge of remaining relevant to the new American Jew by employing several strategies. It is gradually moving away from its traditional, highly centralized allocation system to allow for more donor-directed giving. It is recognizing the interest of younger Jews in more serious engagement with the Jewish tradition by integrating such study into its leadership development programs. Realizing the waning interest of boomers in Holocaust- and Israel-focused programming and appeals, it is reassessing the proportions of monies being sent overseas as compared to the funds allocated locally to strengthen Jewish identity programming. Although some critics argue that these changes are too little, too late, only time will tell the extent to which the quasi-governmental agencies that work on behalf of the Jewish people around the world will capture the loyalties of the new American Jew.

In many ways, synagogues are in a better position to respond to the needs of the boomer generation. They are far less complex organizations than the federations and, with much smaller staffs, can adapt much more quickly to changes called for by their constituencies. Indeed, numerous innovations have been implemented in synagogues over the past twenty years to meet the needs of the boomer generation. Mega-synagogues have tried to respond to the interest in greater intimacy by creating *havurot,* smaller groups of Jews within the congregation that gather for study, prayer, or celebration. Depending on the congregation, the *havurot* have more or less autonomy from the parent body. Increasingly, one can find adult education offerings, including courses on Kabbalah, spirituality, or meditation, in an attempt to speak to the generational interest in a more inward approach to religion. The desire for religious services that are less formal and more participatory have a led to a veritable explosion of "library" or "downstairs" *minyans* (prayer groups) in synagogues across North America. These services are often lay-led and held at the same time as services conducted in the main sanctuary. Although the rabbi may occasionally drop in, the talks and prayers are led by members.

As with the federations, the jury is out on whether these changes are sufficient to capture the loyalties of the new American Jew. It would also be a mistake to underestimate the obstacles to wholesale changes in the way that the American synagogue conducts itself. People are notoriously conservative when it comes to religion; they are resistant to change. Sociologist Charles Liebman has observed that American Jews live with a double standard between the folk religion they practice and the elite religion they want to see represented in their synagogues.[6] Larry Hoffman, co-director of Synagogue 2000, a project designed to help synagogues adapt to the changing needs of the baby boom generation, notes sarcastically that a more appropriate epigram over the ark to the standard "Know before whom you stand" might be "We have always done it this way."

It is hard to criticize this phenomenon too harshly because what draws most people to affiliate with a synagogue is their desire to be part of a "community of memory." The community of memory embodies the most cherished practices and beliefs of the tradition. It is what draws most people to affiliate with synagogues. Nor is it any surprise that synagogues are underwritten and run by members who are drawn to it because they like it. The kind of religious services that will take place and the programming that will be offered will, by and large, be designed to meet the needs of this existing constituency.

Loyalists Versus Dropouts

In Roof's study of the baby boom generation and its patterns of beliefs and religious behavior he calls this existing constituency "loyalists." On many levels, the loyalists are the boomers who were least affected by the cultural trends of the 1960s. They are the least likely to challenge the practices and conventions of the institutions in which they were raised, and their affiliation patterns follow those of their parents. Roof found that loyalists make up 33 percent of the boomer generation. Another 25 percent are characterized as "returnees," individuals who drop out of church or synagogue affiliation only to return as they begin to raise families.

As the returnees begin to come back into the fold of religious institutions, they are likely to parallel the loyalists in terms of taste and disposition—generationally different from their parents but not so radically as to challenge the basic forms and functions of the churches and synagogues that they join. Essentially, because they have relatively low expectations of religious institutions, they also have little investment in trying to change them. During the period of their affiliation with a church or a synagogue, they will accept what the institution offers to serve their immediate needs. Those needs often revolve around life cycle rituals and educational training for young children. Parents often keep the religious institution at arm's length. Unless something especially compelling happens to families during this stage of their lives, many will exit the institution soon after the youngest child reaches the early teen years.

The most interesting category of Roof's survey were the "dropouts," who accounted for 42 percent of the sample. The significance of this category can be best appreciated by realizing that nine out of ten surveyed boomers reported some religious training or association with a religious institution while growing up. (This is similar to the pattern for Jews. Although at any given time only 40 to 50 percent of American Jews are affiliated with a synagogue, some 80 to 85 percent affiliate with a synagogue at some point in their adult lives, usually during the time their chil-

dren are being trained for a bar or bat mitzvah.) These individuals therefore remain outside the orbit of churches and synagogues, not because
they have not been exposed to a religious upbringing but because they
have made a conscious decision not to support or participate in the types
of congregations they were part of as children. Furthermore, though every
generation experiences a significant dropout phenomenon between the
late teens and late twenties, when most young adults are pursuing college
studies and are distancing themselves from the routines of their upbringing, Roof found that the dropout rate of the boomer generation was
30 percent higher than that of the previous generation.[7]

It would be easy, albeit painful, for religious leaders to dismiss this
large segment of the baby boom generation, the dropouts, as unreachable
if we were to ascribe to it a growing secularization and a lack of interest
in matters of the spirit. But that is not the case. The remarkable fact about
these dropouts is that despite their aversion to organized religion, as a
group they have devoted a great amount of time and resources to explore
a variety of spiritual groups and disciplines. These are the people who
have fueled the explosive growth of group therapies like est and Life-
spring, healing centers, New Age communes, ashrams based on Eastern
religious disciplines, yoga and meditation centers, and a variety of self-
help groups. Despite some occasional media portrayals of those who pursue some of these alternative forms of spirituality as people who sever ties
from friends and family and retreat from the world, the vast majority of
this generation's spiritual exploration has been far tamer. One might even
describe the interest as dilettantish. Most dabbled in one or more of the
alternative systems, sometimes as innocently as picking up a book on Zen
or breathing techniques and incorporating suggestions from the book
into their lives. Many engaged in some form of psychotherapy, seeking to
understand themselves better. Some tried meditation in their homes for
short periods each day in an attempt to create an island of tranquillity in
an otherwise hectic life. In short, these "dropouts" are in fact spiritual
seekers.

What boomers are seeking is some practice, belief, or worldview that
gives their lives a greater sense of meaning. In this, the alternatives pursued by dropouts—and by many others of their generation, including
parts of the returnees group, though perhaps to a smaller extent—offer
precisely the commodity that for generations was the sole province of organized religion. Increasingly, boomers have made a distinction between
religion and spirituality. Religion represents a fairly structured and rigid
set of beliefs and practices handed down for centuries in a process controlled by professional clergy. Even boomers who do affiliate with churches
and synagogues have sought to break down the hierarchy in religious

organizations to make them more open to the participatory management style that typifies the boomers' workplace.

In contrast to the experience of institutional religion, spirituality is a way of being in the world. As seekers define it, spirituality offers a framework for understanding themselves and their lives, enabling them to experience their deepest feelings and emotions. Many express an interest in personal and social transformation, in a lifestyle that manifests reverence for nature, in a belief that is more immanent than transcendent so that God can be experienced through many aspects of life, in social justice activities that offer personal fulfillment through commitment to others, and in a longing for healing, harmony, wholeness, and renewal. The fact that boomers have looked to many places to discover this elusive spirituality does not make them unavailable for membership in churches or synagogues. Despite the fact that some observers attributed the dramatic downturn in the membership in mainline Protestant churches in the 1960s and 1970s to the failure of those churches to respond to boomer culture,[8] 70 percent of the dropout sample indicated an openness to joining a religious institution provided that it met their needs.[9]

Two other findings in the Roof study are important to consider for our understanding of the boomer phenomenon in the Jewish context. The first is that the boomer generation has little loyalty to the religions and denominations of their childhood. Raised to be educated consumers in a society offering a dizzying array of choices, boomers have learned to shop around to meet their spiritual needs. Often to the consternation of parents and leaders of conventional religious institutions, boomers have attached themselves to a wide array of "spiritual communities"—yoga classes and groups, feminist groups, men's groups, twelve-step programs, communities practicing Eastern religions, and ecological groups have all offered the baby boom generation spiritual sustenance.

A study of advanced industrial countries revealed widespread acceptance of cultural values that were once deemed to represent the "counterculture."[10] Among these values are egalitarianism, peace, environmentalism, and the pursuit of a higher quality of life, with increased attention paid to the human quest for meaning and belonging. Despite the rapid acceptance of these values in mainstream Western culture, organized religion has been slow to embrace these values because to do so would require reappraisal of long-standing doctrines and practices. Thus the vast majority of churches and synagogues find themselves "behind the curve" in their attempt to appeal to the most influential age cohort in the American population.

The second finding offers a more encouraging prospect for religious institutions. As a generation enters middle age, the polarities that were the currency of its youth tend to soften. Members of the baby boom generation, once quick to reject so much of what their parents and American society represented in the 1960s and 1970s, have aged and acquired precious life experience. Life is now a lot less black and white. The bumps in the road to successful careers and marriages have been humbling. Raising children of their own makes boomers more appreciative of their own parents, who now seem wiser and worthy of greater respect. The aging process itself brings to consciousness one's own mortality and questions of one's legacy. Suddenly religion has a greater appeal.

Indeed, Roof found that even among dropouts, interest in providing appropriate religious training to children, coupled with the boomers' own quest for community and personal meaning, make this constituency ripe for affiliation with churches and synagogues that meet their needs. Contrary to the assumption that the boomers are so individualistic a generation that they would remain forever averse to joining congregations, there is substantial evidence that the generation that experienced strong solidarities and passionate commitments in youth may well find religious institutions the most likely place to recapture those longings as its members enter midlife. The desire to be part of something larger than oneself is as strong in the boomer generation as in any generation before it.[11]

The Hunger

Having looked at the cultural influences that shaped the attitudes and temperaments of the new American Jew, we can now turn to identifying just what this generation is saying about religion and spirituality. These are generational themes that define the likes and dislikes of the new American Jew. It is the prerequisite to understanding why so many Jews have given up on the American synagogue. These eight themes are the key to understanding how the American synagogue might begin to recapture that lost generation.

The Turnoff of the Postwar Suburban Synagogue

The new American Jew tells a generational tale of being totally turned off by the synagogues of their childhood. The parents of the boomer generation built cathedral-style synagogues as status markers in their new suburban neighborhoods. The bigger the synagogue, the higher the status. Rabbis were quickly co-opted into this pecking order as well. A rabbi who could land an eight-hundred-family congregation by the age of forty was deemed to be far more successful than the colleague who was "stuck" in a three-hundred-family congregation at age fifty. Although the suburban synagogues built in the 1950s and 1960s offered impressive facilities and a wide array of services, the boomer generation raised in these synagogues remember them as cold and austere. The larger the synagogue, the less likely that young people would have close personal contact with the rabbi, who delegated "youth work" to junior professional staff.

The most formative experience of boomers in the synagogue centers was their own bar or bat mitzvah. Their parents approached this central life passage consistent with the values that built the synagogues in which the ceremonies took place: the bigger the better. Most adolescents went along with plans for lavish parties that accompanied their passage into Jewish adulthood; but looking back, they recalled the events as a sham.

Adolescents wrestle with a wide range of personal and existential challenges. Their hormones are raging, and they have little to guide them in dealing with their emerging sexuality. They behave and are treated sometimes as children and sometimes as adults, depending on the context, and they are fervently trying to figure out which of the competing voices they are to heed. They are torn between dependence on their parents and a desire to be independent. Their growing intellectual maturity leads them to ask challenging questions about matters of faith, conscience, and social responsibility.

But few boomers remember their bar or bat mitzvah as a time when their involvement with the synagogue helped them sort out these weighty developmental matters. They remember instead a lot of focus on the band, the caterer, and who made the cut for the invitation list. Nor do boomers remember kindly the interminable number of after-school hours they spent in Hebrew school, learning nothing of compelling importance to them. The mismatch between their parents' insistence on attendance and the parents' own disinterest in what went on in the synagogue did not fail to leave its scars.

The issues that begin to intrude on one's consciousness in adolescence rarely go away. They simply resurface in more complex guises. As the baby boomers came into adulthood, synagogues were the last place they would look for spiritual guidance. Spiritual questions they had aplenty; they simply went elsewhere for answers. If anything, they associated the synagogues of their youth with the materialistic values that many of them tried to reject.

A Sense of Exclusion

If participation in the synagogue was experienced by many as shallow and superficial, there were many others who did not even fit in. The "Ozzie and Harriet" model of the American family—a two-parent nuclear family with a couple of children—may have typified the family patterns of postwar America, but it certainly did not represent everyone. Yet the American synagogue of this period was geared almost exclusively to this mom-pop-and-kids standard. Individuals who did not fit this family model had a hard time feeling welcome in the typical suburban synagogue. There were few programs for singles, divorcees, or the elderly, and so these populations were mostly absent from the synagogue.

Even members of the congregation could feel excluded. Most synagogues were slow to respond to the growing feminist consciousness in the 1970s. A handful of Jewish feminists made a compelling case regarding the exclusion of women in Jewish history and in the rabbinic tradition. As Jewish women sought out greater roles within the synagogue, in terms of both ritual participation and lay and clerical leadership, they ran headlong into entrenched male-dominated institutions that only slowly responded to the appeals. The elaborate deliberations that many local and national Jewish institutions had to work through to accommodate Jewish women's desires to participate did little to relieve the sense on the part of thousands of young Jewish women that they seemed to matter less than men did in synagogue settings.[12]

If synagogues seemed slow to respond to the needs of women in the 1970s, the same could be said about the needs of intermarried couples in the 1980s and the needs of gay and lesbian Jews in the 1990s. Each situation raised challenging issues for synagogues and the national movements of which they were part. In the pews, however, these constituencies sensed that they were less than fully welcome.[13] As the baby boom generation matured, fewer and fewer Americans lived in nuclear families. A growing consciousness emerged about populations that had been overlooked—women, the intermarried, the elderly, divorcees, gays and lesbians, singles, the disabled. Some number of Jews from each of these constituencies threw themselves into the struggle for recognition and could sometimes claim modest victories in some synagogues. The vast majority, however, sought out alternative institutions or gave up on Jewish life altogether because they felt that they were not wanted.

Religion Versus Spirituality

One of the ironies of the boomer generation is that the high level of interest in matters spiritual is accompanied by a low level of attachment to things religious. Interest in spirituality increased in the closing decades of the twentieth century even as conventional religious institutions lost members and support. Some have observed that the baby boomers, as members of the most overindulged generation in American history, want to shape religion to their own needs. Unwilling to accept dogmas and doctrines passed down through the generations because they clash with personal belief systems and lifestyle choices, boomers have preferred to seek out New Age spiritual alternatives. Freed of hierarchical structures that dictate which practices are permissible and which are not, boomers approach the smorgasbord of spiritual offerings in contemporary American culture like shoppers at a flea market.

Sometimes it wasn't even a clash of belief systems that drove them away. Many boomers recall being raised in synagogues where prayer and ritual were done by rote. They have little recollection of what the prayers meant or why a particular ritual was practiced. Years spent in Hebrew school attempting to learn Hebrew phonetically was not only frustrating but also failed to convey the beauty of the Hebrew language or the rich meaning of ancient texts. The memorization of some biblical portion that was chanted on the occasion of one's bar or bat mitzvah guaranteed that the enterprise called Judaism was remembered as more about form than about substance.

What spirituality has come to mean to most baby boomers is the attempt to connect one's own life with a sense of larger purpose and meaning. Some who dabble in spirituality through books, support groups, meditation, or forms of individual and group therapy use "God language" more comfortably than others. Most, however, will credit their spiritual explorations with offering them a sense of peace, wholeness, and oneness that would otherwise elude them in a society driven by too much technology, too little time, and few supportive personal relationships. Most boomers do not think that they can get these precious commodities through conventional religious institutions.

Alternative Spiritual Paths

Not all Jews of this generation have spent time in ashrams, on yoga retreats, and in meditation practices, and only a few have dropped out of their previous lives to devote themselves full time to such spiritual searches. For many, the search for fulfillment and greater self-understanding takes on tamer manifestations, including workshops that grew out of the human potential movement, group and individual psychotherapy, and a wide range of self-help groups. Though statistics are hard to come by, many people who have studied alternative spiritual paths, or what Tony Schwartz calls the "American wisdom tradition," consistently remark on the disproportionate numbers of Jews as teachers and students in these settings.[14] It seems inescapable that the generation raised in the synagogues of the 1950s, 1960s, and 1970s emerged with an unquenched thirst for something more spiritual and most concluded that they would not find it within the Jewish community.

Perhaps the most disturbing realization for those trying to understand the religious patterns of Jewish baby boomers is that many of the most serious spiritual seekers of this generation are not to be found in American synagogues. Many rabbis associated with the Jewish Renewal movement spend increasing amounts of time at New Age spiritual centers like the Omega Institute in New York, Spirit Rock in California, the Temple of the Universe in northern Florida, and ashrams associated with one or another Eastern religious practice. They find there thousands of young Jews searching for spirituality. Many are the stories of these rabbis offering *shabbat* services in these settings, which attract Jews who have abandoned the organized Jewish community. The fact that these "dropouts" come to such Jewish services and are often deeply moved by them suggests that there exists a deep, though latent, yearning for a spiritual practice grounded in Jewish tradition. The fact that most of these same Jews would never think of attending a synagogue says much about how seriously synagogues have lost a sizable constituency of young Jewish seekers.

Inclusivity

One of the defining characteristics of the baby boom generation is the growing appreciation of diversity. As technology continues to make our world smaller and more familiar, we begin to realize what a tiny piece of the universe our own lives represent. The search for alternative paths to spiritual fulfillment and wisdom represents a desire to drink fully and deeply from the variegated cup of life. We sense the existence of a truth beyond our own parochial lifestyles and cultures.

This impulse toward the universal often generates such a firm rejection of any particularities that membership in a synagogue represents a violation of principle of the highest order. Many with such a bent of mind will never join a synagogue. Others, however, might reflect similar biases but retain a more nuanced appreciation for the possibilities of experiencing the universal through a faith community rooted in particular ethnic and cultural legacies. To draw such individuals to a synagogue, however, the congregation itself must represent an authentic desire for as much inclusivity as possible.

This is one of the areas where denominational affiliations matter, since the very essence of any historic religious tradition is about boundaries and limits, defining who may be part of the group and who may not. Liberal synagogues can and will be more open to the intermarried or to gay or lesbian Jews than more traditional synagogues. But even more traditional congregations can be aware of constituencies that are typically absent from the American synagogue. Suburban synagogues have not been very open to singles beyond the adolescent years. Rare is the synagogue that makes it possible for deaf, developmentally disabled, or the mentally challenged to participate in services and programs.

The interest in inclusivity goes beyond the fact that as a population, the Jewish community is more heterogeneous than ever before in age, marital status, ethnic makeup, and sexual orientation. In many ways, the generational commitment to inclusivity is an outgrowth of the feminist consciousness of the era. Major strides have been made to reclaim the voices of women in our history as well as see to it that women have an opportunity to provide their insight and leadership in every facet of contemporary life. The same holds true for Jewish history and community today. But equally important is the fact that the hard-earned principles of egalitarianism and inclusivity must necessarily be extended to other overlooked groups as well. Even though total inclusivity will challenge the boundaries of the Jewish community, the generational commitment to the principle makes progress in this area virtually inevitable.

Social Justice

For a significant number of baby boomers, the search for meaning and fulfillment draws them to social or political issues. It grows out of the desire to attach oneself to a movement or to a cause larger than oneself. Relative affluence combined with good conscience motivates many boomers to work on behalf of the poor, the sick, the outcast. Often the cause provides a community of fellow travelers who can offer emotional and personal support as well as a sense that one is contributing to a legacy that will survive one's own mortality—again, the currency of religious institutions.

Many activists take a dim view of religion, for despite all its professions of "right" attitudes, rarely does it result in direct action in the world on the part of "believers." For activists, conventional religion requires too much study, too much sitting, and far too much debating in a world filled with suffering and oppression. In a choice between faith and action, the activist is certain that the moment demands less time in the pew and more time in the street.

For many baby boomers, events in the Middle East in the 1970s and 1980s made participation in the Jewish community even more difficult.

The community had built an impressive advocacy network that amplified the voices of the relatively small Jewish community many times over (most studies put Jews at around 3 percent of the American population). Nearly every institution in the community urged Jews to call and write members of Congress, publish op-ed pieces, write letters to newspaper editors, attend rallies and demonstrations, and otherwise sound off in support of the policies of the state of Israel. Anyone who questioned Israel's policies or who dared to express the view that there may be some justice in the cause of the Palestinians was deemed disloyal and was shunned.

Thousands of American Jews were troubled by Israeli policies regarding settlements in territories captured during the 1967 Six-Day War or by Israel's treatment of Palestinians. For many, this political view was an extension of the Jewish tradition of compassion for the downtrodden and the dispossessed. Identifying with a community that stifled dissenting voices and delegitimized opposing political views was intolerable. Consequently, many Jews distanced themselves from synagogues and the Jewish community in disgust.[15]

In my travels around the country, I have found a handful of synagogues and churches that are renewing the activist spirit of the 1960s, when the religious community became a rallying point for the civil rights movement. The personal stories in this book reveal the interest of Jews in finding a place where they can combine their search for spiritual fulfillment with their commitment to do the work of social justice.

Synagogues and churches will never be the only venue in which people will be able to pursue social justice causes. At the same time, a generation that looks for greater consonance between professions of faith and action in the world will increasingly demand that religious institutions be committed to the work of peace and justice in both word and deed.

Belonging and Communal Support

In *Habits of the Heart,* the classic study of individualism and commitment in American society in the second half of the twentieth century, Robert Bellah and his coauthors note that modernity might best be described as having created a "culture of separation."[16] Greater mobility, technology, and the pursuit of material success have all conspired to cut individuals off from the families, communities, and social contexts that give life meaning. The book's suggested antidote to the syndrome that they call the "poverty of affluence" is the rebuilding of mediating structures between the individual and the state that can become the foundation for a stronger civic fabric. It is what gives individuals, in an ever more complex and technologically driven society, a sense of belonging. Their interviewees suggest that churches and synagogues are among the most compelling of such mediating institutions.

Of course, this becomes true only to the extent that synagogues or churches find ways to encourage and support the creation of interpersonal connections between members. The creation of *havurot* in larger synagogues is the best example of focusing attention on overcoming the "culture of separation" that so many of our generation suffer. *Havurot* consist of groups of five to ten families in a congregation who might celebrate *shabbat* and other holidays together or meet for periodic study. The result is a locus of intimacy between families, an all too rare phenomenon in our day and age.

Robert Wuthnow, one of the preeminent scholars of American religion, has noted the explosion of all sorts of support groups in America populated by members of the baby boom generation.[17] On the sociological level, such groups draw individuals out of themselves and link them to wider social networks that provide much-needed emotional support. On the religious level, when such groups are created in sacred contexts, it allows participants to give voice to experiences of spirituality as part of an unfolding process of self-understanding.

Many synagogues have found other ways to provide similar small-group support for members. Some have created committees that support members in times of crisis, illness, and death. Some have veteran members "adopt" new families to give them a more personal connection to the institution. In some congregations, members are given name tags to wear during services, a long-standing practice in many churches. This not only helps members meet one another but also allows for easy identification of visitors, who receive a badge of a different color. Some rabbis have turned their sermon time into a time of dialogue when attendees at the service can share their thoughts with each other. All of these innovations help make synagogue membership less anonymous and more personally satisfying. It is no coincidence that most synagogues being constructed in the 1980s and 1990s feature seating that ensures some form of semicircular arrangement, a pattern that increases the ability of attendees to see each other's faces and facilitates the ability of congregants to "connect" with one another.

Obviously, some congregations have been quicker to understand the importance of these innovations than others. The American synagogue as an institution became expert at delivering a wide range of programs and services to meet the needs of congregants. The new American Jew is far more interested in a place that pays attention to the relationships between congregants. Learning about the Jewish tradition is of value only to the extent that people in a synagogue are encouraged to relate to one another and support one another in a true community. This entails creating a communal culture that values and promulgates the opening of hands and hearts to one another. All other matters of doctrine and practice flow from that basic principle.

Empowerment

The final theme that typifies the new American Jew is empowerment. Put another way, the baby boom generation is disinclined to defer to hierarchies, be they political, social, or religious.

Many readers will understand this theme as referring to organizational power within the synagogue. Though it is true that some synagogues are controlled by a tight-knit group of longtime members on the governing board, in fact most synagogues are extremely open to the leadership of members who are willing to devote the significant number of volunteer hours necessary to chair a committee or serve on the board. Unlike Jewish federations and secular organizations that make leadership positions contingent on significant financial capability, synagogues have been relatively democratic in that they have been open to the leadership of a wide range of their members.

The more challenging domain of empowerment is in the realm of Judaism itself. For generations, rabbis were the primary expositors of the Jewish tradition. They were familiar with its sacred texts and adept at interpreting and applying Jewish teachings to the challenges of the given time and place. Throughout the centuries, rabbis were the most educated and learned men in the Jewish community. Even in America, rabbis were held in high esteem by virtue of the fact that in a community that valued education, they had more years of advanced study and were more widely read than most of their congregants.

As boomers matured, this was no longer the case. The Jewish community was made up of scientists and doctors, writers and artists, lawyers and therapists, scholars and computer experts. The minute a rabbi made a reference to some field of knowledge other than Judaism, it was likely that someone in the congregation knew enough to offer a correction! Moreover, the explosion of books on Judaica since the 1970s, including translations of long-obscure rabbinical works, made the entire field of Jewish knowledge accessible to a highly educated Jewish public.

Make no mistake, the baby boom generation may represent one of the most Judaically ignorant and Hebraically illiterate group of Jews in the history of Jewish civilization. And yet interest in esoteric bodies of knowledge is extremely high among boomers, and Judaism is just that to them. Given the right environment and the right teachers, boomer Jews have the interest and ability to devour enormous amounts of Jewish information. The challenge, of course, is to create such an environment and to produce the kinds of teachers who can serve as guides to this generation of Jews.

Most critical is to create settings in which Jews are asked what *they* think a particular passage from the Torah says about their lives; what *they* feel Judaism has to say about a contemporary political quandary; what *they* think Judaism has to say about raising their children, loving their spouse, or caring for their parents. Many are the places where rabbis get to weigh in on such matters. Few are the places where Jews are challenged to do the same. But it is in those rare places that something special happens to the Jewish tradition and to the people who are inspired to explore it. It and they become spiritually alive.

The empowerment that the new American Jew seeks is less to be able to negotiate the rabbi's contract than it is to be given the tools to explore an incredibly rich religious tradition. When this happens, not only do they benefit (though that is certainly true) but, more important, the community becomes enriched because suddenly there are multiple voices making the tradition relevant to contemporary life.

○

These are the themes that define new American Jews and their spiritual search. Precious few have found a spiritual home within Judaism.

Some religious institutions have been adept at tapping into this interest in spirituality and have incorporated the most popular elements of spiritual exploration into their synagogues and churches. This is not always easy, as more conservative members of these institutions will invoke tradition, branding such experiments as beyond the pale. Clergy, who often serve as gatekeepers and arbiters of what is and is not acceptable, face a choice between attracting new, younger congregants who want change and satisfying existing members, the loyalists who are already part of the leadership of the institution. Unless a religious institution starts from scratch with a mission to address the baby boom age cohort, existing synagogues and churches are destined to wrestle over each and every innovation that pits religious convention against the interests of a younger generation.

Within the synagogue orbit, individuals who have a substantial investment in Judaism understand why such innovations must be carefully deliberated. But to many baby boomers, often raised with but a token commitment to the Jewish community and to Jewish tradition, there is little understanding of or patience for synagogues that agonize over changes that appear so obvious. Since there are so many spiritual options available in American society today, most pass on joining synagogues and come to satisfy their spiritual needs elsewhere.

It is for this reason that we now turn our attention to the way synagogues have evolved to meet the changing needs of the American Jewish community over time. It is an examination that will bring us face to face with a new paradigm that may be the key to recapturing the hearts and minds of the new American Jew.

3

THE EMERGING
SYNAGOGUE-COMMUNITY

I AM STANDING in the ballroom of the Marriott Hotel in downtown Boston with several hundred Jews, arms linked, some with eyes closed and all swaying to a melody being sung by Debbie Friedman, a singer-songwriter who specializes in contemporary Jewish liturgical music. I have been part of this scene before because I have witnessed Debbie cast her spell over many different audiences. My love for her compositions has resulted in having many of her songs being sung in my own congregation, often eliciting similar reactions from those gathered for prayer.

But this is somehow different. The setting is the 1995 General Assembly (GA) of the Council of Jewish Federations (CJF). The GA is one of the largest gatherings of Jews in Jewish life in America today. In terms of its ability to attract the lay and professional power brokers of the American Jewish community, it has no equal. These are not the people who come to my synagogue. Though many are affiliated with synagogues, as a group they spend far greater amounts of time serving on committees of their local Jewish federations than they do in religious services.

Descriptions of the American Jewish community generally divide up the arenas of Jewish activity into the religious sphere (synagogues and their related schools) and the secular sphere (federations and membership organizations addressing social service, community relations, and overseas needs). Historically, there has been a wide divide between the synagogue world and the world of secular Jewish organizations even as the two spheres share overlapping memberships. There is hardly a community in America that has not seen its share of "turf wars" between the professionals and laypeople who lead those respective institutions. Certainly since the end of World War II, and some would argue even earlier, the locus of power and prestige in the American Jewish community has been with the secular Jewish organizations that have taken responsibility for the interests of the Jewish people, at home and abroad.

During the half-century since the end of the war, the federations have assumed primacy by virtue of their unmatched ability to raise funds and allocate those funds to Israel and other overseas needs and to an array of organizations that serve the local Jewish community in America. It is a world that is driven by a deep commitment to the welfare of the Jewish people. But it is also a world whose makeup is heavily male, whose ambience is business, and whose language is wealth and power.

It was remarkable enough that amid the sessions of the GA devoted to fundraising, endowment funds, the Middle East peace process, intergroup relations in America, and the impact of the U.S. budget on social service needs of the Jewish community, a session was devoted to "healing and spirituality." The topic itself on a GA agenda would have been unthinkable ten years earlier. But even more remarkable was the number of people in attendance and the fact that in the space of an hour, these particular people in this unique setting were singing "And bless us with goodness and mercy and peace; oh hear my prayer to You."

———————— o ————————

There are moments in life that are pregnant with a sense of transition; that one struck me as just such a moment. It symbolized a recognition on the part of a generation of Jews who were adherents of the civil religion of American Jews—ethnic survival and political solidarity—and who worshiped in its temples—federations and secular Jewish organizations—that a new day was dawning. The spirit of the new American Jew had infiltrated the inner sanctum of leadership of the American Jewish community and announced that it was time to shift gears.

Of course, moments such as these only presage change. Institutions change slowly, and whole communities change even more slowly. To a youngish new American Jew who is barely aware of the history of the American Jewish community, joining a synagogue whose organizational culture was shaped by a previous generation of American Jews can be a jolting experience. Before we can chart out a new paradigm for the kind of synagogue that can speak to this new American Jew, we must first understand how the American synagogue got to where it is today.

Three Stages of the American Synagogue

Historically, synagogues played an important role in helping Jews make the transition from immigrant status to becoming full-fledged Americans. An immigrant's arrival in a new country poses myriad challenges. Immigrants are concerned about finding adequate housing, employment, and schooling for their children. Torn from familiar surroundings, they seek out organizations and associations that can help them adjust to their new environment but also provide a touchstone to things that were once familiar to them. For Jews, synagogues were just such institutions. And with the passage of time, as the circumstances of the Jews changed in America, so did the synagogues.

In the course of the growth and evolution of the Jewish community in America, the American synagogue evolved through three stages—the immigrant synagogue, the ethnic synagogue, and the synagogue-center. Each of these stages corresponds to a stage of integration of the American Jewish community.[1]

The Immigrant Synagogue

The immigrant synagogues were those houses of worship first established upon the arrival of the Jews in America. Sephardic Jews were the first to reach American shores in the late 1700s, and they established synagogues in New York City; Newport, Rhode Island; Philadelphia; Charleston, South Carolina; and Savannah, Georgia, all using Sephardic rite and liturgy. German Jews began arriving in the middle of the nineteenth century and established Reform temples similar to those that they knew in their native land. Other than an occasional prayer in Hebrew, the language of the service was German, as were the minutes of the record books and, presumably, the casual conversation among members, for whom English was still a foreign tongue. When Eastern European Jews began arriving in America in the 1880s, they transplanted remnants of the *shteibels* (small neighborhood synagogues) that they knew from the pale of settlement. Familiar with a more traditional service than their German co-religionists, their service was in the traditional Hebrew, but the language of the setting was Yiddish.

Although the synagogues of these three groups differed in significant ways, there were common elements. As the counterpart to the Christian church in America, the synagogue was an acceptable form of social organization and of ethnic differentiation. Though Jews would have their fair share of battles with discrimination and antisemitism in America, the general acceptance of Jews and their synagogues was characterized by the famous letter of George Washington to the Jewish congregation of Newport, in which he stated his high regard for "the stock of Abraham" and pledged that the government over which he presided would "give to bigotry no sanction, to persecution no assistance."

All Jews coming to America would tread the fine line between insularity and assimilation. Their place of origin and denominational preferences would determine the precise balance they would seek out. However, notwithstanding the denominational preferences that would soon emerge, all new immigrants to America faced the challenge of moving from class-based societies, in which church groups worked in close collaboration with the government, to the open and pluralistic American setting. Finding a religious lifestyle, both in the synagogue and in one's personal life, that would allow for the successful transmission of Jewish heritage without impeding integration into American society would be a challenge that not only these immigrants would confront but successive generations of American Jews as well.

The immigrant synagogue, based on the European model, was modest in size and scope and rarely enjoyed the services of any trained rabbi. It was generally located close to where the members lived, often in parts of cities that were densely populated and economically disadvantaged. It succeeded in giving new immigrants a place that was comfortable and familiar when everything else in their lives had changed. Certain immigrant synagogues consisted entirely of Jews who had emigrated from the same town or region in Europe. The immigrant synagogue held sway until around 1920, when the United States put quotas on the number of immigrants coming to its shores.

The Ethnic Synagogue

From 1920 to the end of World War II, Jews were moving from their areas of first settlement to new and somewhat more prosperous destinations. In New York, this meant moving from the Lower East Side to uptown Manhattan, Brooklyn, or the Bronx. In Philadelphia, Jews moved from South Philadelphia and downtown Broad Street to Wynnefield, Mount Airy, West Oak Lane, and the greater Northeast. The Jews of Chicago were moving from the West Side to North Lawndale and Albany Park. The social mobility represented by this migration was atypical for ethnic groups. Most other groups did not move to new areas of settlement until the second generation; many immigrant Jews reached the more affluent sections of the cities during their lifetime.

The ethnic synagogue of the second area of settlement was a larger facility than the immigrant synagogue, and it accommodated many more people. In most cases, the synagogue had a rabbi and perhaps even a *chazan* (cantor). The area was densely populated with Jews, who lived among other ethnic enclaves. Many ancillary Jewish institutions sprang up in this neighborhood, including Jewish community centers and fraternal organizations such as B'nai Brith. The synagogue functioned primarily as a house of worship, and its style tended to be fairly resistant to adaptation. Though the members of the congregation became less and less observant over time, often motivated by their drive to raise their social and economic status, they continued to support the synagogue, which represented a more "authentic" mode of practice. The dichotomy between the "elite" religion of the clergy and the "folk" religion of the people emerged at this time. But even as the ethnic synagogue faced competition from other Jewish groups for the loyalty of Jews, it continued to be an important locus for marking major occasions.

The period immediately following the end of World War II represented a period of explosive economic growth and the birth of the American suburbs. Children and grandchildren of immigrant Jews moved out of the apartments of the city into small, single-family dwellings just outside the city limits. For New Yorkers, this meant Long Island, Westchester County, and the bedroom communities of New Jersey. In Philadelphia, Jews moved to Elkins Park, the Mainline, and Penn Valley. Chicago Jews found themselves buying homes in West Rogers Park and Skokie.

This third area of settlement, the suburban frontier, represented a new lifestyle that came to define an entire era of American life. Caught up in the prosperity of the postwar era, families bought cars and televisions, washers and dryers, and spent their weekends tending gardens and mowing lawns. Much of the civic life of the suburban communities revolved around houses of worship, which provided an extensive array of services to young families. Religious affiliation became part of the suburban lifestyle, and Will Herberg's classic book *Protestant, Catholic, Jew* gave explicit sanction to religion as the most common way that Americans sought out fellowship, associated with others who were like themselves, and engaged in the civic affairs of community and nation.[2] Though Herberg found the "religion" of the suburban house of worship dramatically secular and quite distant from the "authentic" expression of each respective faith, he nonetheless identified the church or synagogue as the institution most representative of the suburban frontier.

The Synagogue-Center

For Jews, the suburbs called for a different kind of synagogue from its precursors, one that could best be labeled the synagogue-center.[3] Seeking to build synagogues comparable to their non-Jewish counterparts, the new institutions offered far more than worship services. The synagogue-center took over the task of Jewish education and the ancillary youth and recreational activities young families desired. It also became the site of most of the Jewish community's social and cultural activities. Wealthier congregations built athletic facilities and swimming pools. Some took on the name "Jewish Center." But even the more modest synagogues in the suburbs sought a certain grandness of scale and aesthetic. For Jews moving into areas that were no longer predominantly Jewish, the synagogue served as a status marker that the Jews had arrived. It spoke of the new socioeconomic station the Jews had achieved and were eager to show off to their Gentile neighbors.

In general, affiliation rates in the suburbs are inversely proportional to the density of the Jewish population: the greater the density, the lower the rate. Whereas the average affiliation rate nationally is 40 to 50 percent, in small towns as many as 90 percent of Jewish families affiliate with a synagogue because it is the only Jewish institution in town. The suburbs surrounding major urban centers with large populations might have rates as low as 25 percent because there are many other options for Jewish associations.

But the synagogue-center's role in the life of the Jewish community has not changed much from that of the ethnic synagogue. Most families join in order to provide their children with a Jewish education culminating in a bar or bat mitzvah service and celebration. Because of the high value placed on that rite of passage, it is estimated that some 85 percent of Jewish families will have an affiliation with a synagogue, at least during their children's school years, although they may drop out after their last child completes the ceremony.

The program of the synagogue-center is heavily child-centered. The disinterest of parents in the content of Jewish education is legendary. Even in synagogues that provide services or adult education programs for parents during the hours of Hebrew school, which may be held one to three days per week for up to six hours, the vast majority of parents will drop off their child for school and never even enter the building. For Jewish baby boomers, the memory of being dropped off for the hated Hebrew school is as commonly mentioned as memories about the Beatles or the Vietnam War.

The typical synagogue-center sees more traffic during the week and on Sundays than on *shabbat*. Men's clubs, sisterhoods, committee meetings, and an array of Jewish organizations that rent or use the facility keep the synagogue-center busy throughout the week. The late Friday night service became the service of choice for most who attended at all. It supplanted *shabbat* morning as the main service because of its shorter length and the fact that it competed less with myriad chores and activities that turn up on the Saturday morning calendar. Many Friday nights feature or honor some subgroup of the congregation, which helps guarantee attendance. Often a guest speaker may be invited. On Saturday morning, many of the larger suburban synagogue-centers will have large crowds for a bar or bat mitzvah, but the majority of the attendees will be guests of the celebrating family. When there is no bar or bat mitzvah, the Saturday morning crowd is sparse, with few regular worshipers.

Services are primarily clergy-led. The rabbi serves as the master of ceremonies, and a cantor leads the singing of the prayers. In some synagogues, the cantor is accompanied by a choir or an organ (or both). Depending on the degree of traditionalism of the congregation, there will be English selections that worshipers may be invited to read together or responsively with the rabbi. Because the Hebrew skills of most members are poor, there is little participation during the Hebrew portions of the service. When the Torah is read, it is usually done by one of the clergy or a designated reader paid to offer the service. By virtue of the architecture of most synagogue-centers—which has the *bima*, the ark to house the Torahs, and the clergy lecterns in front—and the top-down conduct of worship, services can be described as "high church." Members in attendance are relative passive recipients of a service prepared and delivered by the clergy.

In the suburban Jewish community of the second half of the twentieth century, the synagogue is the "retail outlet" that can most easily identify the Jews of the community. This is not to say that synagogues see their members on any regular basis. However, the array of services keeps a significant percentage of the identifying Jewish community on its membership roles. Although there is occasional friction between the synagogue world and the world of secular Jewish organizations, the leaders of most synagogues welcome the partnership with the agencies of Jewish life, whose work they value highly. As a result, the synagogue is an important base from which a host of secular Jewish organizations succeed in raising money. In many ways, the synagogue-center is an extension of the civil religion of ethnic identification described in Chapter Two. The lay and clerical leaders are willing representatives and advocates for an agenda that they fully embrace.

Although the rabbi plays a central role in the life of the synagogue, it is rare that the rabbi exerts leadership in the wider community in the way that rabbis like Abba Hillel Silver and Stephen Wise did before World War II. The public leadership role in the postwar era passed to Jews of wealth whose commitment of time and dollars brought them into the top echelons of the Jewish organizational establishment. Many of these same Jews became significant donors to public officials, providing them access and influence that benefited the Jewish community. A new class of professionally trained Jewish communal servants came to direct the day-to-day operations of the organizations, though they serve at the pleasure (and sometimes the whim) of their wealthy lay leaders.

What emerges during this period, then, is a certain division of labor between the secular Jewish organizations and the synagogue world that together meets the needs of the Jewish community. The secular Jewish organizations work on behalf of the welfare and safety of Jews at home and abroad. The state of Israel and endangered Jewish communities around the world are particularly compelling issues, given the "never again" mentality of a generation of Jews so traumatized by the Holocaust. The synagogue tends to the "inner life" of Jews, educating children, offering social and cultural opportunities for members, and providing the setting for the marking of sacred seasons and sacred moments in the lives of the Jews. But because to Jews of the postwar era the ethnic survival agenda is paramount, it is that agenda that is the focus of most of the energy of synagogue members. The agenda of the inner life gets only secondary attention.

Signs of Crisis

Demographic data collected in numerous community surveys and national studies over the past three decades reveal a portrait of a Jewish community whose numbers are dropping and whose lifestyles are increasingly distant from historic patterns of Jewish behavior. In the twenty years between a 1971 national study and the 1990 National Jewish Population Survey (NJPS) conducted by the Council of Jewish Federations, synagogue affiliation dropped from 48 percent to 41 percent. There was also a shift during this time in terms of denominational preference. Conservative Judaism represented 42 percent of affiliated families in 1971; Reform, 33 percent; Orthodox, 11 percent. In 1990, Reform affiliation had become the choice of the largest percentage of affiliated families, 38 percent, with Conservatives at 35 percent and Orthodox at 6 percent.[4]

This trend is generally characterized as growing Jewish "minimalism." It is supported by other data, which show that by any ritual measure (such as keeping kosher, fasting on Yom Kippur, or lighting Chanukah candles), Jews are becoming less and less observant over time. The 1990 NJPS study found that only 17 percent of "core Jews" (meaning those who identified as Jews as opposed to those who may have separated in some way from the Jewish community) lit *shabbat* candles with any regularity. More than a third of these same core Jewish households admitted placing a Christmas tree in their homes during the winter holiday season!

Intermarriage has generally served as the bellwether measurement of Jewish assimilation. If anything, the data in this area have raised even greater concerns than the data regarding synagogue affiliation and observance. Until 1940, only 2 to 3 percent of American Jews married someone who was not born a Jew. In the early 1960s, that rate went to 17 percent. By the 1970s, it was in the 30 percent range. The 1990 NJPS study revealed that the intermarriage rate had surpassed the 50 percent mark. Some sociologists have challenged the way that these numbers were determined. Others have argued that intermarriage may represent a potential gain for Jews, since the partner adhering to the minority religion (Judaism) is likely to have a greater influence on the life patterns of the household. In such a situation, it takes only one Jewish parent to produce Jewish offspring, not necessarily two. Still, studies over two generations indicate that children raised in interfaith families are consistently less tied to Judaism and to the Jewish community than their counterparts from households with two Jewish parents.

From a sociological perspective, the trend toward assimilation is a natural consequence of living in an open, pluralistic society. Over the past decades, Jews have become increasingly accepted in American society. Aside from a few high-profile incidents given wide media coverage, formal and informal manifestations of discrimination against Jews have practically disappeared. Overt acts of antisemitism are condemned by a broad spectrum of Americans as deviant behavior and are prosecuted by authorities as crimes. In such an environment, the need for Jews to maintain insular social and religious arrangements has diminished.

The same phenomenon has affected every other European ethnic group that came to America and has been taken in stride. Except that in the Jewish community there is an obsession with survival. The obsession is motivated by many factors: nostalgia for the religious forms of previous generations, a response to the tragedy of the Holocaust, and inspiration from the reborn Jewish state of Israel, the very existence of which represents an assertive identification with the history and the future of the Jewish people. Against this backdrop, the panic over evidence of American Jewish assimilation is palpable among the people most committed to Jewish continuity. In such an environment of anxiety about the viability of the Jewish community, there is a lot of finger-pointing. The synagogue-center of the suburban frontier gets more than its share of blame for the attrition.

The synagogue-center was created by a generation of Jews enjoying the first fruits of socioeconomic success in America. Although the Jews who helped establish these synagogues were desirous of some continuity in the content of the religious patterns of worship of their childhood, the synagogues they created were far more significant as markers of social status than as institutions of serious Jewish learning, observance, and spirituality. The American Jews who moved to suburbia in the postwar period were flush with both prosperity and options that they could hardly have dreamed of in the Depression years of a decade earlier. The American dream had come within their grasp, and they were more eager than ever to court the approval and acceptance of their Gentile neighbors. These thoughts stirred the passion to build large and beautiful structures that would not only provide religious services but also showcase the material success of member families. Public officials attended the groundbreakings and dedications of new buildings and wings to symbolize the growing importance of the Jewish community in civic life. Congregational leaders and members were more interested in having their rabbi represent their community at interfaith and civic functions than they were in having the rabbi come to their home to discuss their personal commitment to study, worship, and observance. If anything, congregants preferred to keep Jewish practice at arm's length and to experience Judaism vicariously through their rabbis instead of making onerous commitments themselves to religious lifestyles. Such commitments were seen as obstacles to economic aspirations and to full integration into their new communities.

The Critique of the Synagogue-Center

The generation of baby boomers that was raised in these synagogue-centers was quick to reject the values that were implicit in the way that those institutions functioned. They pointed to the hypocrisy of their parents who dropped them off at Hebrew school and attended services only on the High Holydays. They mocked their own bar or bat mitzvah celebrations for being long on ostentation and short on religious significance.

They pointed to their own lack of Hebraic and Judaic competency and used it as an indictment of their Jewish education. To the extent that this generation was raised in an age of great social turmoil and unrest, few carried memories of their synagogues' or of their rabbis' being particularly relevant to the social and political issues that mattered to them.

In a major study of Reform temples conducted by the Union of American Hebrew Congregations in the early 1970s, several themes emerged that represented a critique of the way that the typical synagogue-center functioned.[5] Members reported that their congregations did not provide an adequate ideological basis for them to understand how to be a Jew in contemporary America, nor did they receive enough direct, firsthand experience on how to practice their Judaism on a day-to-day basis. The most often cited shortcoming, however, was the perceived lack of an experience of belonging to a community. People joined their temples to receive one or more of the services it provided, but rarely, if ever, did they feel welcomed or embraced by the people who made up the institution. It was rare for members to report a sense of emotional attachment to or investment in a congregation. The report concluded that Reform temples must reengineer themselves as places where Jews can connect with other Jews in an environment of mutual caring.

Some twenty years later, the Central Conference of American Rabbis, the professional association of the Reform rabbinate, brought together a representative sample of Reform Jews to learn their reactions to the worship experience in their temples. These interviewees complained about the prayerbook, its language, and its content. They admitted having difficulty with the Hebrew passages, and they found the English prayers "banal," "mindless," and "unevocative." Even those who regularly attended worship services complained of uncompelling music, a lack of passion and emotion, and no experience of connecting to other human beings.[6]

A different critique was leveled at the synagogue-centers of the Conservative movement. The very institutions that attracted the lion's share of Jews who moved to the suburbs after World War II were losing both their least committed and their most committed youth. The least committed were more inclined to join Reform temples when they married and started families, drawn by the lower expectations regarding observance and the fewer hours demanded of children attending religious schools. More painful, however, was the fact that many of the most engaged Jewish youth, those who took an active part in the movement's stellar youth movement, United Synagogue Youth (USY), and camp system, Ramah, found it hard to return to the style of worship of their childhood synagogues. In USY and Ramah settings, youth were encouraged to take ownership of the services. Many Conservative youth were more than capable to chant the service, give a *d'var torah* (talk about the biblical portion of the week), and read from the Torah. The energy created at numerous USY conventions and *shabbatot* at Ramah was nowhere to be found in their parents' synagogues, where the service was still conducted from the top down, with the clergy leading and worshipers looking passively on. Many of these youth "superstars" of the Conservative movement found themselves seeking out Orthodox *shuls* and *minyanim* (prayer groups) as they became young adults.

When Jews were geographically concentrated in one area, a synagogue could retain allegiance by providing an array of services and clubs that Jews wanted (such as Hebrew schools, burial societies, men's clubs, and sisterhoods). But as Jews enjoyed growing prosperity and increased mobility, they became less dependent on the synagogue for their sense of place in American society. New multimillion-dollar Jewish community centers offered programs and facilities that the synagogue-centers could hardly match. The leadership role of the rabbi was threatened as well. As noted earlier, a new class of professionally trained Jewish communal workers had emerged that was better informed and closer to the issues that mattered to Jews. Scholars teaching Jewish studies at American universities and colleges supplanted rabbis as the leading experts on Jewish history, culture, and texts. And the majority of Jews coming to the synagogue for High Holyday services or on special occasions had minimal connection to the institution at other times and didn't even know the rabbi or the small nucleus of members who attended services on a regular basis.[7]

In some ways, it is hard to fault rabbis and synagogue leaders with creating institutions that were based on ethnic loyalties and not on religious piety. They were responding to their constituency. Whenever surveys are conducted about the religious beliefs and practices of Americans, Jews score far below their Christian counterparts. In response to the question "Do you believe in God?" 95 to 98 percent of all Americans (to cite a range of results from nearly a dozen surveys) say yes, but Jews generally score between 65 and 75 percent. Some 80 percent of American Christians are members of churches, whereas Jewish affiliation rates run below 50 percent. Between 40 and 50 percent of American Christians claim to attend worship services on a regular basis; only 10 percent of Jews make that claim. In contrast to the tenacity that the Jewish community has displayed in the public square working for the welfare of the Jewish people, the relative weakness of American Jewish religiosity is a striking phenomenon.

In interfaith settings, one can find Christians speaking with ease about their faith in God, their relationship with Jesus, and the power of prayer. Jews squirm and talk about their feelings of connection to other Jews and their identification with Jewish history. This contrasting take on religious identity reflects in part the different emphasis each faith community places on theological matters. But it also reveals the focus in the Jewish community on matters of group survival over matters of the spirit. For much of the twentieth century, this focus on survival met the needs of the American Jewish community on many levels. But as Jews came to enjoy greater material success and social acceptance in America and threats to Jews overseas receded, the apparatus of the Jewish community was increasingly out of sync with the needs of American Jews. Ironically, the American synagogue-center did not know how to respond to Jews who finally wanted to talk about their inner life. The gap became painfully obvious, for when new American Jews finally started to ask religious and spiritual questions, they were fairly convinced that answers were not to be found in synagogues.

Judaism Meets the Counterculture

It was in the late 1960s, amid the turmoil of the antiwar movement and the stirrings of a youth counterculture, that the seeds were planted for a Jewish revival and a new era of Jewish life. The *havurah* movement marked the first organized response by the baby boom generation to a form of synagogue organization that no longer met its needs. Beginning in 1968, in places like Boston, New York, Philadelphia, and Washington, D.C., small fellowships began to spring up, sponsoring Jewish prayer and study. Most of the early *havurot* had strong, charismatic leaders who helped organize these experiments in Jewish religious fellowship. These groups were decidedly antiestablishment and were disinclined to adopt the institutional trappings of conventional synagogues. Jews sought out *havurot* as an alternative to the synagogues that they had grown up in and were loath to join. The *havurot* had no rabbis, no buildings, and only the loosest of governing structures. They attracted students, young adults, and independent spirits who wanted to experiment with Jewish ritual, prayer, and study in ways that were unlikely to happen in most synagogues.

The generation of Jews that created *havurot* felt that the highly centralized, authoritarian, and bureaucratic synagogue-centers created by their parents and in which many of them were raised stifled the initiative and imagination that could make Judaism come alive and be relevant. These Jews turned their backs on the synagogue-centers and instead created small Jewish fellowships that offered a strong sense of community, high levels of participation, an egalitarian and democratic ethic, and a renewed sense of spirituality.[8]

The *havurah* represented an implicit critique by these new American Jews of all that was wrong with the synagogue-center. It was too focused on social conventions and the attempt to blend into the American suburban frontier. Its organization was more corporate than communal, run by boards of directors who talked about marketing and the bottom line. Worship was a performance by professional clergy, reducing the laity to passive, observer roles. One Conservative rabbi, understanding better than most of his colleagues the failure of the synagogue-center to meet the needs of the younger generation, noted: "Our services of readings in fine English, correct musical renditions by professional cantors and choirs, and decorous and dignified rabbis in elegant gowns arouse disdain and contempt in our young people. They want excitement and noise, improvisation and emotion, creativity and sensitivity, informality and spontaneity."[9]

The bible of the *havurah* movement was *The Jewish Catalog*. Written by Michael and Sharon Strassfeld and Richard Siegel—themselves among the founders and leaders of the fledgling *havurah* movement—*The Jewish Catalog* was the Jewish version of *The Whole Earth Catalog*, so symbolic of the countercultural spirit of the 1960s. The book (followed by two sequels), provided an alternative way to understand the basic teachings of the Jewish heritage. More important, it offered guidance and advice on how to create a "do-it-yourself" Judaism. Although rabbis were among the contributors to the volume, the implicit message of *The Jewish Catalog* was, "You don't need a synagogue or a rabbi to experience authentic Judaism."

In the succeeding two decades, the movement grew into a loose confederation of over 250 *havurot* around the country. A national organization was formed in 1980 called the National Havurah Coordinating Committee, and it sponsored an annual summer conference, the Havurah Institute. The movement was staunchly nondenominational (some describe it as "transdenominational"), and the style of each affiliate was as varied as the leadership that emerged in each locale. The total number of Jews represented by the *havurah* movement was negligible as a percentage of the American Jewish community, but the intensity of the affiliation of its members stood in stark contrast to the hundreds of thousands of Jews who held nominal memberships in synagogues across the country.

It was impossible for rabbis, and for the Jewish community in general, not to take notice. Some synagogues tried to create *havurot* within their own institutions, hoping to capture the spirit of fellowship and relationship that seemed to thrive in small, independent *havurot* and that was so lacking in synagogues with hundreds of anonymous members.[10] Rabbis watched with keen interest as *havurot* began to develop their own prayer books and innovative rituals. Some rabbis experimented with the forms and innovations of the *havurot,* with varied success. Most synagogues, run by individuals with vested interests in familiar forms and customs, were resistant to wholesale change.

The *havurah* was no panacea to the spiritual lethargy of the American Jewish community. As the young pioneers of *havurot* grew older and married, they found that the *havurah* could not always meet their needs. Teachers and schools were needed to train their children. Rabbis were sought out for marriages and other life-cycle needs. Many *havurot* had trouble sustaining the high levels of energy of their early years as founding personalities moved on, drawn by personal and professional opportunities. The very lack of institutional structure that was so attractive to the first generation of the *havurot* proved to be a built-in weakness as well.

Notwithstanding some of the attrition that was inevitable in the *havurah* movement as members aged, the spirit that the movement engendered had a profound effect on the Jewish community. New institutions sprang up out of a desire to create alternatives in the Jewish community. Many of these were founded and led by individuals of the generation that had challenged the conventions of American society. They were willing to explore ways to redefine how Judaism could be observed and practiced in an age that valued egalitarianism over authority, substance over form, and community over denominational labels.

Other alternative interpretations of Judaism challenged the synagogue's monopoly on the way Jews experienced their religious lives. A spate of books offering a feminist interpretation of Judaism spawned women's prayer and spirituality groups throughout the country. Jewish feminists, challenging the lack of egalitarianism in Jewish religious practice, offered up radical reinterpretations of the entire Jewish tradition. A growing assertiveness in the homosexual community led to the founding of dozens of gay and lesbian synagogues to meet the needs of that particular constituency.

By the late 1970s, the label "Jewish Renewal" came to be applied to the array of new organizations, people, and prayer groups spawned by the spirit of the *havurah* movement. In 1978, B'nai Or (later renamed P'nai Or, a change from "children of light" to "faces of light") was founded by Rabbi Zalman Schachter-Shalomi in Philadelphia to train teachers and rabbis to serve the loosely defined Jewish Renewal community. Soon Reb

Zalman, as he was known, began offering private rabbinical ordination to individuals whom he felt could serve the Jewish community in the renewal mode. In the 1990s, a series of institutions and projects associated with Jewish Renewal came together under an organizational umbrella called Aleph, the Alliance for Jewish Renewal.

In the 1980s and 1990s, retreat centers sprang up around the country, the best known being Elat Chayim in upstate New York. Elat Chayim, like many other such centers, attracted thousands of Jews wishing to deepen their Jewish knowledge and explore a spiritually compelling brand of Judaism through short-term intensive workshops and courses.[11]

By the mid-1990s, tens of thousands of Jews had been exposed to a new style of Jewish study, prayer, and living through the conferences, retreats, classes, and prayer groups in this network of alternative institutions. Even the more established Jewish community caught the spirit. The Center for Jewish Learning and Leadership (CLAL), founded in 1974 by a progressive Orthodox rabbi named Irving Greenberg, brought together an interdenominational faculty that deepened the Judaic knowledge of thousands of leaders in the federation leadership structure. The Wexner Heritage Program targeted young Jewish leaders for a similar type of intensive Jewish study. The United Jewish Appeal, picking up on the burgeoning interest in programs with strong Jewish content, began to feature young, charismatic teachers of Judaism in programs for its young leadership divisions.

Just as the synagogue had so long programmed for the public agenda of the Jewish community, the secular Jewish world was beginning to program for the inner life of American Jews. The impact of the baby boom generation was beginning to be felt. Recognizing the weakening pull of the Holocaust-and-Israel approach to Jewish life, the central funding arm of the Jewish community took up the cause of Jewish continuity, and it was all about study, prayer, and intensified Jewish living. To the consternation of many pulpit rabbis, young adults that they could not attract to their synagogues were attending classes and workshops on Judaism sponsored by self-described secular Jewish organizations. The institutional lines that had long defined the American Jewish community were shifting. It was these developments that formed the context for the hundreds of people who stood, arm in arm, responding to the singing of Debbie Friedman in the improbable setting of a CJF General Assembly in 1995.

o

There is a wide cultural chasm between the Jews who retreat to New Age–inspired Elat Chayim and the yuppie Jews who are the emerging leaders of the federation world. Yet these Jews were part of the same generation, and the approach to Judaism that attracted them represented a style that was decidedly different from that of conventional synagogues. It was participatory and spontaneous. It encouraged a vigorous yet loving challenge of the dictates of Jewish tradition. It was lyrical, musical, and poetic. It engendered serious study. It put a premium on spirituality.

But the vast majority of these Jews returned to their home communities and found their enthusiasm and energy quickly extinguished. Their most regular contact with Jewish life was through the synagogues of the Reform, Conservative, and Orthodox movements, where it proved difficult to change the styles that were so deeply ingrained within these institutions. The generation of Jews who came of age in the sixties and seventies, the baby boomers, was a generation that was ready to dance in the aisles; their synagogues offered them responsive readings.

A New Paradigm

Can the American synagogue transform itself to address the spiritual needs and interests of new American Jews? The answer is a resounding yes, but it won't be quick and it won't be easy. This book suggests a new paradigm for the American synagogue that I call the "synagogue-community."[12] The synagogue-community is a paradigm that is just now beginning to emerge as synagogue-centers realize that time is passing them by. The failure of synagogue-centers to evolve into synagogue-communities will have dire consequences, not only for those institutions but also for the American Jewish community as a whole as new American Jews find places outside of the Jewish community to fulfill their spiritual needs. This exodus of new American Jews from the Jewish community is already taking place. But it needn't be that way.

The synagogue-community marks a fourth phase in the evolution of the American synagogue. It represents a synthesis of two competing models of the past few decades—the synagogue-center and the *havurah*. The synagogue-community captures the spirit of the *havurah* in its decidedly low-church style with an emphasis on participation, informality, contemporary music, and spontaneity. However, recognizing the shortcomings of the *havurah*, it offers much more structure. Synagogue-communities may have rabbis, cantors, and professional educators. They may have their own building and school, which in turn require substantial dues collection and ancillary fundraising. But all of this is done in the service of a community that is very much in tune with the eight generational themes set forth in Chapter Two.

If the model strikes the Jewish community as new and unprecedented, it shouldn't. The Christian community, which spends a lot more time and resources trying to understand its constituency and shaping institutions that respond to it, has been working on counterpart models for years. First, noting the decline of mainline Protestant churches and the rise of evangelical churches over the past few decades, it became clear that Christian baby boomers would respond enthusiastically to churches that made high demands on their time and energy. They were leaving churches that catered to a permissive and relativistic ethic and joining churches that offered clear creedal formulations and expected congregants to abide by a certain code of conduct.[13] Second, Christian boomers longed to find in churches a sense of community in an increasingly mobile and transient world. They wanted their ministers to offer them inspiration and spiritual guidance.[14] Third and finally, the most successful of the new-paradigm churches of this generation moved away from pews, robed clergy, stained-glass windows, and organs. They addressed the "hope deficit" that so many Americans are experiencing today. And they understood that in an age of consumerism, the one thing that money can't buy but people long for is a sense of religious passion and ecstasy.[15]

The synagogue-community must strive to do all of these things because new American Jews are asking for precisely the kinds of things expressed by their Christian counterparts. We are, after all, products of the same generation and the same culture. There was a time when Jews were sufficiently differentiated from non-Jews in American society so that what held for one group did not necessarily hold for the other. That day is long past. We must, however, cast the characteristics of the synagogue-community into a Jewish key. The synagogue-community will be distinguished by its functioning in four areas: organizational culture, spiritual leadership, articulation of mission, and framing of serious Judaism.

Organizational Culture

The organizational culture of any institution affects everything that happens in it. It is the hardest thing to establish and the hardest to change. The synagogue-community will succeed in attracting new American Jews only to the extent that it reflects the eight generational themes set out in Chapter Two. Decision making has to be inclusive and democratic. The atmosphere must be casual and fun. Education must be maximally interactive and provide practical guidance for daily living. Worship needs to speak to the heart and not shy away from demonstrative expressions of joy and celebration. Ritual roles and organizational leadership must be as egalitarian as religious principles allow and must not be accorded on the basis of wealth alone. No effort should be spared in creating opportunities for small-group and one-on-one interactions to counteract the anonymity of large institutions. Finally, mechanisms must be instituted to invite the participation of members at whatever level they deem appropriate, be it in religious services, on committees, or in outreach to others.

Spiritual Leadership

Any system that does not permit strong leadership to emerge can never reach its full potential.[16] This is as true of synagogues as of any other setting. The corporate organizational model that governs synagogues is dysfunctional. The very lay leaders who see to it that the rabbi fulfills his or her contractual obligations and dutifully reports to the board are the first ones to be impoverished, because they regard their rabbi not as a spiritual leader but as an employee. Of course, fiduciary responsibilities cannot be overlooked, but those and many other managerial issues can be dealt with creatively. The more important point here is that some individual must provide vision, inspiration, teaching, and guidance. In most synagogues, this should be the rabbi. If the rabbi is true to the principle of the synagogue-community's organizational culture, he or she will be adept at empowering others to emerge as leaders in the system as well. The rabbi, as leader, will be the chief articulator of the community's mission and a catalyst for maximizing the creativity of every member of the congregation. By virtue of his or her standing in the community, the rabbi will also give license to do the hard things that have to be done, be it taking a controversial action on an issue of social conscience or standing up for a principle that everyone else in the community is prepared to abandon.

Articulation of Mission

The synagogue-community must state what it stands for. It cannot be all things to all people. If it tries to be, it will be nothing at all. Ideally on the one hand, if the institution seeks to be consistent with the principles of its organizational culture, it may enlist members of the community to help draft the mission statement of the synagogue-community. On the other hand, if the spiritual leadership model of the rabbi is such that he or she feels it important to articulate a mission for the community, the statement may emerge that way. The mission statement should express the approach that the community takes to the basic tenets of Judaism, such as God, Torah, and Israel. It should articulate how it seeks to serve its own membership as well as the world at large. Finally, it should be clear about what it expects of individuals who want to join the community. Although synagogue-communities will differ in how they promulgate and enforce the tenets of their particular mission statement, all should hold up that statement to members as the ideal to strive for. Synagogue programs should seek to advance one or more of the principles of the mission statement. Finally, the mission statement should serve as a screening device that will help people decide whether this is a community they wish to join.

Framing of Serious Judaism

Perhaps the most damning indictment of American Judaism on the part of new American Jews is that it is trite, superficial, and irrelevant. Not a few Jewish boomers hold just such a view. What is so alarming about the indictment is that there is so much evidence that Judaism provides an extraordinary framework for encountering the modern world, with a heritage that is wise, deep, and directly applicable to the challenges that Jews face today. The synagogue-community has got to deliver this kind of Judaism. It will not come in catchy sound bites, nor will it be mastered over tea on sisterhood sabbath. It will require time, study, and discipline. If the synagogue-community demands this kind of commitment, Jews will rise to the occasion. If most Jews aren't interested, that is fine for now. When the Jews on the sidelines see the impact that full engagement with the Jewish tradition has on their friends and colleagues, they will gravitate to the synagogue-community because there are so few other places in America to find spiritual grounding in a tradition that goes back thousands of years. This is the kind of serious Judaism that will be the hallmark of the synagogue-community and has the potential to bring about a renaissance in American Judaism.

o

At this point, you may be crying out, "Show me the money!" Is this a dream, or does this synagogue-community exist? The answer to both questions is yes. Although the American Jewish community still has a long way to go to transition from the synagogue-center model to the new-paradigm synagogue-community, what follows are profiles of four synagogues that are on the cutting edge, putting this new paradigm into practice. The spiritual autobiographies of various members of these four synagogues testify to the ability of these congregations to attract new American Jews to their ranks. The profiles demonstrate not only that the paradigm can work but also that it knows no denominational boundaries.

PART TWO

A REFORM CONGREGATION WRESTLING WITH GOD

4

NATE'S PATH

A LETTER HAS COME in the mail from the rabbi asking Nate Grad if he would like to contribute an essay about his "return" to Judaism. Nate can't find the letter actually, doesn't remember where he's put it, and yet the question it has posed stays with him, and he keeps thinking about it. Has he returned? True, on most Saturday mornings, he sets his alarm and heads up to Sudbury, the next town north, where "his" synagogue—Beth El ("House of God"), Larry Kushner, Rabbi—is located. He knows not to bother to have breakfast—he can grab one of the bagels they've put out for the congregants, a cup of coffee, some weeks even juice. The first time he ever came here—he was with his son David—he'd been startled not to see a service happening. Instead a group of people were sitting around a large square table in the sanctuary, lit by a wall of clear glass windows, picking over some passages of that week's "portion"—sometimes arguing about it, sometimes reflecting on personal meaning. To Nate, it was like a kind of dream-synagogue, where, if the rabbi said something, you could argue with him. And then a service started later. People threw candy at a new bride and groom who were called to the Torah. When a new baby was brought up, people stood in all parts of the room to propose blessings: "May she have a beautiful face." "May she be

Nate Grad is the fictional stand-in for Alan Feldman, a poet whose work has appeared in the *Atlantic Monthly,* the *New Yorker,* and many other publications. Feldman chairs the English Department at Framingham State College in Massachusetts and for many years has taught advanced creative writing at the Radcliffe Seminars. Feldman says that writing about Nate seems to help him stand outside himself, enabling him to write a clearer version of his own character and experience.

kind." What struck Nate was the input. You could be a spectator, or you could put in your two cents' worth. You could share your thoughts.

So, Nate reflected, some old bread he'd cast on the waters was floating back to him tenfold. Years earlier, he'd taught the rabbi's daughter, Noa, at the local college, and then she'd gone off to Brown. A week before he'd first gone to Beth El, when Davy kept asking, "Did you call the rabbi yet?" Nate had called the Kushners and actually spoken to the rabbi's wife, Karen. "This isn't Harold Kushner's house, by the way. It's *Larry* Kushner." Nate couldn't believe it. It was like a script. Nate recalled that Noa had once told him that her father, a rabbi who wrote books, was always being confused with another local rabbi, Harold Kushner, who also wrote books, best-sellers. So when strangers called, the first thing these Kushners always said was that this wasn't Harold Kushner's house.

"No, I want Larry Kushner," Nate said. "I was once Noa's teacher. Contemporary European and American Literature. Years ago. How is Noa?"

Noa, it turned out, had taken a year off to travel around the world before entering rabbinical school. Nate couldn't quite imagine her quoting from Milan Kundera and John Berger and Marguerite Duras in her future sermons. He'd probably taught her all the wrong things. Nate couldn't tell whether Karen was just being polite, but she did seem to remember that her daughter had enjoyed the course.

Larry had a high and, to Nate's ear, distinctly un-rabbinic voice. It was more the shrill voice of a comedian. So far, so good. "Look," Nate explained to Larry. "My wife was raised a socialist, and I was over-parochialized. Neither one of us has had anything to do with a synagogue. We don't like them. But our son, who's almost sixteen and has fairly serious learning disabilities—I mean, it's been hard enough to get him to learn to read English—has told us he's decided he wants to become a bar mitzvah. So I was wondering if, maybe, I could bring him by sometime, maybe even on a Thursday, and he could be called to the Torah. I mean, that's essentially what the ceremony is, right?"

For years now, Nate had been telling people how Larry had answered him. Sure, if Nate wanted to bring him by, that was fine. But don't send out any invitations. Larry Kushner's synagogue wasn't for rent. To have a real bar mitzvah there was a whole lot involved. Well, Nate had said, he and Carolyn didn't really want to get involved. His wife was an artist. He was a teacher of literature and a poet. He had enough of a spiritual life reading *Anna Karenina*.

"Listen, can I tell you something?" Nate's rendition of Larry saying this gave the question a sort of Talmudic inflection, that rising melody of the smart-assed Jewish question, but the truth was Larry had probably said what he'd said forcibly. He was fisher of men, yes, but he made use, too, of a sort of Zen shock tactic. "This isn't about your son. This is about you. This is *your* coming of age."

Well, that was sensible, Nate remembered thinking. It answered the absurdity he'd grown up with, the notion that you became a man on the day of your bar mitzvah. Hah. Maybe he'd reached puberty by then, but his erection was just about the only part of him (except maybe his vocabulary) that might have been considered grown up. But now, yes, his own coming of age. That made sense. He was in that in-between generation, with a father nearing eighty and a son growing up. The responsible one. Why, he was even a department chair. And he figured he earned enough money to pay for the party Davy wanted. Yes, Nate remembered thinking, maybe this bar mitzvah was about confirming his adulthood, even if his own had not been.

Nate broke the news to David. "He says we can't just bring you by. You've got to learn enough Hebrew to read three verses in the Torah. You've got to be in a class. *We've* got to be in a class. It's a whole big deal."

"Fine," said David. Having badgered Nate to call, the boy had been standing in the kitchen waiting for Nate to get off the phone. He repeated what he'd often said before, that the idea had come to him because of the twentieth wedding anniversary celebration Nate and Carolyn had planned. Nate was going to read his poems; Carolyn was going to have an art show; even his sister, Elizabeth, was going to fly in from the University of Chicago and perform some of her songs. But what was Davy supposed to do? Sure, he'd be there, but what, exactly, was going to be his part? No, he wanted some occasion of his own, a ceremony where he could stand up in front of all his friends and family so they could see he was growing up. "It's not even the presents, really, Dad. I swear. I mean, most kids do it just for that. Sure, I'd like presents, but that's not the main thing for me."

And that proved to be true, too. With amazing consistency, David worked night after night after dinner studying the Hebrew alphabet with Nate. Nate wrote a poem about it:

> Why does he want to learn Hebrew anyway,
> When no one's a believer around here, and even ordinary English
> Comes out scrambled? And why does he lean against me
> Like a much younger child when we sit side by side in the booth?
> (He's sixteen, has a faint mustache, and food stuck in his braces.)
> And what would he hear if I told him what they told us to say
> At the learning disabilities conference, that I wish

He didn't have to struggle so hard, but that I love him?
I am trying to read each word backward, the way he does,
Putting the squiggles together into sounds, for his sake, though
it's not easy.
They didn't say so at the conference, but this must be
One of the features reserved for the next world:
That with the boy leaning against him, the father can enter the
son's mind,
The swarm of letters massing toward some revelation,
And the son can sit above himself like his own father,
The whole field clear for the first time,
So the son thinks, *At last, everything is where I can find it,*
And it's all happening as easily as tadpoles turn into frogs

Somehow reading in the wrong direction seemed not as difficult for
David as Nate had feared. Well, the boy was motivated. And the bar mitzvah had been terrific, not a dry eye in the house. Nate and Carolyn had
even enjoyed the classes for parents and the weekend away with the rabbi
and the other families whose children were becoming bar and bat mitzvah that same year.

And a little child shall lead thee, Nate thinks, not sure what scripture
that's from, Jewish or Christian. *And he shall be called emperor, mighty
counselor, king of kings, Almighty God.* Nate's misquoting from Han-
del's *Messiah?* Anyway, as of that day, it was impossible to think of Davy
as merely a child. He had stood up there beaming so fiercely, so eagerly
delivering the speech Nate had managed to get him to write by taking dic-
tation at the computer. It was all stuff Davy had really said, but it sounded
so grown up when he read it slowly and distinctly to all those people:

> Just as Moses has to let the Israelites take responsibility for living in-
> dependently, my parents have had to recognize my maturity as I've
> grown up. I've had to assume responsibility for daily chores and take
> responsibility for my own money as I grow up. I've also had to
> take responsibility to stand up for myself and say what I believe in,
> and let my emotions flow through me so other people can know what
> I feel. I've had to be responsible for following up on daily friendship
> with companions I get along with. In the near future, I will be re-
> sponsible for driving a car, filling out my income tax, moving out,
> being independent, living on a boat, in a house, or in a cabin—I'm not
> sure where. But I know I'll be there without my parents.

The Israelites need to follow up on the rules they have been given. I do too. I must be honest and polite to each person who crosses my path. I must remember cleanliness—just as the Israelites must remember to keep themselves pure—I must never run away from reality, or be unkind or disrespectful to others. Those laws my parents gave me are passed on to me, and will be carried through the life that I live. As I begin to set off on my own, I would like my parents to say to me: Follow in the footsteps we have set down for you. And I would like to say to them that I can be trusted in all the years in my future to keep my priorities straight and to keep my life flowing along the right path.

The whole idea of comparing the Israelites before Moses' death to himself may have been suggested by Lorel, the cantor, but it was a concept Davy absolutely understood. This declaration of maturity was in back of the whole effort. Nate had been very moved, almost unable to deliver his own blessing of Davy aloud without becoming choked with tears.

The real surprise had come later, though. Nate didn't think it would be seemly to drop synagogue membership right after the bar mitzvah. But neither did he think he'd start going regularly again, the way he did when he was a boy. The truth was, though, Davy's bar mitzvah had led Nate to a recognition of his own state of belief. That is, he *did* believe. Or rather he believed that his version of belief was probably what real belief felt like. In part, of course, it came from a recognition of powerlessness. Just try raising a child who will never read beyond the fifth-grade level and entrusting such a child to the world, as Davy was asserting they would have to. That would be a leap of faith. But somehow Davy's bar mitzvah had made Nate recognize that he had that faith. And there was more, also from Davy. Nate had always thought one's humanity came from one's imputed intelligence. Davy, over long years, had taught him that one's humanity came from—well, from one's humanity. That a soul was something everyone had, however eloquently or simply that soul might speak to others.

Yes, Nate believed. Oh sure, "belief" felt like a mere construct too. Nate knew all about the existential vision of the world's absurdity—that's the stuff he talked to Noa about in his class years back—but he discovered he also knew how the world was infused with the invisible and often seemingly ineffectual but utterly transforming presence of God manifesting itself through human hands and words, like Davy's speech, for one. A construct, sure. But once Nate caught it (or found it), it seemed to stay with him. He thought of something Larry had written about asking a high school girl whether she thought she had a self. She thought about it and said that yes, of course she did. And he then asked her if she could prove she had a self. "Oh," she said. "I see what you mean." So, yes, God was the self of the world—as there, or not there, as a self was in a person. Nate, as it happened, felt quite palpably that he had a self, one that was still learning too, learning even from his own son, and was equally certain that the world had such a self as well, just as tortured and complicated as Nate's own, to be sure. More so a few billion times, as it happened.

So Nate has become a Jew who goes to synagogue, not that he'd ever stopped considering himself a Jew. Even Carolyn, bred a socialist, who thinks religion mainly separates people—even she acknowledged her ethnic roots and is sometimes interested in what can be learned when the two of them attend together. And Nate has recognized himself as a believing person. Pasternak once said that he put religious ideas into *Doctor Zhivago* the way one puts stoves into a house, to warm it up. But for Nate, it is as though only with these ideas can he say more about the world than he's said up to this moment.

So *has* he "returned"? he wonders, each time he tries to get to the bagels on Saturday morning. A few faces he recognizes and he wishes them *shabbat shalom*. But mainly he still feels on the edge of the crowd. Even his belief, he suspects, makes him odd. He doesn't seem to have earned it at all, so maybe it's specious? And anyway, it's too personal to speak about even in a laid-back, liberal place like this.

Last year, Larry was teaching Hebrew grammar and the class was picking through one or two sentences of the original Torah each week. How much there was to think about! Something new every week! And this year they've been looking at a few sentences of Rashi. Nate loses patience with Rashi, who seems so literal-minded. But then there is his remark about lentils, how the "red red" Esau gulped down (in exchange for his birthright) was actually a funeral meal because lentils are round and round foods are eaten at a feast of mourning because, said Rashi, mourning comes into our lives in a cycle.

So Nate behaves exactly as he did before, except that he has added this weekly assignation. He shows up at synagogue Saturday mornings. He leaves before the singing service. The class is what he wants, and the little division between weeks, a pause to think in the largest way, and then back to the as-usual. He's certain it won't make him a better man. He was a good enough man before. He's certain he'll be no less afraid to die. Every third thought he has—he's paraphrasing the new Philip Roth novel, which quoted Shakespeare in its epigraph—is about death anyway. No different now. But suddenly the universe, which was always filled with darkness, is also filled with light, an essential, organizing ingredient, even though he can't put his hand on it. And all the members of his wonderful, newfound synagogue, as well as the rabbi, particularly the rabbi, are messengers, the angels walking up from earth to heaven and back down again, just to show Nate how this can happen even in ordinary life. And they have nothing to do with the cringing, frequently hypocritical Jews of his childhood temple and the sententious rabbi who spoke to them so eloquently and never allowed questions. Though of course they're just the same sorts of human beings. Surely it is Nate who has changed. He sees the faltering holiness in others, of which normal hypocrisy is just a part. No matter what others might think, for Nate, Larry, with his shrill voice and his jokes, is a real messenger. And Nate has become a messenger too. And everything he does now, everything he writes too, has somehow become the message.

So Nate continues to write his own individual Torah, just as he would have anyway if he'd remained a completely secular Jew. It was all planned, he is sure, somewhere in his DNA perhaps, or perhaps in God's.

Larry once said that the best thing he ever wrote, which no one paid attention to, was about how it's impossible to think about slavery and be sad without thinking about the Exodus and rejoicing and how it's impossible to think about the Promised Land without thinking of the Diaspora and how it's impossible to think of the Holocaust without thinking, too, of the creation of the state of Israel and on and on. When we see all that God has in store for us, we move beyond tragedy or comedy into pure mirthless, tearless vision. Larry wonders—and Nate wonders—why that didn't just explain everything to everyone, why in fact Nate or Larry or anyone should ever have to write another word. It's probably that those who see this vision don't need to be told and those who can't see it can't be told.

It could be that Nate's failure to reconnect with Judaism until his older child—who received no bat mitzvah or Jewish education—was already off to college is a terrible loss; it could be that, via his younger child, Davy, this failure, and Nate's regret, led to an amazing redemption. In truth, all of that is true, Nate realizes. So when he thinks of his son, he neither rejoices nor grieves—just the way he thinks God must think about the world.

5

CONGREGATION BETH EL
SUDBURY, MASSACHUSETTS

IT IS NOT UNUSUAL for parents to have their first encounter with a synagogue as an adult when one of their children approaches the age for a bar or bat mitzvah. Typically, the synagogue is happy to enroll the new family as members. Although the synagogue's expectations of both student and parents will vary widely, it is rare that the three- to five-year stint as synagogue members affects the family so deeply that it results in a change of well-established patterns of living that never included much in the way of Jewish learning, practice, or affiliation.

Nate Grad was not so different from thousands of fathers like him before. Perhaps a bit more educated than the average. Certainly more leery and cynical, as is the wont of an academic. Which makes it all the more telling that Nate was available to be dramatically affected by his encounter with Congregation Beth El and its rabbi, Larry Kushner. At a time when many Jewish leaders are willing to write off growing numbers of alienated and disaffected Jews, it is worth paying attention to the institutions that seem to know how to draw such Jews into their respective universes.

○

Congregation Beth El's origins were similar to those of many congregations in the suburbs surrounding major metropolitan areas.[1] Located twenty-five miles west of Boston, the communities around Sudbury, Massachusetts, attracted families seeking more affordable housing and more land even as many commuted to the urban center for their jobs. In 1962, twenty-three families organized the first Jewish congregation in the area under the name Congregation Beth El.

The local Methodist church provided Beth El with its first home, and a local stockbroker, Albert Yanow, served as part-time rabbi for the congregation's first two years. As the congregation began to grow, Rabbi David Neiman, a local Bible professor, was retained to provide religious leadership to the fledgling group. By 1968, the families of Beth El had bought a piece of property in the heart of Sudbury and in another two years had raised enough money to construct its own building.

The building represented a coming of age for the congregation, which now served over one hundred member households. Having a permanent home precipitated two major decisions—to affiliate with a national denomination and to hire a full-time rabbi. As the only Jewish congregation in the area, its members came from a wide range of beliefs and practices. There were advocates for affiliation with each of the four denominations of American Jewish life, though the Reform option had the greatest support. A compromise was struck: Beth El would affiliate with the Reform movement's Union of American Hebrew Congregations (UAHC), with the proviso that the congregation would sponsor *shabbat* morning worship as well as Friday night services, it would maintain a kosher kitchen, and it would observe the second day of Rosh Hashanah. All three of these practices were more traditional than the norm in Reform congregations.

In the same year as the affiliation issue was decided, 1971, Rabbi Lawrence Kushner was hired as the congregation's first full-time rabbi. Only twenty-eight years old, he had served as the rabbinic fellow in residence at Congregation Solel in Highland Park, Illinois, under Rabbi Arnold Jacob Wolf, one of the most innovative rabbis in the Reform movement. Kushner wasted no time bringing new ideas and a fresh spirit to Beth El. His penchant for the mystical was conveyed by the introduction during worship of *niggunim*, wordless melodies in the tradition of the Hasidim. He organized retreats in remote settings away from the distractions of home and chores to give families the full experience of *shabbat*. His skills as a teacher and storyteller quickly engaged the adults and children of the young congregation.

Empowerment

Rabbi Kushner was committed to having congregants play a significant role in the religious life of the community. This led to the creation of a variety of new forms and expressions over the years. The Ritual Committee created its own supplement to the High Holyday *machzor* (prayer book). A Friday night service was created that wove together a sacred meal, music, readings, and worship. Different members brought to the congregation melodies and musical contributions that they had learned in summer camp or at other congregations. These members would often share their talents with the congregation in the context of a worship service. Beyond the aesthetic contribution, it began to send the message that the *bima* (ritual center stage in a sanctuary) was not the exclusive province of professional clergy.

Not everyone was thrilled with the innovations of the new rabbi. In particular, as Kushner pushed for higher levels of individual involvement, some members balked. Three years after his arrival, Kushner won renewal of his contract by a single vote. In the shakeout over the direction of the growing congregation, the dissenters left to form a second temple in Sudbury. But as is so often the case after a controversy, the departure of the most strident dissenters led to a period of unparalleled creativity and a project that would bring Beth El national attention.

The spirit that Larry Kushner brought to Beth El, especially in the realm of prayer and devotion, was hardly the kind of worship service that was standard in the Reform movement. Thus it was no surprise that the members found the Union Prayer Book, the UAHC-issued standard, wanting in many respects. A much better reflection of the spiritual impulses of the community were the prayer books that bar and bat mitzvah families would occasionally customize for their service. Larry Kushner's great interest in prayer led to his teaching of a course on liturgy for several years. Members of the class, challenged by the course and noting the gap between the forms of prayer that they desired and the Union Prayer Book, decided to create their own prayer book. Ironically, although Kushner's class and the style of worship that he introduced to Beth El gave impetus to the creation of this prayer book committee, it was hardly his idea. In fact, Kushner had proposed that the congregation adopt the traditional prayer book of David de Sola Pool, a book that is mostly used in Orthodox synagogues. The members of Beth El, however, had other ideas.

Thirty of them began work on the new prayer book, which eventually was published in 1975 under the title *Vetaher Libenu* ("Purify Our Hearts"), edited by Nancy and Peter Gossels. Five years later, *Vetaher Libenu II* was issued. Edited by Nancy Gossels and Joan Kaye, it was more notable than its predecessor in one significant way. The editorial committee had decided that the exclusive male imagery used to describe God in the traditional liturgy was unacceptable. It led, they felt, to a form of idolatry. Their solution was to retain the traditional Hebrew language, though they added the names of the four matriarchs to the three patriarchs in the *Amidah* (standing prayer). At the same time, the English translation alternated the pronouns *He* and *She* when referring to God. It also avoided the use of the medieval metaphor of God as King. The standard translation of the blessing formula was changed from "Blessed art Thou, Lord our God, King of the Universe" to "Holy One of Blessing, Your Presence fills Creation."

The new prayer book was hailed as the first nonsexist prayer book in Jewish history. Beth El's office fielded requests from all over the world for copies of the privately printed book. Of course *Vetaher Libenu II* also became the *siddur* (prayer book) for the congregation. But perhaps the most remarkable part of the creation of the prayer book was the fact that the rabbi was not part of the committee that created it.

o

The Right Place

When my husband, Peter, and I were "temple-shopping" seventeen years ago, we happened to attend High Holyday services at Congregation Beth El. There we heard for the first time the words of a young, dynamic rabbi and prayed from a loose-leaf *machzor* that had been written by members of the congregation. We knew we had come to the right place.

It was a far cry from the source of my own Jewish roots: a small, blue-collar mill town in northeastern Connecticut where a handful of Jews maintained an Orthodox *shul* yet could afford neither a rabbi nor a religious school. I came to Beth El with no formal Jewish education but with a deep sense of Jewish identity, which I attribute with love to my parents.

Though I blush to admit it, my knowledge of Judaism was so minimal that during one of my first encounters with Rabbi Kushner, I interrupted a discourse on the Torah to ask him what exactly the Torah was. (He teased me about that for a long time!)

I'm not sure whether it was because of the ingenuousness of that question or some deeper, mystical insight, but some time later the rabbi suggested that I consider joining the Ritual Committee. I was stunned. Never mind that I had never studied Torah or that I couldn't tell an *aleph* from a *bet;* I knew almost nothing about a prayer service. (I would soon learn that at Beth El there are no prerequisites, or even limits, to what you may do as long as you are willing to study, to learn, and to labor to reach your goal.)

In the early spring of 1980, a committee that had been working for nine months to revise and expand the first edition of our *shabbat siddur* met and listened to coeditor Joan Kaye read an article that suggested that using masculine metaphors alone to describe God was idolatrous. The same committee had earlier rejected a proposal to do an entirely nonsexist *siddur* because it seemed more politically fashionable than theologically sound at the time. Now came the realization that such exclusive use of male imagery was unacceptable on theological grounds!

By evening's end, Joan, Peter, and I, along with committee members Bill Adelson, Mark Bloomberg, Adeane Bregman, Aleta Cane, and Gerry Dicker, agreed that we would have to re-edit the entire *siddur.* Not only would we have to change not only the masculine and feudal epithets for God, but we would also have to find language that would reestablish the dignity of women and have meaning for our children as well. It was an overwhelming and frightening moment. But it was also exhilarating. For where else but at Beth El could a group of laypeople assume such an awesome responsibility? We had made a momentous decision without congregational or rabbinic approval. Yet in our hearts, we had made the only decision we could make.

The birth of *Vetaher Libenu II* six months later turned out to be a historic event: the first nonsexist *siddur* ever published. It received publicity all over the country. Its appearance was even noted on the front page of the *Wall Street Journal!* Most important, the congregation welcomed it warmly. Eight years later, *Vetaher Libenu* is in its sixth printing, and thousands of copies have been sold worldwide to Christians as well as Jews.

For Beth El is the kind of place where such growth is possible, a place that challenges our minds and hearts while it encourages, nurtures, and supports great dreams of daring.

It is indeed the right place.

[Nancy Gossels's recollection excerpted from *The First Twenty-Five Years: Congregation Beth El of the Sudbury River Valley,* Congregation Beth El, p. 68.]

o

Even though Larry Kushner to this day thinks that the *Vetaher Libenu* writers might have done even better if they'd had extensive exposure to more traditional prayer books, he is staunchly proud of what his members created. He deliberately kept his distance from the prayer book projects. When presented with drafts of sections that included questions of taking one direction or the other, he would offer his opinion and then say, "Whatever you do will be fine."

This is perhaps the best example of what Larry Kushner brought to Beth El: empowerment of his congregants. Kushner's rabbinate has been characterized by one central organizing principle: the job of a rabbi is to teach the members of the congregation how to run their congregation without rabbinic help. The rabbi must be sufficiently restrained so that the members have the room to experiment, fail, learn, and·grow. The rabbi has to resist the temptation of regarding the congregation as a personal possession or fiefdom. Kushner has gone so far as to leave congregational committee meetings early so as to take his opinion out of the mix.

"Larry," as nearly everyone calls him, was raised in a classical Reform temple, Beth El of Detroit. He was turned off by what he perceived as a congregation that was lacking in serious religious content, driven by people seeking social status and pretentious in the extreme. The very architecture of the large, cathedral-like temple tended to constrain the human quality of relationships within that space.

Kushner credits his mentor, Arnold Jacob Wolf, with showing him that one could challenge conventional synagogue practices, with positive results. It opened up many of the possibilities that he would see flower in Sudbury. The most central lesson that Kushner took away from his years in Chicago with Wolf was that the primary goal of synagogues was to get the membership to engage in three "primary Jewish acts"—holy study, communal prayer, and good deeds. These are the very acts prescribed in the section of the Mishnah known as *Pirke Avot*, or *Ethics of Our Ancestors—Torah, avodah,* and *gemilut chasadim*.

A rabbi's job, Kushner came to believe, is to teach, guide, and enable congregants to become ever more proficient in these three areas. All other activities that take up congregants' time, energy, and talent are secondary at best, and, at worst, harmful in that they detract from the central mission of the synagogue. This approach to synagogue life has also led Kushner to keep the congregation's various business, administrative, and financial matters at arm's length. Whereas other rabbis might see these areas as central to the health of the community, to Kushner they are a distraction.

The creation of *Vetaher Libenu* was only the most celebrated example of Beth El's actualization of Larry Kushner's two-part philosophy of empowerment and primary Jewish acts. The Ritual Committee also wrote a prayer book for summer services (*Beyn Hashmashot,* 1978), a prayer book for a house of mourning (*Limnot Yameinu,* 1980), a daily prayer book (*Kanfay Shachar,* 1987), and a Rosh Hashanah *machzor* (*Chadesh Yameinu,* 1997).

The congregation also created its own *hevrah kaddisha,* a burial society that attended to all of the ritual requirements and needs of the family of mourners. Members of the congregation lead all the evening *shiva minyanim* (prayer services required in a house of mourning), the rabbi preferring to spend pastoral time with the family during the quieter daytime hours.

Social Action

The congregation took the initiative as well in the realm of social action. In the early 1970s, two members of Beth El founded Action for Soviet Jewry, which became part of the network of organizations working throughout the United States to obtain the right for Soviet Jews to emigrate. The congregationally based Soviet Jewry committee adopted a refusenik family and sponsored travel into the Soviet Union to provide Soviet Jews with aid, comfort, and teaching. For years, a chair stood vacant on the *bima* to symbolize the inability of adopted refusenik Vitaly Rubin to leave Russia and to serve as a reminder to all who came to worship at Beth El of the community's commitment to Jewish sisters and brothers overseas.

Nor was the congregation's activism limited to Jewish causes. In the mid-1970s, amid the publicity surrounding the refugees from Vietnam who had become "boat people," many of whom were drowning at sea as they tried to escape the political terror of their native land, Beth El reached out a helping hand. Through the International Rescue Committee, Beth El took responsibility for the Trans, a Vietnamese family of four that had been languishing in a refugee camp in Malaysia for several months after escaping from Vietnam. The congregation rented and furnished an apartment in nearby Marlboro, where a Vietnamese community existed. Over the course of four years, members of Beth El provided medical services, child care, and drivers for the family's two toddlers and a job for the father as a maintenance man. After the family had become acclimated to America and acquired some proficiency in English, the congregation loaned them funds to relocate to the warmer climate of New Orleans and to purchase a shrimping boat so that the father could pursue his profession of choice.

In 1987, activism and consciousness raising by several members led to a congregation resolution declaring itself a sanctuary for illegal aliens from Central America who were in danger of being deported back to their countries of origin by the federal government. It linked Beth El with a social justice movement that was much more popular in Christian churches than in synagogues and for which Beth El received a national award from the umbrella organization of Reform congregations, the Union of American

Hebrew Congregations. Although the resolution did not call for allowing illegal aliens to live in the temple itself (as happened in some churches), it did urge members of Beth El to take illegal aliens into their homes.

In fact, in March 1988, the Arias-Brizuela family, fleeing persecution in El Salvador and coming to this country without proper papers, was offered residence in the home of one of Congregation Beth El's families. With congregational financial and moral support, the Salvadorans soon moved into a subsidized apartment in nearby Framingham, and Beth El members helped find jobs for both parents in a nursing home in Sudbury. Gradually, the family became self-sufficient, found permanent employment, and succeeded in acquiring legal status from the Immigration and Naturalization Service.

The congregation's Social Action Committee regularly volunteers at an interfaith soup kitchen serving the homeless population of Boston. Another outlet for the congregation's social justice impulse is a *tzedakah* collective formed for families of Beth El in the late 1970s. Membership in the collective required a contribution of 2 percent of one's gross income to a fund that would then be allocated to charities deemed most worthy by group decision. The process has led to growing consciousness about the wide array of worthy causes deserving of support as well as the difficult decisions required to determine how best to allocate limited resources to so many worthwhile organizations.

All of these activities were seen as extensions of the community's commitment to engage in the holy work of *tikkun olam*, "repair of the world." Still, not all Beth El's members are satisfied with its social action program. Intervention on behalf of refugees seemed to be the high-water mark in congregational activism. Some members, aware of the strong social action bent of the national Reform movement, feel that Beth El's efforts fall short of full engagement on issues of political and social importance. Some speculate that it is because the congregation is located far from an urban center and so is somewhat out of touch with the cutting-edge issues of the moment. Others believe that social action simply takes a back seat to the congregation's intensive focus on matters of prayer and study.

Learning

Learning, one of Rabbi Kushner's "primary Jewish acts," is one of the central pillars in the life of Congregation Beth El. As in many synagogues, Sunday mornings become a focal point for the community's learning time together. What distinguishes Beth El from many other congregations, however, is the number of adults who attend on Sunday mornings, in addition to the three hundred or more youth who are there for religious school.

Adults and children participate in a *shacharit* (morning) service, many with *tallit* and *tefillin* (prayer shawl and phylacteries); parents of children in kindergarten through second grade are engaged in a family education program; other adults attend the popular "bagel talks" on topics of current interest; and for several months each semester, bar and bat mitzvah students and their parents attend a class with the rabbi that culminates in a retreat.

The hiring in 1990 of a key professional staff member, Lorel Zar-Kessler, vastly expanded Beth El's offerings. Although her official title is music director, Lorel has emerged as an assistant rabbi, assuming pastoral and teaching functions in addition to leading services. One of the ambitious projects Lorel spearheaded was the launch of an adult literacy program. The two-year program was designed to offer more comprehensive studies for adults interested in something akin to an adult bar or bat mitzvah. Meeting every other week, the program offers a range of courses, including Bible, theology, life cycle, liturgy, history, and classical texts. Graduates of the course can go on to learn how to read Torah. Ten to fifteen adults enroll in the program each year.

Beth El's culture of learning extends to its young people. The school boasts an amazing retention rate for its teenagers: fully 85 percent of Beth El's teens remain part of the regular educational program through their senior year. Monday night pizza and study has become a fixture with the youth, and a regular program of retreats keeps the students closely bonded with one another.

---

o

Tikkun Olam, Repairing the World

I remember it was some time in the late seventies; I had been a member of Beth El for only a few years. I had been going to all of Rabbi Kushner's classes, so I guess that's how I got on his "list." He sent me a packet from Chai Impact (a Jewish social action center) that contained a list of suggested social action issues for congregations to tackle. According to the rabbi, if I could choose just one and get ten other people to join me, "the Messiah will come." Of course, he didn't give me any clues as to how to make this happen.

I chose the Vietnamese boat people because they reminded me of the boatloads of Jews turned away from the world's shores during the Second World War.

It was more difficult than we ever imagined: the red tape, the countless phone calls, translators, cultural misunderstandings, all kinds of traumas we hadn't even begun to anticipate. But despite all the trials and tribulations, it worked. Here was a family that had been uprooted from a tiny fishing village in Vietnam. And with our help and love, they virtually rebuilt their lives. They learned English. They learned how to get along. They even made a decision to move to New Orleans and fish! We still hear from them occasionally, and their accomplishments continue to amaze us.

Through the years, I've watched Beth El go from imagining a world free of nuclear stockpiles to creating an international Rainbow Covenant that demanded concrete action from the world leaders to ensure the survival of our planet. I've watched us go from imagining a world free of starvation to working in the soup kitchens of Sunday's Bread and sending emergency funds to starving Cambodians and disenfranchised Ethiopian Jews. I've watched us go from imagining a world free of refugee camps to actively supporting Project Going Home, a repatriation of Salvadoran refugees from Honduras. Through our actions, we've made the entire world a Jewish issue, not just our small corner of it.

I feel very strongly that this reaching out beyond ourselves, this commitment to repairing the world—to *tikkun olam*—is what makes us a holy community. For Beth El to maintain its integrity as a Jewish congregation, we can never be content merely to imagine a just world. We must join hands with the world at large to make it happen.

[Esta (Bloomenthal) Avasalu's recollection from *The First Twenty-Five Years: Congregation Beth El of the Sudbury River Valley*, Congregation Beth El, pp. 52–53.]

○

Five Scenes from Beth El

Scene 1: Erev Rosh Hashanah 5741. It is my first time here. I walk into the sanctuary, and the bell and sirens go off. Ten-foot-tall neon lights, bright orange and red, point straight at my head saying, "*Goy! . . . Not Jewish! . . . Goy! . . . Not Jewish!*"

Scene 2: Shabbat, 23 Sivan 5743. I am in the foyer, standing at the lectern in my prayer shawl. Giving a *d'var torah*. I am a Jew. A Jew who speaks of Jacob, my namesake. Yaakov. No sirens, no lights. I am a Jew, but I am still strange. Surely God was in this place, but I did not know it back then, just like my namesake. I know more now. But this struggle is not done.

Scene 3: 1 Tammuz 5743. I am married as a Jew. Anita and I stand beneath the *chuppah*. This Beth El spins with wine and music and dancing and the laughter of friends. I dare to jokingly call my non-Jewish friends "the *goyim.*" The walls feel mine; the chairs feel mine. The funny little hat sits comfortably on my head. Still, I struggle. Is this what being Jewish is?

Scene 4: Rosh Hashanah 5744. Trembling, I stand before the congregation and read, haltingly, my portion. In Hebrew. I don't know what the words mean, but I memorized the sounds well enough to sound like I know what I'm doing. When I am done, the adrenaline relaxes. Kushner yells, "Another Beth El bar mitzvah!" It feels good, but it will surely take a lifetime to learn Hebrew. Am I still a Jew if I don't learn it? Or a pretend Jew?

Scene 5: 10 Kislev 5746. My nineteen-day-old daughter is in my arms. Anita and I both rock her to keep her quiet through the naming. It doesn't work. Kushner holds her and puts his little finger in her mouth, rocking like a Hasid. It works. She quiets. A miracle. My daughter is born a Jew. I've come full circle. Under this roof, on this *bima*. So far from the first time, when it seemed I used a rock for a pillow and struggled with a strange God and didn't know the holiness that dwelt here. I still struggle. But this place is mine. I belong.

[Jim Ball's recollection from *The First Twenty-Five Years: Congregation Beth El of the Sudbury River Valley,* Congregation Beth El, p. 64.]

The Rabbinic Factor

Larry Kushner is, both philosophically and temperamentally, non-authoritarian. His commitment to the empowerment of the members of Beth El has clearly unleashed a level of energy and commitment that is rare in congregations of any denominational label. And yet there is no mistaking his centrality to the institution.

Few American rabbis have so clearly articulated a philosophy for how congregations should operate, and Beth El has been his laboratory. And even though few rabbis have implemented Kushner's formula, Beth El serves as living proof that the prescription not only works but has given rise to one of the most vital Jewish congregations in America. Some rabbis might measure their effectiveness on the basis of how many projects or aspects of the congregation revolve around them; Kushner's yardstick would be how many projects are thriving on the initiative and energy of members of the congregation.

Notwithstanding Kushner's personal feeling that no rabbi should ever refer to the congregation where they work as "my congregation," to the outside world, Beth El is "Larry Kushner's synagogue." This is not so much a repudiation of Kushner's empowerment philosophy as it is a function of the fact that Kushner has emerged as one of the most noted American writers and thinkers in the field of Jewish spirituality. Indeed, Kushner was addressing the topic twenty years before it became popular in the American Jewish community. Kushner's interest in spirituality and mysticism has animated his rabbinate and shaped Congregation Beth El's approach to Jewish life.

Kushner's first book appeared in 1975. *The Book of Letters: A Mystical Alef-Bait* featured Larry's own calligraphy of each of the twenty-two letters (*otiyot*) of the Hebrew alphabet, accompanied by his commentary on the significance of each letter and key Hebrew terms beginning with the letter. In his introduction, he wrote, "The *otiyot* are more than just the signs for sounds. They are symbols whose shape and name, placement in the alphabet and words they begin put them each at the center of a unique spiritual constellation. They are themselves holy. They are vessels carrying within the light of the Boundless One."[2]

The Book of Letters became a classic of Jewish mystical and meditational literature; a second edition was issued in 1990. Several other books followed. *Honey from the Rock: Visions of Jewish Mystical Renewal* appeared in 1977 and presented the lay reader with a primer on how to integrate the insights of Kabbalah to everyday life. *The River of Light: Spirituality, Judaism, Consciousness* (1981) is Kushner's most ambitious book, seeking to offer a contemporary theology of Judaism, linking the classical themes of creation, revelation, and redemption to self-realization, consciousness, and personal transformation. *God Was in This Place and I, I Did Not Know: Finding Self, Spirituality, and Ultimate Meaning* (1991) analyzes one line from the Bible—the words Jacob uttered after his dream of the ladder of angels (Genesis 28:16)—from the perspective of seven different rabbinic commentators. Each becomes a prism through which Kushner addresses a different aspect of human awareness and religious consciousness.

Significant parts of each book found their earliest expression in Kushner's sermons, classes, and conversations at Beth El. It was not an accident that Jews seeking a place to explore a more spiritual and mystical approach to Judaism gravitated to Beth El on the strength of Larry Kushner's growing reputation. The fact that it draws members from more than fifty ZIP codes testifies to the intensity of commitment to Kushner and Beth El. It also suggests how few and far between are the places where Jews can feed their spiritual hunger.

Membership Growth

Beth El's growth over the past twenty-five years, while steady, has been modest. Several factors account for this. First, relatively small numbers of Jews live in Sudbury and the surrounding areas. Second, the congregation has not marketed itself in any significant way. The leadership of the congregation has never set size as a measure of its success and has been more than satisfied with people coming to the congregation based on word of mouth recommendations and driven by their own desire to be part of this unique congregation. Third and finally, the dues of Beth El are unusually high. Using a tiered dues structure, families with incomes over $100,000 will pay $2,200 a year, exclusive of religious school fees (1999 dues levels). Although families with lower incomes pay less, the dues burden for members of Beth El are well above the national norm.

Congregational leaders have also resisted pressure to recruit members in order to accommodate budgetary needs. They prefer to allow the congregation to grow at a natural pace, attracting Jews who are interested in the core values of Beth El. The congregation takes great pride in the fact that such a high percentage of members joined Beth El because they wanted God to become a larger part of their lives. Consistent with that philosophy, greater emphasis is placed on "inreach"—getting existing members to become full participants in the community—than on outreach.

In 1996, after a two-year long-range planning process, the board of Beth El decided to cap its membership at four hundred fifty households. The decision was based on the congregation's unwillingness to shoulder the financial obligations involved in growing larger: expanded facilities, a second rabbi, additional professional staff. The decision revealed several key principles that had taken root in the community.

Larry Kushner promoted a form of inclusive elitism. Although any Jew was welcome to the congregation (and non-Jews if they were married to Jews), the community felt that the quality of its program should be sufficient to attract people to membership. Beth El came to enjoy its reputation as a place for "serious Jews." The high dues structure added to the perception that if you were serious about what was happening at Beth El, you would be willing to pay the price to be part of it. That not everyone bought in was just fine with Beth El's leadership; the ones who did were committing themselves to be "challenged Jewishly," regardless of their previous level of knowledge or commitment. Thus working to bring members to ever higher levels of Jewish literacy was the focus, not adding member households. As the community expanded beyond three hundred families, concern also grew that involvement, as measured by voluntarism, attendance at services, and participation in programs and activities, was not keeping pace.

Although the high dues level contributed to Beth El's elitist reputation, the pricing was actually more driven by the community's commitment to egalitarianism. The congregation's leadership strongly objected to the kind of caste system that results when synagogues give special recognition to large donors. At Beth El, there are no plaques singling out benefactors for capital improvements or program sponsorship. Members point with great pride to a $100,000 endowment that was raised in the 1980s to support congregational programming. All donations were made anonymously.

The leadership believes that plaques divide congregants, in effect establishing a hierarchy of influential individuals that is inimical to the commitment to having an across-the-board buy in to the health and welfare of the temple. Congregational leaders are aware that their approach may well have generated less money than might have been raised using more conventional fundraising and recognition strategies. The high dues structure has been one way to compensate.

Finally, the prospect of unchecked growth at Beth El potentially undermined the sense of intimacy among members that had come to be so cherished, especially among members of long standing.

Community Involvement

Notwithstanding Larry Kushner's growing reputation, one of the keys to the community's success has been that the most prized aspects of life at Beth El do not center around the rabbi. Members acknowledge that people join Beth El because they are attracted by Kushner's charisma, extraordinary teaching skills, and disarmingly effective ability to create moving worship experiences. Typically, however, within a year or two of becoming members, most report that what keeps them fulfilled and satisfied with their Beth El experience are their relationships with others in the community and programs run by laypeople.

Though far less recognized than his writing and teaching on matters of Jewish spirituality, this phenomenon is Kushner's greatest contribution to Congregation Beth El. Numerous members will recount how Larry would approach them to lead one project or another long before they felt that they had adequate knowledge or expertise in the area, only to find themselves accepting the rabbi's offer. Year after year, Beth El's programmatic diversity was a function of Kushner's behind-the-scenes recruitment efforts. Over the years, it became clear that to lead a project at Beth El represented a true opportunity to give shape to one's own understanding of how Judaism might be played out in the context of a living, breathing community of fellow Jews.

Kushner genuinely relishes creativity and spontaneity. It is more important to him than promoting a rabbinic role that might have set him up as a spiritual guru—a role that many would probably have been happy for him to assume. At Beth El, he became a catalyst for creativity by planting seeds and then backing off. In return, congregants quickly learned that Kushner meant what he preached—the congregation belonged to the congregants. They would ultimately be the architects of their Jewish lives. And still, what made the implementation of this strategy of empowerment work was Kushner's uncanny ability to "read the souls" of his congregants, knowing who might be willing and capable to take on a project even as they believed the given project was well beyond their reach.

The prayer book efforts are perhaps the best-known example, but many other projects undertaken by the laity at Beth El have had a direct affect on the religious character of the temple. Members regularly lead *shabbat* services when there is no bar or bat mitzvah. Many members have been trained to read Torah and Haftarah. Some members offer courses as part of the menu of adult education offerings. A handful of members are selected to serve as *gabbaim,* essentially ritual enablers. These *gabbaim* help families prepare for the bar or bat mitzvah of their son or daughter. They deliver talks on the weekly Torah readings. They may lead the Torah service instead of the rabbi. Although questions about the quality and competency of these individuals are occasionally raised, the program is deemed valuable and continues.

One of the more interesting creative outlets for the congregation is a journal called *Lichora* ("On the Face of It"). Appearing quarterly, with writing and editorial responsibilities rotating among Beth El members, it features articles, poetry, and book reviews, primarily on religious themes. One member offers an interpretation of a particular Torah portion while another recalls memories (both good and bad) of growing up Jewish. One mother recounts her trip to Kathmandu to meet her son's Buddhist master and make peace with the spiritual path her son has chosen. A regular feature of the journal is ongoing debate on issues under discussion in the congregation. It is clear that the congregation puts great value on the ability to express dissenting views in the most public of ways.

There are many lay-initiated and lay-run projects. On Thursday mornings, one can walk into Beth El and find a lay-led morning *minyan,* with both men and women wearing *tefillin,* a fairly uncommon practice among Reform Jews. One member has coordinated an annual poetry festival each year, bringing in nationally known poets for readings. One of the highlights of Beth El's program calendar is a Purim extravaganza that features a musical parody production written by members of the congregation. Over the years, members could choose from a variety of special-interest groups launched by fellow members, including a men's spirituality group, a post-*shabbat* morning lunch and study group, and a growing array of *havurot* that shared social and religious occasions in home settings out of a desire to maintain feelings of intimacy even as the congregation grew in size.

Not every project launched by laypeople at Beth El has met with success. Some work for a time and then come to an end. Kushner is philosophical about the successes and failures of lay-initiated synagogue projects. He does not believe that programs define the success of a congregation; rather, a successful community is one in which laypeople feel empowered to try out new ideas without interference from elected or self-appointed gatekeepers.

The Worship Experience

The central communal experience at Beth El is *shabbat* services, and it is here that Larry Kushner has provided a unique signature. Inspired by the immediacy of the God experience he describes in his books on theology, he has created a worship experience that allows people to experience the power of the moment, a sense of "everyday miracles" (the theme, by the way, of a book Kushner wrote for children). Many who attend services at Beth El recount how often they have that very feeling. It is a place where "there is a lot of laughing and a lot of crying."

Larry Kushner detests convention. One senses a hidden pleasure when first-time attendees note how "unrabbinic" he appears. He is short; his voice is high-pitched. He might lead services in jeans or in a suit and tie. The worshiper who expects ongoing stage direction from the rabbi will be surprised. Most of the liturgy is led by Lorel Zar-Kessler, the musical director. Though not formally trained as a cantor, her voice, knowledge of the service, and presence command attention.

The Beth El building, though modest, lends itself well to the service that Larry Kushner has created. The large central hall has no fixed seats, and the configuration will change based on the service. At the Friday night service, the chairs wrap around a central table at which the service leaders will be sitting. (It conjures up images of a *rebbe*'s *tisch,* a hasidic custom during which the hasidic master is seated at a table and his devotees sit around the table listening to the rebbe's words of Torah.) The table might accommodate twenty persons. Additional people will sit on the periphery of the table on three sides.

On *shabbat* morning, the forty to fifty regulars might be joined by one hundred or one hundred fifty bar or bat mitzvah guests. The chairs will be set in three facing sections with the reader's table serving as the lectern for rabbi, cantor, and Torah reading. Kushner feels that part of the worship experience is to look into the faces of your fellow worshipers, not at the backs of their heads. The raised *bima* area is used only to access the ark and the Torah scrolls.

Larry Kushner recoils at any trappings that might smack of "an imperial rabbinate," which he feels has discouraged soulful, participatory worship. The music complements Kushner's style in that it invites the participation of all in attendance. For years, Larry led the chanting, which also gave him the ability to control the mood and pace of worship. The addition of Lorel Zar-Kessler in 1990 added a more aesthetic dimension to the music. The melodies at a service alternate between soulful, wordless *niggunim* and hand-clapping, upbeat singing. Lorel's radiating smile is its own invitation to join in.

Occasionally, Larry will encourage personal styles of devotion. During the *Amidah,* he directs congregants to pray the words, in English or Hebrew, in an audible, conversational tone. It evokes the *davening* buzz that is typical of Orthodox congregations but almost never in evidence in Reform settings. Some worshipers cover their heads with the *tallit,* as Larry typically does. Some leave the sanctuary for the five or so minutes, exiting to a lovely side garden where they offer their devotion surrounded by nature.

On a typical *shabbat* morning before the service, about sixty people gather from 9:00 to 10:15 A.M. for Torah study over coffee and bagels. They split into three separate study groups, one led by the rabbi, one by Lorel, and one by lay members of the congregation. The study itself is framed with liturgy, opening with the morning blessings of *shabbat* and concluding with *Kaddish* (which is the liturgical break between two parts of the service). It gives the study the feel of being more integrated with the service, although it takes place in classrooms down the hall from the main sanctuary. At 10:30, some of those who gathered for study will leave, and others will arrive for the service.

The *shabbat* celebration at Beth El has changed over the years. In the 1970s, Friday night services attracted the larger crowd, perhaps one hundred people. A different constituency, slightly fewer in number, would come on *shabbat* mornings. But as the popularity of home-based *shabbat* evening observances and *shabbat* morning study groups has grown, the number of people attending Beth El services on Friday night and *shabbat* morning are now about equal.

On Friday nights, Kushner will usually give a sermon. Occasionally, he might introduce a particularly provocative topic and have worshipers break into small groups for discussion. He is particularly noted for taking the most ordinary of daily occurrences and offering a spiritual understanding of them. On Saturday morning, Kushner will offer a *d'var torah* on the weekly Bible selection, although it is not uncommon for a member to interrupt the talk with an observation or an objection, which Kushner welcomes. Often he will conclude his *d'var torah* by relating it to the bar or bat mitzvah student of the morning.

Although Kushner expresses some disappointment over the fact that more members do not make the *shabbat* morning service part of their routine, he adamantly refuses to "market" Beth El's worship services to his membership. He is disdainful of the gimmicks used by many synagogues to swell attendance on designated days, whether it is by "honoring" some subset of the congregation (as on "sisterhood sabbath") or allowing a Hebrew school class to lead a service, thereby ensuring that the students' parents will be in attendance. Nor will he advertise his sermon titles, despite his talks being much beloved by congregants. In his view, people should come out of a desire to pray. Period.

Kushner similarly resists holding out some standard to judge how committed his members are to Jewish life. It's not that it doesn't matter to him whether or not they are observing *shabbat,* engaging in Jewish study, or doing *mitzvot* (good deeds prescribed by Jewish tradition). On the contrary, he has structured his rabbinate to encourage these primary Jewish acts. But he refuses to be a scorekeeper of Jewish observance. He wants members to be responsible to themselves for their Jewish lives. He doesn't want members apologizing to him for not coming to temple for three months. He wants them "to tell themselves the truth."

Despite his having consistently encouraged his congregants to take responsibility for their own Jewish lives, Kushner admits that it was often difficult to separate his ego from the congregation and the lives of his congregants. It is not that he isn't invested in the outcome of a given congregational decision or the ability of a congregant to reach a new level of Jewish competence; it is simply that he sees his job as providing the context and the tools for Jewish things to happen in their lives. He is convinced that the community will be healthier in the long run with a rabbi who is not "guilting" people into higher levels of Jewish involvement.

○

Praying with Chairs

There are no pews at Beth El. The sanctuary, which is about the size of a high school gym, has bare white walls and a gracefully arching redwood ceiling. While the absence of pews isn't the most important reason my husband and I joined this congregation of 270 families, I think it was the first clue that the Reform synagogue I had wandered into three years ago was unlike any other I had ever attended. . . .

I want to tell you how we pray with chairs at Beth El. During Friday night *shabbat* services, a portion of the synagogue's folding chairs are arranged in rows around a *shabbos tisch*—a large, cloth-covered table that holds candles, challah, and wine. We greet the sabbath by looking not at the backs of heads but by meeting each other's eyes across a table. We begin, always, by singing a *niggun,* a wordless melody. Without the barrier of words, nearly everyone opens his or her mouth in song. The tune is so simple that even first-time guests to Beth El commonly join in. Rabbi Lawrence Kushner—the bearded, balding, boyish forty-one-year-old rabbi of Beth El for fourteen years —often explains that a *niggun* provides a way "to get from where you are to where you want to be." Through its simple repetition, it forces the analytical, critical side of yourself to shut down and opens you to other ways of knowing and being present.

Before the *Amidah,* the standing individual prayer, Rabbi Kushner encourages people to pray audibly, "so your own ears will hear what your mouth is saying, otherwise you'll read the prayer book the way you read everything else." Then, in order to "bring your whole body into your prayers," we are asked to find a spot in the room that will enable us to fully concentrate on the words of our mouths and the meditations of our hearts. Some people simply stand where they are, but others move to find a space of their own, apart from everyone else. The chairs shift and rattle around as we stand and sit, leave our places and take them again. . . .

The reason I belong to Beth El really does have something to do with the chairs. I've noticed that people who attend services regularly don't sit in the same seats—or even the same part of the sanctuary—

from one week to the next. Maybe this is a kind of acknowledgment that people, buffeted by the demands of family and work, are not the same from one week to the next. After a service at Beth El, the chairs are never quite where they were when the congregation walked into the sanctuary; hopefully, neither are we.

[Anita Diamant, "Why I Daven Where I Daven," *Reform Judaism*, Fall 1995, pp. 16–17.] Copyright © Anita Diamant, used by permission of the author.

○

Some Truths About Congregations

• Members of a congregation ought to selfishly and routinely demand that the congregation provide them with the instruments (teachers, classes, books, colloquia, programs, etc.) they need in order to grow as Jews. In many congregations, unfortunately, this order is reversed. Leaders who have not clarified their own religious goals are supposed to set policies for other members who themselves have not yet even determined that they need to come around at all. Here is the proper sequence: first comes religious growing, then comes effective congregational policy.

• There is no evidence whatever to support the notion that people who are drawn into the congregation for an innocuous non-religious event such as gourmet cooking, move on to activities of more primary religious worth any sooner than if they had been left alone to discover their own inevitable and personal religious agendas and timetables. Indeed, there is substantial data to suggest that congregations which run many "basement" activities, in hopes of getting people from there onto upper floors, only wind up adding on to the basement.

• The chief goal of a rabbi is to teach the members of the congregation how to run their congregation without rabbinic help. The rabbi must tell them what he or she knows and then persuade, cajole and even trick them into doing what they want to do with their congregation. The congregation belongs to them; but only when they realize that their rabbi will not "do it" for them can they (and it) begin to realize their full creative and religious potential. In the imagery of Lurianic Kabbalah, as Eugene Borowitz has wisely suggested, this is called *tsimtsum*, or voluntary self-contraction, resulting in the creation of a space within which people have room to experiment, fail, learn and grow.

[Excerpted from Rabbi Lawrence Kushner, "The Tent Peg Business: Some Truths About Congregations," *New Traditions*, Spring 1984, pp. 87–92.]

A Different Drum

In Larry Kushner's twenty-five years at Beth El, the congregation has gone from one that was seen as a maverick operation to one that has an enviable reputation for innovation. By many Jewish measures, the congregation has been an unbridled success. Yet the congregation's leadership notes that the "beautiful people" never belonged to Beth El. It is an observation said with more pride than regret. If Jews use their associations with synagogues to network with other successful individuals, Beth El has not attempted to provide such a context. One leader of the congregation observed incredulously that few people at Beth El even inquire about the professions of fellow congregants. Certainly Beth El, as a matter of policy, has refused to offer any form of recognition on the basis of ability to contribute financially to the temple. The leadership lives comfortably with the consequences of this policy.

Just as Beth El avoids some of the more conventional aspects of American synagogue culture, it also defies the conventional forms of American Reform Judaism. Although the majority of members are from Reform Jewish backgrounds, Beth El boasts a much higher percentage of members from more traditional Jewish backgrounds than other Reform congregations do. One reason is that its approach to worship is more Hebraic and more participatory than the typical Reform service. Beth El's laid-back and spontaneous style is the antithesis of the highly decorous and formal services that characterize the leading congregations of the Reform movement.

One of the highlights of Beth El's year is the service for Simchat Torah, which marks the beginning of the annual Torah-reading cycle. No event better exemplifies Kushner's desire to make prayer into a joyous and spontaneous experience. Some years ago, he introduced the tradition of unrolling the entire Torah scroll, having it held aloft by a circle of hundreds of congregants. Kushner then literally walks people through the Torah's narrative, pointing out the highlights on the parchment held aloft in the room. Adding to the spirit of the festival is dancing to a klezmer band during the joy-filled evening.

A strong common denominator among Beth El's members is dislike for the congregations of their respective childhoods, which cover the gamut from Orthodox to Reform. Part of the draw of Beth El is the disarming way that Larry Kushner challenges conventional religious forms and thinking. People who join this congregation are likely to concur with the implicit critique of American synagogue life that Beth El represents.

Larry Kushner is proud to be a Reform Jew and cherishes Beth El's association with the Reform movement. He has served as an adjunct professor at the New York branch of Hebrew Union College, the Reform seminary, and has held leadership positions in the national organizations of the movement. Yet many Beth El members say they joined the congregation *despite* its Reform affiliation. Years ago, Kushner coined the term "Reconservadox" to describe his approach to Jewish life, and that probably has more resonance for his members than the Reform label. But the label that most congregants apply, with pride, is "different."

Ironically, even though Larry Kushner has more to do with this difference than any other individual, he recognizes that it has bred a certain aloofness in his congregants toward the rest of the Jewish world. He admits that in the early years, he cast the organized Jewish community as "the problem," for which Beth El would be a constructive antidote. The attitude bred a form of insularity that Kushner now sees as not entirely healthy. His own interest in having Beth El serve as a model for other congregations has been somewhat undermined by the fact that so few of Beth El's members have gone on to play significant roles in the Reform movement or in the greater Boston Jewish community.

It is not that Beth El is a secret. Larry Kushner's growing popularity as a lecturer all around the country and the prayer book series produced by the congregation have both made Beth El one of the best-known congregations in the Jewish community. Kushner has chaired the committee on liturgy and worship for the Union of American Hebrew Congregations, the national lay umbrella for the Reform movement. He is invited to do an annual retreat for the Rabbinical Assembly, the national rabbinical umbrella for the Conservative movement, on the topic of empowerment. He serves on the faculty of Hebrew Union College in New York, which trains Reform rabbis.

Still, the Beth El approach has not been widely copied. First of all, not much energy goes into promoting Beth El as a model for other congregations to emulate. Part of this is a reflection of Beth El's historic insularity, made more acute by its location outside of a major urban center. Part of it is also a sense that Beth El's success is not inherently obvious; in fact, there has not been a time in Beth El's history when the leadership did not feel overwhelmed by the crises of the moment. Only in retrospect do the participants realize what a special creation they have wrought.

Kushner is keenly aware of the gap between the enthusiastic reception his ideas about congregational life receive and the failure of rabbis and congregational leaders to replicate what he has accomplished at Beth El.

The most common reason they give him is also perhaps the most honest: "We don't know how to do it." Indeed, congregations are patterned social and cultural institutions with deep roots in their community. Such relationships are incredibly hard to change. Even when brand-new congregations start out, the founders will pattern them on synagogues with which they are familiar. And that only serves to perpetuate the conventional structure of board, rabbi, and congregation, patterned in ways entirely different from what Kushner would consider healthy.

Rabbis in pulpits for more than a few years would have a hard time changing the patterns of relationships that exist and in which they are embroiled. New rabbis, just starting out, rarely have the skills to implement, much less manage, a program that leads to so many widely scattered centers of power. Kushner himself thinks that if he were to assume a new pulpit, it might take five years or longer to implement the mode of functioning that is a natural part of the communal culture at Beth El. Most rabbis, he feels, are too busy and too insecure to try to undertake his empowerment design. He concludes that the most effective way of replicating a synagogue like Beth El is for a rabbi with solid years of experience and a clear idea of what he or she wants to create, to start a congregation from scratch.

At various times, members of Beth El have thought about seeding a new congregation or creating a rabbinic fellows program. Neither has ever come to fruition. Veteran members are convinced that the organizational culture is so deeply rooted at Beth El that any successor rabbi would have to conform to the tenets Larry Kushner has so successfully promulgated. But it is not at all clear if Kushner's principles, no matter how lucidly they are articulated, can in and of themselves transform other congregations into Beth El of Sudbury.

6

JOAN'S PATH

I AM A "PROFESSIONAL JEW." My days are filled with the constant struggles and great joys that come from bringing Jewish learning to a community of people, many of whom are just learning about their Judaism. Some resist attempts to reach them. Others are just incredibly eager to learn. It is my life's work. My world is framed by the Jewish calendar: my year begins with Rosh Hashanah and is punctuated by the festivals; my week ends with *shabbat*, a day of rest and renewal without which I could not function the other six days. Judaism is at the core of my being; it defines who I am.

It was not always that way. My father was strongly opposed to religious education. He felt that the main purpose it served was to give children an exaggerated sense of their own importance and to prejudice them against people of other faiths. We grew up in Brooklyn, in the midst of a totally Jewish community, celebrating Christmas complete with tree-decorating, hanging stockings, and a big family party. Holiday memories from my childhood are waking up on Christmas morning and opening the presents heaped under the tree or opening our apartment door on Easter and discovering the basket from the "Easter bunny." When I was eight, one of my friends told me that I was Jewish, but the word had no meaning for me. As I entered adolescence, I went though my first "religious phase," probably brought on by wanting to be like my friends, all of whom were Jewish and went to synagogue on the High Holydays. The

Joan Kaye, executive director of the Board of Jewish Education of Orange County, California, is an adjunct faculty member at the University of Judaism, serving as a consultant at the Whizin Institute for Jewish Family Life. She is the coauthor of *The Parent Connection* and several high school curricula including "Why Be Good?" and "The Power to Lead." She is the mother of two grown daughters.

family Christmas tree was banished to the maid's room (after all, it wouldn't be fair to deprive her of her holiday!). And I was allowed to have a Chanukah menorah in my room. I even insisted on going to confirmation classes. Unfortunately, I have only two memories of that class: the first is of kids shooting water pistols at the ceiling while the rabbi, each week, tried in vain to discover the source of the "leak"; the second is of people being chosen for speaking parts in the confirmation ceremony based on their parents' level of participation (primarily financial) in the synagogue. My experiences with religious services over the next several years were no more inspiring. Eventually, I just stopped going.

Despite all this, somewhere along the way I managed to pick up some pretty strong feelings about being Jewish as well as a kind of vague yearning for a spiritual life. I never had any inclination to search for it outside of Judaism. My sister, who joined her first synagogue as a young, single woman, sent her son to day school for several years and is currently a member of a very active *havurah* at a right-of-center Conservative synagogue (she doesn't read Hebrew but insists that she is more comfortable in a "traditional" service), and I puzzle frequently over where our strong attachment to Judaism could possibly have come from. We've searched our childhood memories but never found anything that could answer the question.

For me, this attachment was initially played out through my desire and that of my then husband to bring up our children as Jews, providing them with an understanding of Jewish traditions, customs, and history. We were thrilled to discover an alternate religious school that was not attached to a synagogue and focused on history and culture. Because of the long waiting list, each of my daughters was registered within a week of her birth. When it actually came time for my older daughter to start attending, however, due to a combination of pressure from my former mother-in-law and enticement from two good friends who had inexplicably given up our Friday night bridge games to start having "Friday night dinners" (whatever they were) and attending services, we joined Beth El. I was convinced to go to High Holyday services by the argument of "doing it for the children." We observed the major holidays at home with elaborate meals and occasional prayers. In my mind, however, the major difference between Rosh Hashanah and Thanksgiving was that the former required two days of cooking. In short, I was doing a lot of things that were meaningless to me, mainly in order to provide my kids with something that I had never experienced and knew practically nothing about.

Then my husband lost his job. We had no disposable income to spend on going out. I had noticed an adult education course in the synagogue bulletin titled something like "Folktales of the Jewish People," and since it was free and seemed potentially more entertaining than the current season's TV shows, we decided to go.

"Folktales" turned out to be *midrash*, but it wouldn't have mattered what the subject was because Larry Kushner teaches souls, not texts. And within an hour of entering that classroom, I knew I was embarked on a journey. That journey would change my life in ways I couldn't even begin to imagine.

Going to class led to going to services on Friday nights, which led to joining a Hebrew class so that I could participate in the services. (There was no transliteration in the Beth El prayer book. Larry's theory was that providing transliteration was a disincentive to learning Hebrew.) Just as *"mitzvah goreret mitzvah"* (one good deed leads to another), each new experience led to a thirst for more and deeper experiences. I was taking Larry's class in modern Jewish thought and struggling with such thinkers as Borowitz, Fackenheim, Rosenzweig, Buber, and, of course, Kushner. I was intrigued by the concept of "covenantal theology," which offered a Judaism that spoke to my rational as well as my spiritual self. What was the real meaning of being in a covenantal relationship with God? What did it mean for me and my family and the community in which I lived? My search for the answers to those questions changed from the vague yearning of my adolescence to what would be the major quest of my life.

I immersed myself in Jewish study and Jewish living. I joined the *shabbat* morning Torah study group. There were about ten of us, mostly men, who would spend three hours every *shabbat* morning studying Torah with the aid of English commentaries and bottles of cheap Scotch. For three years, this provided a very intense learning experience with the only distraction being the occasional bar or bat mitzvah, which pulled the rabbi away. This was in the days before Beth El had a regular *shabbat* morning service or many kids of bar or bat mitzvah age. What I learned on those mornings became the core of my Jewish knowledge; the people with whom I studied became my teachers. For me, a young mother who didn't work outside the home, starved for intellectual as well as spiritual stimulation, Beth El provided an incredible feast—and I gorged myself.

A group of us, along with Larry and his family, truly lived what is my understanding of the essence of Reform Judaism—to study the tradition and to partake in the widest possible range of Jewish experiences in order to make informed decisions about both practice and belief. We embarked on Larry's gradual "five-step program" for becoming kosher. We joined a *havurah* of young families who were committed to Jewish growth and, specifically, to *shabbat* observance. My husband and I would go to services Friday night; we would study Torah on *shabbat* morning; and in the afternoon, our *havurah* would gather for study, *seudat shlishit* (the late afternoon meal on the sabbath), and *havdalah* (the ritual marking the end of the sabbath). Perhaps this period was best symbolized by a metaphor of Arnold Wolf's in which the *mitzvot* form a path of precious and semiprecious stones. As we walk along it, we try picking up the ones that seem to "call" to us. Sometimes they are too heavy and we have to put them down again; sometimes they become a part of our lives. In either case, regardless of whether or not we choose to carry them with us, we recognize their absolute value.

Our lives were enmeshed with the synagogue. We studied there, we prayed there, and we participated in its management. At one point, seven of the eight adults in our *havurah* were serving as chairs of major synagogue committees. Beth El was a place in which, if you noticed a lack, you filled it. When I went to Larry and asked why we didn't have services on Passover morning, he handed me a copy of a family service he'd written as a student rabbi and told me to write my own. And somehow I did. It was as if there had been this incredible hole inside of me that I didn't know existed until I started filling it. My hunger was voracious—and apparently insatiable. The more that Judaism became part of my life, the more all-encompassing I needed it to be.

After I lost a local school board election, Larry convinced me to become chair of the Beth El school committee. In my second year in the job, we hired Les Bronstein, and together Les and I turned the school upside down, creating a modern version of the traditional *cheder* (elementary school) where the only texts used in the school were a *chumash* (Bible) and a *siddur* (prayer book). The next year, I convinced Les to let me teach. Our curriculum was *parashat hashavua* (the weekly Bible reading), and I would study for hours to prepare for each fourth-grade class I taught. As an English teacher, I had loved the classroom but hated the preparation; as a religious school teacher, my preparation was a religious act, and I loved every minute of what I did. It didn't take very long for me to realize that my future career lay not in returning to the classroom as an English teacher or continuing my studies to obtain a doctorate in educational administration (my long-term plan for after my children grew up) but in becoming a Jewish educator. Within a year, I had applied to the Hornstein program in Jewish communal service at Brandeis University, the final step in achieving complete congruence between my professional and personal lives.

During my first four years at Beth El, I learned more than I had ever learned or ever would learn in any comparable period in my life. I existed at a level of spirituality in which I truly felt that I "walked with God." The Presence of the Holy One suffused my existence, inspiring not only me but my students and my friends as well. Though the feeling varied from a kind of background awareness to moments of great intensity, it was never entirely absent during these years.

The more I learned and grew, the more I wanted to know and experience. Little by little, I started going beyond Beth El to get my needs met. At first, it was just Hebrew that I couldn't get at Beth El, so I registered for the *ulpan* (intensive Hebrew course) at Boston Hebrew College, where I studied three times a week for three years, eventually spending six weeks at Ulpan Akiva in Netanya, Israel. Then it was *davening*. Friday nights continued to be wonderful, but the *shabbat* morning Torah study group had expanded and changed from intensive study to a pleasant lunch after the now frequent bar and bat mitzvahs, with lots of families and small children running around.

I began to attend Havurat Shalom, an independent group of Jews without professional clergy engaged in regular prayer and study, on a regular basis. I learned to *daven* during those *shabbat* and festival mornings in Somerville. And I brought what I learned back to Beth El, where a small group of us struggled to establish a *shabbat* morning *minyan*. Larry would participate if he was in town, but from the beginning, it was entirely lay-led. We took turns leading the *davening,* reading Torah, and giving *divrei torah* (talks on the weekly biblical portion). It took nearly ten years (as well as a new congregant who was committed to leading it every week and had the Hebrew ability and beautiful voice necessary to make it work) before it was established. It is wonderful for me to visit now and to listen to the different melodies that are part of the service and remember how that one was from Havurat Shalom and this one Riki Lipitz taught us when she was our cantor and the Sephardic melody is one that Les brought and on and on. It is an eclectic service that demonstrates the best of Beth El, where laypeople are empowered to create what they need and individual contributions are woven into a communal whole.

Vetaher Libenu, the Beth El *siddur,* is another example of that. The prayer book was put together by a committee of laypeople from Beth El and was published in 1975. After five years of use, it began to feel increasingly inadequate to many of the people most involved in religious services. It didn't reflect the greater sophistication and knowledge of our maturing congregation; it didn't have a *shabbat* morning service. When Nancy Gossels and I volunteered to redo it, we envisioned a book that would reflect who we were as a congregation. At that time, we were reading Torah on Friday night, but the traditional Torah service reflects the mood of *shabbat* morning, so we experimented with creating a service that would have the softness and mystical feeling of *leil shabbat* (Friday evening). We tried out several with the congregation until we felt we had gotten exactly what we wanted. We took the form of *kabbalat shabbat* (the Friday evening liturgy) but chose not the traditional psalms but those which more closely reflected Beth El's theology. And we made choices also based on what we knew. For example, we chose among sections of the Hallel (Psalms 113–118) based on what melodies the congregation knew how to sing. And then, halfway into our work, we had a revelation. After nearly a year of editing and writing, Nancy and I realized that we were becoming increasingly uncomfortable with the male imagery that we had been using—so uncomfortable that we came to our committee and proposed the then (it was 1980) radical idea of gender-neutral language. With their enthusiastic approval, we re-edited what we had done and proceeded to write a *siddur* that truly reflected the beliefs, language, and theology of the congregation.

The completion of the *siddur* coincided with the beginning of my third and last year as the director of the Brandeis Jewish Education program, a Sunday school meeting on the Brandeis campus. Brandeis became a wonderful resource for me as I continued my personal search. What I found were amazing opportunities for intellectual study and growth. I took courses both in the Near Eastern and Judaic Studies department and at Hebrew College. A friend and I hired an Orthodox rabbi to teach us Mishnah. I studied *Sefer Aggadah* (a compilation of midrashic texts) with Rabbi Al Axelrod, the director of Brandeis Hillel, in a class for Brandeis faculty and staff.

But there was no class in which I could study what it all meant, no place to continue my quest for personal meaning. Larry's classes at Beth El were for beginners. No matter what the subject, since Larry taught people, not texts, and there were always new people, the class always raised the same introductory issues. The disclaimer that goes along with every class or service at Beth El: "no previous knowledge required" is very true. The unfortunate corollary is that no previous knowledge is desired. It became increasingly frustrating to sit through classes where people were beginning their search for their own entrance into Judaism and didn't care about, much less understand, the issues that I needed to raise. It was hard to attend services led by people who not only had no clue about the structure of the *siddur* but also felt no need to learn.

Each year it became more difficult to find what I needed at Beth El until eventually it became clear that despite all my efforts to get my needs fulfilled, it was no longer possible for me to do it there. In those first few

years, I lived at a spiritual peak that was impossible to sustain. Some of it
may have been due to the newness and excitement of discovering Judaism
for the first time. It seems clear to me that two other factors were critical
to my period of intense Jewish spirituality—an extraordinary teacher like
Larry Kushner, who could help me climb to successive rungs of the Jewish spiritual ladder, and a community of people who wanted to live in-
tensely Jewish lives as liberal Jews.

Larry changed my life. He introduced me to the beauty and awe and
richness of Judaism, and he opened doors that I eagerly entered. But after
I had conquered the ground floor, I never found an elevator or an escala-
tor or even a flight of steep stairs to get beyond it. God knows I tried.
There was a moment when Larry and a group of other rabbis, including
Art Green and Max Ticktin and Zalman Schachter-Shalomi decided to
create a seminary without walls. Each of the rabbis invited one or two students to Fellowship Farm in Philadelphia to explore what it would mean
to create such a place. Studying with Art and Max was amazing; when we
davened with Zalman, it felt as if we were literally knocking on the gates
of heaven. When we mapped out a course of study, I knew I had found
the teachers that I needed and the next level I had been looking for—but
it somehow fell apart and never proceeded beyond that initial experience.

It took me a long time to learn that you can't do it without a community—a community for which I am still searching. When I first became
involved in Judaism, I was part of a group of people learning and growing together, and that was wonderful. But it didn't last. The people who
regularly attended services at Beth El constituted a community where I
could see the same people and catch up on things—but only on Friday
nights. My extended family, who were nominally Jewish, referred to me
as a "born-again Jew" and didn't quite know what to make of me. I still
remember the shock of receiving an invitation to my uncle's eightieth
birthday party. It was on Sukkot on *shabbat* in a Chinese restaurant. I was
terribly offended until I realized that for my family, neither *shabbat* nor
Sukkot nor *kashrut* (dietary laws) had any meaning whatsoever. They
weren't purposely ignoring things that I felt were important; it would just
never occur to them to think of those things. And yet when my grandmother died and I arrived in New York for the funeral, my father told me
that he wanted me to conduct it, to make it a "Jewish" funeral. There I
was on Friday evening, preparing to conduct a funeral on Sunday from a
house in which there was not a single Jewish book! On Saturday, we
walked to the local bookstore, where I frantically tried to memorize some
passages (I would neither write nor touch money on *shabbat*). Saturday
evening, I called Boston, and Nancy Gossels dictated to me some readings

from the *Kaddish* section of *Vetaher Libenu*. And on Sunday morning, I conducted the first funeral in the Silber family in which Hebrew words were spoken.

I grew up at Beth El. Though I came there as an adult, it was where I passed through my Jewish childhood and adolescence and came into maturity, and for a long time, it was all I knew of Judaism. In its eclectic nature, it was a place like no other. It still is. The services at Beth El have a quality I haven't been able to find anyplace else. And that leaves me homeless. I belong to three synagogues now in Southern California (where I moved nine years ago to become director of the Orange County Bureau of Jewish Education). I joined a Conservative one for times when I feel the need for a full service, a Reconstructionist one at which I can create new rituals with my friends, and a Reform one because I am philosophically a Reform Jew. The sad truth is that the only synagogue in town where I find the *davening* to be both creative and traditional is the Orthodox synagogue, but to me, the *mechitzah*—the wall separating the men from the women in Orthodox sanctuaries—interferes with the inspiration.

I became a synagogue Jew at Beth El. The synagogue was the center of my social, spiritual, and volunteer activities. I now belong to three synagogues and I don't feel at home in any of them. I'm actually somewhat astounded that I, the professional Jew, who should know all there is to know about this stuff, have not been able to figure out how to become meaningfully involved. At Beth El, the ritual committee wrote a *siddur*, struggled with conflicts between human needs and *halacha* (Jewish law), and created new ways of celebrating ancient holidays. When I joined the Conservative synagogue here, I volunteered to *lein* (chant) Torah, help with services, be a member of the ritual committee. They welcomed me and gave me lots of opportunities to practice my ritual skills in the synagogue. I tried attending ritual committee meetings because, for me, wrestling with the meaning of ritual and how it would be worked out in the congregation was central to my congregational life. But the focus was on what the *Shulchan Aruch* (code of Jewish law) had to say about the issue at hand. At the Reform synagogue, the ritual committee deals with logistics; the Reconstructionist synagogue doesn't have a ritual committee because the rabbi takes care of all that.

The community that I need, one that will allow me to observe traditions in a liberal setting, doesn't seem to exist. And without community, I find it increasingly difficult to maintain any meaningful level of observance. My search falters, slows to an almost imperceptible level. But then something touches me, I find a renewed surge of energy, and I give it "one more try." I go into Los Angeles for one of the *minyan* services; I take a class at the University of Judaism. Last year, I traveled three thousand miles to return to Beth El for Rosh Hashanah. Although I kept telling myself that it was a mistake to try to recapture an idealized past, that "you can't go home again," I was elated that my heart turned out to be wiser than my head.

It was wonderful. The cantor, Lorel Zar-Kessler, has a beautiful voice that she uses not to perform but to get everyone to participate. Even sitting in the last row of the *shul* is OK because everyone around you is singing. Lorel gave the *drash* (talk) on the second day and talked about her struggles with "what it means to be commanded." Those were once my struggles. And I started to think that I was again ready to engage in that struggle.

I came back to California with renewed energy and hope and invited a group of ten friends and acquaintances to join the struggle with me. We started by reading Fackenheim, a voice that speaks to many of us philosophically. We combined this with the study of Abraham Chill's book *The Mitzvot* to be sure we were rooted in the tradition. I am under no illusions about the ability to fashion the Beth El of my early experiences in sunny California. Revisiting the place of my Jewish birth is not the same as re-creating it. But knowing of the fulfillment that is possible when one finds true community in a Jewish context is just enough to keep me trying.

PART THREE

AN ORTHODOX COMMUNITY THAT WELCOMES A PLURALITY OF VOICES

7

CAROLE'S PATH

I KNEW THAT I WAS JEWISH growing up—but it was not until adulthood that I realized that my parents were concerned about keeping me that way.

Ours was essentially a secular household in a predominantly Jewish but non-Orthodox neighborhood. Not only didn't we keep the kosher food laws, but we savored ham and pork, and my mother served milk with steak. Although I remember my grandmother lighting sabbath candles, my mother never practiced the ritual because my father was afraid of fire.

We celebrated only two Jewish holidays in any real way, Chanukah and Passover. On Chanukah, my mother lit the eight-branched menorah and we received the requisite gold coins filled with chocolate. We played dreidel games using raisins as tokens. But we also put stockings up on the wall and filled them with candies and oranges at Christmas. My grandmother gave me a music book of Christmas carols because a version of my name was on the cover. I recall the joy with which this Carole learned to play those carols on the piano.

At Passover time, we invited some family relatives to an abbreviated *seder* using a Haggadah distributed by our local Workmen's Circle chapter. As a child, I thought this *seder* ran very long. In the fall, when the Jewish New Year came around, my friends and I would dress up in fancy

Carole Oshinsky is a librarian who serves as the manager for publications and information resources at the National Center for Children in Poverty at the Joseph L. Mailman School of Public Health at Columbia University in New York City. She is also active in Jewish communal organizations, currently serving as public relations chair for the Riverdale Jewish Women's Forum, a group formed to facilitate dialogue among women from all streams of Judaism. She and her husband, Sy, have raised three children, one of whom now makes his home in Israel.

clothes and loiter outside our community's Orthodox synagogue. But we never went in—and neither did my parents. I remember one Yom Kippur when, all dressed up, we trekked to a distant neighborhood to sample a new food from Italy—pizza. Sukkot was a time for my sister and me to sit in public school while all of our Jewish neighbors absented themselves for the holiday.

My father professed to be an atheist. He had spent spare time in his youth giving socialist speeches on street corners and helping to organize unions. I thought that he didn't believe in G-d. My grandmother wanted us to have some kind of Jewish education, but my father would not allow us to attend the nearby Orthodox Hebrew school (Talmud Torah) because of his own negative childhood experiences in *cheder* (elementary Jewish school). In the end, my father never celebrated his bar mitzvah because my grandfather took him out of *cheder* after the teacher hit him. Undoubtedly, this had a formative impact on my father's attitude toward Judaism.

As a compromise, my sister and I were allowed to attend the local after-school Yiddish school, *shule,* sponsored by the Workmen's Circle movement. Though I enjoyed learning Yiddish songs, I resented having to sit through classes in Bible and to memorize Hebrew and Yiddish words. The fact that my parents used Yiddish as a secret language to hide things from me did not motivate me to study hard. I never did the homework, but somehow I managed to pass the final exams and receive a certificate in Yiddish and Hebrew at age thirteen. My parents made me a party to mark my "bat mitzvah."

Two positive experiences I had in *shule* were the annual Chanukah play and the public celebration of the third *seder.* I recall one play in which I hammed it up as a mother covered with flour, serving latkes to her family. I loved the music of the Passover *seder* and the fact that my family was sharing the celebration with me.

Another positive Jewish communal experience in our neighborhood was the annual bazaar, where plump old ladies served their homemade knishes and other Jewish delicacies. I also cherished the summers our family spent at Venice Beach in California. There my paternal grandmother, who made kosher pickles, showed off her grandchildren to the other old Jewish ladies in her circle of friends.

These contacts and experiences made me comfortable among Jews. In fact, in my Bronx neighborhood, nearly all of my friends were Jewish, too. But I was nervous around those who actively practiced their religion. I wasn't motivated to learn more about Judaism as a religion or to seek out spiritual avenues of expression. I viewed Judaism as a cultural heritage that I pretty much took for granted.

In my college years, I occasionally attended Hillel programs on campus, but I avoided religious services. I enjoyed listening to the lectures the Ethical Cultural Society broadcast every Sunday morning on the radio, in the days before television. Yet I was never attracted to other religions.

My road to Orthodox Jewish observance was fairly direct. The first step was marrying a Jewish man—in fact, I had dated Jewish men exclusively. I have often wondered why non-Jewish men never appealed to me as they did to some of my friends. My husband came from a more traditional, observant Jewish family. His parents kept a kosher home, attended synagogue on holidays and occasional sabbaths, and held a bar mitzvah celebration for their son. But his parents also ate in nonkosher restaurants and traveled on the sabbath. This was partly due to the hard economic times they lived through when they came to the United States before World War II.

I married at twenty, while still in college, and upon graduation went to work in a publishing house. Before our children arrived, we used to spend Jewish holidays with my husband's parents, attending their Orthodox synagogue and sleeping in their house. I think that these brief contacts with religious observance whet my appetite for something more, but I couldn't identify it at the time. There was just this feeling that life was unfocused and without deep meaning. We were doing all the typical newlywed activities: taking our first trip to Europe, buying furniture, moving two long train rides away from our parents in the Bronx to a garden apartment in Queens, and making new friends.

I first realized that my parents cared deeply about their Jewishness when our first child, a boy, was born. We were a modern family and were going to have a modern circumcision—in the hospital, performed by a doctor. I was shocked to learn that this was unacceptable to my father. He insisted on a proper Jewish ritual *brit* performed by a *mohel*. And we complied.

Soon after, we met an Orthodox family in our new community, and we began to spend a lot of time together, pushing baby carriages, learning to be parents, sharing dinners. This family seemed to have an inner peace, a direction and rhythm to life that we lacked. I watched with fascination as the wife prepared for the sabbath, shopping at the nearby kosher butcher, buying challah and cake at the bakery. Their sabbath table was always beautifully set, and their home was alive with songs and wonderful food smells emanating from the kitchen.

That initial spark of religious interest was further nurtured on a weekend several years later spent away from our two young children. We went on a Jewish marriage encounter—a phenomenon of the late 1970s that is still practiced today. At a nearby Holiday Inn, we and about fifty other couples—without tennis rackets, entertainment, or television—learned to "communicate" better with our spouses and to explore our feelings about marriage, family, careers, and Judaism. The open sessions were led by three experienced couples. One of the couples included a rabbi.

The rabbi on this weekend broke all of my stereotypes about what a spiritual leader was like. He was a young, clean-shaven man with blond hair and a beautiful wife. He also dressed for each session in a colorful shirt and matching head covering (*kippa*). In the session on what part Judaism played in their lives, the three couples shared how they had become enriched by Jewish observance. These couples may have been from Reform or Conservative backgrounds, but their obvious deep emotional attachment to the sabbath and the synagogue filled me with envy and pulled me along to the next level of my spiritual quest, affiliating with a synagogue.

I came back from that marriage encounter weekend not only with new skills for communicating with my spouse but also with a rekindled desire to learn more about being Jewish. By this time, we had moved back to the Bronx to a new high-rise community called Co-op City. Serendipitously, a friend asked me to go with her to a Bible study class at the local Conservative synagogue. I accepted and found a wonderful teacher, Elias Bloch, who opened my eyes not only to the world of Midrash (stories that expand on events mentioned briefly in the Bible) but also to Judaism's ethical system of law. As the culmination of a year of study, the class prepared to lead a Friday night service in the synagogue. I remember proudly saying my part, with my family looking on. After this, I began to attend Saturday morning services, occasionally accompanied by my spouse. But I still felt the need to know more.

My husband and I attended monthly follow-up meetings with a small group from our marriage encounter weekend. Judaism was a frequent topic of discussion. We started separating our dishes into meat and dairy; we put our children into after-school Hebrew classes at an Orthodox synagogue, and I joined the parents' association. We started observing some of the sabbath rituals. We especially grew to love the Friday night meal, with its emphasis on the family sitting together, singing, and thanking G-d. I began to see how Jewish practice elevated the ordinary details of our life to sacred acts.

Another incident in my family at that time confirmed for me how deeply my parents did care about Judaism. A close relative married a non-Jewish man, and my parents could not bring themselves to attend the wedding. I saw their pain and felt their sadness at the values that had not been transmitted. They were confused when the bride announced that she would give her male children a *brit milah* (ritual circumcision) but have any female child baptized.

When my father died suddenly the following summer, the Jewish rituals for death and mourning comforted me and my family. I went to say *Kaddish* (the memorial prayer) at the Young Israel synagogue early in the morning, and the old men in attendance welcomed me. This outpouring of support from religious Jews and the growing strength of our spiritual needs led us, the following fall, to enroll our children in a Jewish day school located on the other side of the Bronx. But the young families in Co-op City were moving away to houses in the suburbs, and the community was being torn apart by a rent strike. We felt that we needed a change, and I wanted to move to a community where I could learn more about my Judaism and have our children attend a Jewish day school closer to home.

Some parents from the day school our children attended heard about our search for a house and referred us to a section of Westchester that was within walking distance of the school and also home to two Orthodox synagogues, both with long histories. We spent a weekend in this community, checking out the congregations and looking at homes. Within two months, we had purchased a four-bedroom colonial on a quiet, tree-lined street, with a dining room appropriate for large *seders,* and joined one of the synagogues. We loved being so close to the day school, participating in educational Sundays and occasional weekend retreats to help parents grow religiously. Our lives became molded by the Jewish and the Hebrew day school calendars. We so looked forward to the sabbath each week, we really meant it when we said, "Thank G-d it's Friday." We based our activities around Jewish holidays and school events, and we relished Passover and Rosh Hashanah each year as special celebrations of being Jewish and gathering the family together.

As we grew in observance, the synagogue we joined shrank in attendance and activities. Apparently, we had come at the end of an exciting period overseen by a dynamic young rabbi. When he left the community shortly before we moved in, much of the dynamism went with him, and many young families stopped coming to services. I became disillusioned with the synagogue. We had not yet fully adopted an Orthodox lifestyle in that we still ate nonkosher food when away from home and traveled to family celebrations on *shabbat.* Thus we were open to other forms of affiliation and even went to a Reform temple for a Saturday morning service to see what it was like.

Suddenly, a young rabbi was hired by the other Orthodox synagogue in the community. He reached out to the young families and started a small annex of the *shul* closer to our home to attract young families.

Every other Saturday afternoon, he invited men and women to a talk in his apartment; on alternate weeks, his young wife led a class for women on *kashrut*. Their warmth as a couple was like a beacon inviting us to become more religiously observant. The rabbi gave a talk about why women should observe the laws of family purity and attend a *mikvah* (ritual bath) each month. He explained that each month that a menstruating women does not become pregnant, a potential child is lost, and she and her husband mourn for that lost life by abstaining from a physical relationship with each other for about twelve days. I was motivated to accept this aspect of Jewish religious observance. This period of abstinence, though stressful on the physical level, also led to greater verbal closeness with my husband, and each monthly visit to the *mikvah* marked the beginning of a regular honeymoon period in our lives as a couple.

We were very distressed when the synagogue closed the annex and, as a result, the rabbi and his wife moved to another community. By then the young families had allied with some older congregational families and unaffiliated families, and we decided to start our own synagogue. We spent a year without an official rabbi, meeting in a nearby parochial school classroom. While a number of rabbis from the surrounding areas said we could call on them, only one, an Orthodox rabbi from a synagogue three miles away, offered to serve as our temporary spiritual leader. He was Rabbi Avi Weiss of the Hebrew Institute of Riverdale (HIR). For six months, Rabbi Weiss came up to Westchester every few weeks on the sabbath to speak to us and to run special programs. Finally, our search bore fruit, and we were lucky enough to attract an experienced, dynamic Orthodox rabbi from a Connecticut congregation that had switched from Conservative to Orthodox under his guidance.

Rabbi Barry Freundel was returning to Yeshiva University to complete his doctorate in medieval Jewish history and was looking for a part-time pulpit nearby—just what we had to offer. During the three years he spent in our community, we established our congregation at a nearby home for the Jewish aged. On Sabbath afternoons, with our children playing at our feet, we would sit on the lawn and embark on intellectual journeys in Jewish law and contemporary issues. Jewish holidays as well as each sabbath service featured lay cantors from our congregation chanting the prayers. The rabbi made us part of his family, inviting us to his wedding and sharing the births of two children with us, all the while gently moving us to grow religiously. It was with him that we spent our first all-night learning session on Shavuot (the holiday of the giving of the Ten Commandments to the Jewish people).

Equally important for me, he opened up the idea of women having a greater role to play in public Jewish ritual. He allowed women to speak before the congregation when a girl became a bat mitzvah. Women could dance with the Torah on the holiday of Simchat Torah (completion of the annual Bible reading cycle) and kiss it as it was carried through the women's section. A woman was permitted to be an officer of the congregation as well. This took place in the mid-1980s, when women's prayer groups were few in number and no national organizations existed to lend us support.

By the time Rabbi Freundel left New York, our family had become fully observant Orthodox Jews. Two of our children had been welcomed into adulthood. We had become used to a small, nurturing synagogue where members looked forward to coming together each week to pray, discuss, eat, talk, and carry out plans to reach out to the surrounding community in acts of *chesed* (kindness), such as delivering Purim baskets to elderly residents.

Despite valiant efforts to keep the structure and style of our congregation intact, we had to disband a few years later, and so once again my husband and I went synagogue-hunting. We still had one child in elementary school and wanted a synagogue that neighborhood children attended. We turned to the local Young Israel affiliate, but it did not have the same intellectual and outreach environment as our previous synagogue. Attendance at Jewish education institutes for women, such as Drisha, and numerous days of learning over the years sharpened my Jewish knowledge so that I could feel comfortable in almost any Jewish environment. But I was still not happy about our spiritual lives.

As our children became teenagers, we gained the freedom to walk farther on Saturday morning. We were drawn to Rabbi Avi Weiss's synagogue, the Hebrew Institute of Riverdale, first by the monthly women's prayer group that met there, second by his warmth in making each of his congregants feel that he cared about them, and third by the *ruach* (joy) the members displayed while praying.

Perhaps it was the Shlomo Carlebach tunes that enraptured us and made me want to sing along with the *shaliach tzibbur*, as the cantor is called at the HIR; perhaps it was the way that Rabbi Weiss frequently gathered in my husband and other men to dance with him during especially joyous parts of Friday night services welcoming in the sabbath; perhaps it was seeing the Torah handed to a woman to carry on sabbath mornings through the woman's section and then being one of those women who carried it lovingly; perhaps it was the joint readings and explanations by men and women of the books of Esther on Purim and Ruth on Shavuot; perhaps it was the array of classes on all different levels of Jewish knowledge, held year round; perhaps it was the beginner's service, which meets on Saturday mornings; perhaps it was the talks at the end of the afternoon before the close of the sabbath—talks, attended by men and women together, one on the biblical portion of the week and on the oral and written law (Talmud); perhaps it was the participation by children in the *havdalah* service, which closes the sabbath in the synagogue; perhaps it was the rabbi's philosophy of the congregation as one community, not broken up into early prayer sections, teen groups, or young marrieds; perhaps it was the wonderful assistant rabbi and the educational director, all different from Rabbi Weiss but showing the same intensity of caring about us as individuals and as Jews; perhaps it was Rabbi Weiss's strong concern about all Jews and the world community and his willingness to speak up about issues that upset him; perhaps it was the homeless shelter the HIR sponsored, the programs for retarded adults and developmentally handicapped children, the group visits to area hospitals and nursing homes before Jewish holidays.

Maybe it was all these factors that made me finally realize I had found my spiritual home at the HIR, a place where I could continue to grow in Jewish observance and knowledge along with my family, a place that makes me proud to be Jewish, a place that acts on my concerns for my fellow Jews and the rest of humanity. The table of my Jewish experience is now fully set: a rich, religious home life supported by my husband and children and daughter-in-law, mother, and sister; an uplifting synagogue experience each week; and a deep sense of faith in the wisdom of Jewish teachings and the value of Jewish observance.

8

THE HEBREW INSTITUTE
OF RIVERDALE
BRONX, NEW YORK

MY DESIRE TO FIND one synagogue from each of the major denominations in American Jewish life to profile was almost frustrated when it came to Orthodoxy. Though I was sent to an Orthodox *yeshiva* as a child and I grew up in an observant home, my own path had moved in decidedly more liberal directions as an adult. I was dependent on the advice and recommendations of friends and colleagues who would recommend that I explore one Orthodox *shul* and then another. Following each lead meticulously, I would contact the rabbi and explain my project. I am not sure, to this day, whether the reserve with which my approaches were met were real or imagined. I visited several communities and began the interview process with rabbis and leading lay members of the congregation. In some cases, the members of the community were not sufficiently forthcoming in sharing their personal stories with me. In other cases, I came to realize that the synagogue did not meet the criteria that I had set for a true synagogue-community.

In retrospect, it is not surprising that the synagogue that Carole Oshinsky found was the one I also uncovered. Although many Orthodox synagogues will welcome Jews who are *baalei teshuvah* (Jews from less traditional backgrounds who come to embrace an Orthodox faith and lifestyle), few Orthodox synagogues are as welcoming of Jews from all backgrounds, regardless of their level of commitment, when they walk through the door. Carole Oshinsky found what hundreds of other Jews have found at the Hebrew Institute of Riverdale—a synagogue that called itself a *bayit* (house) and was a true home.[1]

—————— o ——————

Most people hear about the Hebrew Institute of Riverdale because of the activism and, some would say, notoriety of its rabbi, Avi Weiss. However, one need spend but a little time in the community to discover one of the most exciting Orthodox congregations in the country. Not surprisingly, it is also a congregation that has been willing to redefine the parameters of Orthodox Judaism.

In the mid-1960s, the Hebrew Institute of University Heights, in the New York City borough of the Bronx, found its neighborhood deteriorating and many Jews moving away. A handful of members, led by Fred Katz, who had been the president of the Orthodox *shul* for thirty-six years, decided to move the congregation to Riverdale, a nearby community in the Bronx that was attracting young families.

Property was bought in Riverdale, but there were too few members to support the building of a facility, so the thirty or so families from University Heights began attending the Riverdale Jewish Center, the largest and wealthiest Orthodox synagogue in the area. In 1971, it was decided to rent space in the basement of the Whitehall apartment building in Riverdale for High Holyday services. Cantor Israel Flusberg, who had served as the *chazan* in University Heights and had himself moved to Riverdale, became a link for the congregation in transition between the old neighborhood and the new. He, along with a rabbi hired just for the occasion, Rabbi Herbert Dobrinsky, led the High Holyday services in 1971 and again in 1972. During the rest of the year, twenty to forty regular worshipers attended services in the Whitehall building, led by Cantor Flusberg.

The last full-time rabbi, Maurice Lamm, had left when the congregation closed its doors in University Heights. But after the 1972 High Holyday services, the community set out to find a new permanent spiritual leader. Avi Weiss, a young rabbi who was serving a community in Monsey, New York, was hired. Soon after Rabbi Weiss's arrival in January 1973, younger families began to attend services at the reconstituted Hebrew Institute of Riverdale (HIR).

There quickly developed a clash between many of the older members who had come over from University Heights and the new, younger constituency led by the new rabbi. The flashpoint was the style of *davening* led by Cantor Flusberg. The formal cantorial style was not what Avi Weiss imagined for his new congregation, and the cantor was forced out, leading to the resignation of many of his supporters from the old neighborhood. With new, younger leadership and a new direction charted, the HIR began to grow. By 1974, the congregation had to rent the social hall of the Whitehall building to accommodate a crowd that typically was about one hundred fifty on a regular *shabbat*. That same year, the property that was originally bought in Riverdale was sold to enable the purchase of a more desirable site on Henry Hudson Parkway.

The house bought at 3700 Henry Hudson Parkway in 1975 was to become the *bayit* for the Hebrew Institute of Riverdale. It would house administrative offices for the congregation, although it was never adequate for anything but ancillary worship services and small classes. The congregation continued to use the social hall at Whitehall for their main services. Even the rabbi would find his home study more conducive to his work than the *bayit*.

In 1979, the congregation, which now numbered some two hundred households, completed the shell of its sanctuary and social hall adjacent to the *bayit*, enabling the congregation to conduct the majority of its programs in its own facilities. It would be another eight years before the sanctuary would be dedicated, by which time the size of the congregation had doubled. The sanctuary and *bayit* still serve the HIR community, which today consists of more than six hundred households, though frequently the facility is incapable of holding all of the people in attendance at certain services and programs.

○

Klal Yisrael, the Community of Israel

It was the Sunday night before Rosh Hashanah in 1998. The Hebrew Institute of Riverdale had extended an invitation to neighboring synagogues to join in a communal learning program. Members of the local Reform, Conservative, and Orthodox congregations began pouring in. Groups of three to five were combined at random and given an English translation of Genesis 21 to study. It is the portion that recounts the story of the *Akedah,* the binding of Isaac. Traditionally read on the second day of Rosh Hashanah, it raises questions about faith, sacrifice, blind obedience, filial piety, and more.

The number of attendees soon overflowed the social hall where the program was intended to take place. Three, four, five hundred people eventually gathered, and groups were finding corners in which to study in classrooms, the sanctuary, and the adjacent *bayit*. The campus was abuzz with Jews from different backgrounds studying Torah together. Most had never met one another. Given the polarization in

the Jewish community, it is unlikely that most had much regard or respect for Jews affiliated with movements other than their own.

At the appointed time, everyone convened in the sanctuary, where
Rabbi Jonathan Rosenblatt of the Riverdale Jewish Center (Orthodox), Rabbi Barry Dov Katz of Adath Israel (Conservative), Rabbi
Steven Franklin (Reform), and Rabbi Avi Weiss of the HIR (Orthodox) each provided their own interpretations of the biblical passage
just studied. The presentations were followed by questions from the
audience. Torah study had brought together these disparate Jews,
leaving everyone with a strong sense of *klal Yisrael,* communal solidarity. The evening was worth more than a hundred sermons on re-
specting difference and honoring fellow Jews.

[Recalled by Hillel Jaffe, interview, July 16, 1999.]

o

Overcoming Orthodox Conformity

As an Orthodox community, *halacha* is, and should be, our guide as
the manifestation of God's will in our everyday lives. In order to establish Jewish norms, we ask for a certain level of practice. Yet the
trend goes beyond *halachic* norms. In the Orthodox community in
5758 (1997–1998) there is a certain message that conformity is to be
valued. Dress a certain way, wear a certain type of *kippa,* read certain
books—what most Orthodox *shuls* in 5758 are becoming are highly
successful melting pots where different people merge into one pattern.

This is where the HIR stands apart. Our *bayit* stands out because
we are not a melting pot—we are a place that encourages a plurality
of voices. We want to explore our inner selves and find our own
unique way. We want to touch others, without losing our special
flavor. This manifests itself on many levels. In our public dialogues on
issues such as theology and Israeli politics—no viewpoint is verboten.
Our members range from people who learned to read Hebrew at birth
to those who learned last week, from those who don black hats for
shabbat to those who find spirituality by wearing a tennis shirt and
sneakers to *shul.*

We are encouraged to be unique and have our own interests, and
our *shul* celebrates this in a public way. This message comes from the
top down. Rabbi Weiss, by showing complete love for all people and
all Jews, has sent the message that no matter where you are from, no
matter what your interest, you are embraced and loved in our *bayit.*
Everyone, regardless of background, is embraced and accepted but at

the same time encouraged to grow and strive spiritually. Although increased observance is encouraged, it is not a prerequisite to being an integral part of our *bayit*.

[Recollection of Rabbi Aaron Frank for the twenty-fifth anniversary of the HIR. Rabbi Frank came to HIR in 1996 and now serves as the associate rabbi.]

Open Orthodoxy

To understand the Hebrew Institute of Riverdale requires an understanding of the current state of Orthodox Judaism in America. Though many Jews outside the community are inclined to paint Orthodox Jewry with a broad brush, Orthodoxy in fact encompasses a much wider spectrum of belief and practice than any of the other denominations of American Jewish life. The Judaism taught and practiced at the HIR is what Avi Weiss calls "open Orthodoxy" or modern Orthodoxy, and it has been framed as an alternative to more right-wing expressions of other branches of Orthodox Judaism. It is based on several key tenets.

Open Orthodoxy seeks to expose Jews to Torah values instead of imposing them on adherents. It seeks to afford women a central role in the synagogue, school, and community. Given that *halachic* standards require separation between men and women and designate men as the primary actors in the conduct of public worship, a handful of communities that subscribe to open Orthodoxy have created women's prayer groups and women's study groups, thereby allowing women a level of Jewish participation that is rare in the Orthodox world.

Open Orthodoxy infuses the existence of the state of Israel with religious meaning. Whereas Orthodox Jews farther to the right feel that the coming of the Messiah is the prerequisite for seeing Israel as the fulfillment of the Divine Promise, adherents of open Orthodoxy subscribe to the teachings of religious Zionism, which holds that through the modern state of Israel, Jews can create the kind of society that the Torah envisions and offer that as a model to the world.

Finally, even though its primary focus is on other Jews, open Orthodoxy is willing to work with non-Jews and to embrace a universal agenda regarding issues of global and social concern. From this perspective, even though one's first loyalty may be to other Jews and the issues that directly affect them, the understanding that every human being is created in the image of God (*tzelem Elohim*) leads the adherents of open Orthodoxy to act on issues like hunger, homelessness, or AIDS, even as these problems primarily affect non-Jews. The same perspective encourages a more welcoming attitude toward non-Orthodox Jews than might be the case in other parts of the Orthodox world.

Unquestionably, over the past two decades, the Orthodox Right has grown in numbers and confidence while modern Orthodoxy has felt itself on the defensive. But one finds no defensiveness at the Hebrew Institute of Riverdale. As noted, the congregation now exceeds six hundred households, and its myriad programs reach thousands more. Even more significant, Avi Weiss has created a community of remarkable spiritual depth, perhaps unparalleled in the American Jewish community.

Outreach, HIR-Style

Not coincidentally the theme at the HIR is openness. It is a form of outreach, but not in the conventional sense. Many synagogues do outreach as a way to build membership. In the Orthodox world, there is also a commitment to *kiruv,* bringing Jews closer to Orthodoxy. As practiced prominently by the Lubavitcher Hasidim as well as many other Orthodox organizations and synagogues, *kiruv* generates a constituency of *baalei teshuvah,* Jews who come from a nonobservant lifestyle to embrace Orthodoxy and its regimens.

Neither of these expressions of outreach describe what Avi Weiss has modeled. Outreach is part of Weiss's theology and, in turn, the core of what makes the Hebrew Institute of Riverdale tick. Weiss does not even like the term *outreach.* It implies that one party believes that she or he has something special to offer and is seeking to share it with others who lack it. For Weiss, outreach is a mutual interaction in which both parties are elevated to a higher level of Jewish consciousness as they learn from each other. Seeing it as an "encounter" (Weiss's preferred term), the mutual exchange can lead both parties to benefit and to acquire a deep respect for each other. The purpose of the encounter is not necessarily to get others to join the synagogue or to bring them to religious observance but to "light a spiritual fire" that allows those who are being touched to chart their own religious direction.

Fortunately, the staff of the HIR has grown to give Weiss's outreach vision a programmatic form. Beginning in 1983, the congregational budget provided for a second rabbi. In 1986, the position of executive director was created to handle the growing administrative and scheduling challenges. In the mid-1990s, a third full-time rabbi was added to work primarily with youth and education. A fourth rabbi was added several years later to oversee a *kollel,* an intensive text-learning program to train modern Orthodox rabbis. All of the rabbis, along with several rabbinic interns, provide pastoral services, fulfill teaching duties, and occasionally preach from the pulpit in the congregation.

Weiss articulates his philosophy of outreach quite clearly, and his actions speak even louder than his words. His outreach agenda has expanded as he identifies more and more disparate groups that he wants to touch.

For example, for years Weiss has visited the apartment complexes that dot the Riverdale landscape to visit the elderly who cannot easily walk to the synagogue. On Chanukah, he and his rabbinic staff go to each complex to light candles for the residents who may not be able to do it on their own. The HIR organizes regular visits to Montefiore Hospital and the nearby Fairfield Nursing Home as a way to fulfill the *mitzvah* of *bikkur cholim*, visiting the sick, and thereby bringing fellowship to the aged and infirm. In addition, more than two hundred nonmember families come to the HIR for a hot lunch program and bus trips to shopping areas, museums, and concerts. As the services increased, the HIR was able to secure funding from the social service department of the city of New York to professionalize some outreach to the elderly, but many outreach activities continue to be provided by the Hebrew Institute.

Rabbi Weiss and the HIR community view serving the unaffiliated in the area as part of their mandate. Every Passover, there is a free *seder* for members of the community. The congregation collects clothing for distribution to Russian immigrants and other needy Jews in the Bronx. And on the late afternoon of the two days of Rosh Hashanah and on Yom Kippur, there is a free religious service for the community. Hundreds attend, and the rabbis offer a program customized for those who know little, if anything, about the Jewish tradition.

For most congregations, the selling of seats for major holidays is a prime source of revenue. The cost of a Passover *seder* can be so high—$30 to $40 per person—that many committed Jews must think twice before paying for the privilege of partaking in a communal celebration. But at the HIR, no money is required. Nor is membership in the congregation pushed. In 1998, for the first time, attendees at High Holyday services were offered the opportunity to join the congregation, and approximately eighty families did so.

Another major outreach tool is the Jewish Youth Encounter Program (JYEP). Funded in part by the Gruss Fund, a New York-based foundation supporting Jewish education, this program offers children regular Jewish educational encounters from kindergarten through twelfth grade. Staffed by one of the congregation's rabbis, Aaron Frank, it provides more than one hundred children with the only Jewish exposure they will ever get, at a nominal cost. In grade 4 or 5, each student is assigned a big brother or big sister from the congregation who will spend about an hour each week tutoring the child in Hebrew, for a modest stipend. During these years, parents are gradually brought into the programming as well through holiday celebrations and *shabbat* dinners.

Any student in the JYEP program can request a bar or bat mitzvah without obligation. Many arrange for a private ceremony for family and friends, but the service takes place in the HIR facility, and one of the rabbis officiates. If a family would like to have the bar or bat mitzvah as part of the regular service on *shabbat,* that too can be arranged, regardless of the membership status of the family.

Many of the families that participate in JYEP have little or no Jewish background. It is impossible to tell whether the attraction to them is the low, subsidized cost of the educational exposure or the openness of the approach. But despite some fears that the program might be a scheme to "lure Jews to Orthodoxy," the experience is authentic and sincere. One participant noted that in light of her weak Jewish background and her husband's antipathy to institutional Judaism, she has been overwhelmed by the warm acceptance her family has found at the HIR.

One of the most remarkable examples of outreach is a monthly program done by the congregation for the physically and mentally challenged. Called "Special Friends," the program has received both city and state funding, which has allowed for the hiring of a professional social worker. Though not all of the attendees are Jewish, Rabbi Weiss interacts with the group with songs, stories, and dance, weaving in both universal and Jewish themes of love and caring.

This sensitivity to the physically challenged also led the congregation to enhance its own accessibility. A member of the community was in a car accident that left him in a wheelchair. Called to bless the Torah one *shabbat* morning, he declined the honor because he felt that it would be undignified to have his wheelchair lifted up to the raised *bima*. This act so upset the congregation and its leaders that they built a ramp to the *bima* so that physically challenged individuals would not be denied full access to all the sacred corners of the prayer space. The fact that this modification to the interior of the sanctuary required the sacrifice of precious seating area only reinforced the message that the community would not place potential revenue or convenience above principle.

All of the HIR's programs are explicitly understood by the congregation as ways to live out the Jewish value to regard every person as made in the image of God. It is no coincidence that the HIR attracts a wider array of people than most Orthodox synagogues. The outreach efforts result in many different people gravitating to the *shul*. The unaffiliated, the elderly, the non-Orthodox, and the physically and mentally challenged can all be found in a service on a typical *shabbat*. No one feels judged; all feel welcome.

A Community Synagogue

The outreach has two other consequences as well. One is that it is hard to quantify the HIR community in the way most synagogues do—by number of dues-paying households. Hundreds, perhaps thousands, of Jews in the greater Riverdale area consider the HIR their Jewish home even though they pay no dues. One unaffiliated Jew whose only appearance at the HIR was an annual visit to the free High Holyday service came forward during the congregation's last building campaign and committed half a million dollars to the effort!

The tremendous emphasis placed on outreach to the unaffiliated is typified by a bimonthly newspaper put out by the Hebrew Institute called the *Riverdale Jewish Encounter*. The articles are written primarily by the rabbis of the Hebrew Institute. All of the synagogues in the area, regardless of denomination, are listed, with addresses and phone numbers, a clear attempt to encourage unaffiliated Jews to make a spiritual connection somewhere. Ads in the four-page publication announce a full range of programs and opportunities that are available at the HIR free of charge.

In the monthly newsletter, the HIR can publicize a Saturday evening coffee house with music and entertainment, a Friday night program of story and song in the spirit of the outreach High Holyday service, Hebrew crash courses, dinners themed to Jewish festivals, and programs for local singles. In many ways, the Hebrew Institute functions very much like a Jewish community center in the sense that it has taken on the responsibility to program for the community at large. Many small Jewish communities rely on the major congregation in town to provide community-wide programming. What is so unique about the Riverdale phenomenon is that the Hebrew Institute is hardly the largest or wealthiest congregation in the neighborhood. Its sponsorship of such an array of programs for Jews in the vicinity without any particular membership push can only be understood as an implementation of a deep sense of mission to meet the needs of *klal Yisrael*, the broader Jewish community.

The second consequence of the outreach emphasis at the HIR is the effect that it has on the core membership. Many members who were raised in Orthodox synagogues note how challenging and sometimes even

uncomfortable it is to be part of the HIR. The typical Orthodox synagogue is much more homogeneous, either attracting like-minded and like-
practicing Jews or having an atmosphere that subtly (or sometimes not
so subtly) encourages conformity to a certain worldview (*hashkafa*) and
lifestyle.

Many Jews are drawn to the HIR initially by the outreach programs,
but they return because of the community's nonjudgmental attitude about
each Jew's respective level of observance. The community is well aware
that some who come to the HIR on *shabbat* have driven a car to get there.
Others cannot read Hebrew. Still others are totally nonobservant.

For twenty-five years, Avi Weiss has preached the *mitzvah* of *ahavat
Yisrael,* the love of the Jewish people. He sees all Jews as part of his family, which means that we must love them for who they are and not for
what they do or do not do. HIR members act accordingly. Not only does
this philosophy account for the HIR's many outreach activities, but it also
makes the community one of great openness, tremendous warmth, and
love extended to all, simply because they are Jews. It is also this philosophy that makes Weiss and the Hebrew Institute open to Conservative, Reconstructionist, and Reform Jews and their rabbis. At a time of great
tension between Orthodox and non-Orthodox Judaism—precipitated by
debate in Israel over the "Who is a Jew?" question—Weiss actively sought
out opportunities to join with the other movements as a way to signal the
unity of the Jewish people. It was Weiss who initiated a joint Simchat
Torah celebration with local non-Orthodox synagogues in Riverdale.
And it was Weiss who reached out to non-Orthodox colleagues for a pa-
rade and party to celebrate the fiftieth anniversary of the state of Israel.
Weiss was also one of the only Orthodox rabbis willing to set foot into
the Reform Temple Emanuel in New York for a community-wide com-
memoration of Yom ha-Shoah (Holocaust Remembrance Day). On the
Sunday night between Rosh Hashanah and Yom Kippur in 1998, Weiss
organized a community-wide study session on the story of the binding of
Isaac (Genesis 22) featuring a panel of Orthodox, Conservative, and Reform rabbis as well as text study in small groups composed without regard for denominational affiliation.

To participate at the HIR is to encounter all types of Jews. And they are
there because the message from the rabbis and from the leadership is
"This is your home too. You don't have to be like us to be here." There
are not too many synagogues where an observant Jew wearing a black hat
(representing a more extreme form of observance) might be sitting next
to a nonobservant Jew wearing a sport shirt and sneakers who has come
to the HIR to seek out his roots.

Certain Jews have left the HIR out of fear that their own level of observance and propriety might be diluted by the mix of people attracted to the congregation, but those who stay feel that they have been inwardly strengthened by the outreach. They rejoice in the heterogeneity that Rabbi Weiss's theology has spawned.

The Prayer Experience

If the challenge in liberal congregations is to provide participants in the prayer experience with enough knowledge of the structure and language of the service so that they can experience it to the fullest, the challenge in an Orthodox synagogue is to get participants to a place where their routinized knowledge of the service doesn't serve as a barrier to true *kavanah* (prayer intentionality). The HIR accomplishes this in several ways. First, there is little tolerance for the chatter that is commonplace in most Orthodox synagogues. The rabbi will step forward to the reader's table and stop the service if he feels there is too much talking, preventing the cantor from continuing with the chanting until he is satisfied with the attention level.

Second, the rabbi will stop a service momentarily to highlight why a prayer that is about to be recited is especially important or appropriate on that particular day. He'll end with an admonition—"now listen very carefully." For many, it works.

The third and perhaps most important reason for the very spiritual *davening* that takes place at the HIR is Dr. Eli Kranzler. A therapist during the week, Kranzler has served as the cantor of the Hebrew Institute since 1986. He is a student of the melodies of Shlomo Carlebach, a guitar-playing rabbi who composed hundreds of Hasidic-style prayers that are now sung in Jewish communities throughout the world. Not only are the melodies enticingly singable, but Kranzler offers them in a soft, mellow, and inviting voice. His repetition of the refrain in a wordless rhythm encourages even those unfamiliar with the Hebrew to join in. His energetic drumbeat on the reader's table is the cue for worshipers to clap hands and, on occasion, to link arms and break into a circular dance. Rabbi Weiss is most often the lead clapper or dancer, giving permission for overt expressions of joy that is rare in other synagogues of any denomination.

Several years ago, Kranzler expanded his Carlebach-inspired *davening* to the Friday evening service. Not customarily a well-attended service because many people have an elaborate *shabbat* celebration at home, the service began to attract hundreds of younger Jews from Riverdale and beyond eager to participate in a service filled with song and joy. Among the attendees are over one hundred women, a remarkable phenomenon for an Orthodox community.

There are two exceptional features to the design and layout of the sanctuary itself. The first is the placement of the *bima,* traditionally the place for the ark housing the scrolls and seating for officiants at the service. At the HIR, the focal point of the service is a table (*shulchan*) placed in the center of the sanctuary. It is from here that the Torah is read and the *chazan* leads the service. The *bima* is regarded as a place of honor reserved for seating the rabbi and other dignitaries. When the rabbi or a guest speaks, it is from a lectern placed between the ark and the reader's table. For all other parts of the service, the rabbi roams the men's section of the sanctuary, imparting hugs, pats on the back, and kisses. Particular attention is focused on newcomers, who receive an added share of the rabbi's attention.

The Role of Women

The second exceptional feature of the sanctuary is that the women's section and the men's section are side by side, with a full view of the leaders of the service and those on the other side of the *mechitzah* (divider). Although most Orthodox synagogues have a higher *mechitzah,* with the women's section often far from the front of the synagogue, at the HIR the men and women could swap sections with no change in proximity to the service.

Avi Weiss and his colleague, Rabbi Saul Berman, have been the leading voices in the Orthodox community advocating for an increased role for women in Jewish life. Though stopping short of the egalitarianism, prevalent now in most of the non-Orthodox Jewish world, that would count women in a *minyan,* allow them to officiate at services, and allow them to be ordained as rabbis, the proponents of open Orthodoxy encourage women's prayer groups, serious Jewish study, and equal status with men in providing leadership to the institutions of Jewish life, including the synagogue.

All of these elements are in evidence at the HIR. Once a month, a women's prayer group meets on *shabbat* morning. Avi Weiss's book, *Women at Prayer,* sets the *halachic* parameters for such gatherings. And while women coming from a more liberal background would bristle at the notion that women can assume all ritual roles in a service only because there are no men present, the women's prayer group provides participants with opportunities for Jewish involvement that would be hard to find in other places in the Orthodox world. The women's prayer group also provides the context to allow young women to celebrate a bat mitzvah in a manner equivalent to their male counterparts, even if it does not take place as part of the main service.

The desire to reach out to women in the community is telegraphed in other ways as well. During the main service, Rabbi Weiss seems to go out of his way to face the women's section as much as the men's section when he speaks. His use of gender-sensitive language is a rarity in Orthodox circles. Nor does he restrict the handling of the Torah by women. A few Orthodox synagogues have started allowing women to carry the Torah on Simchat Torah; the Hebrew Institute passes the Torah to the women's section every *shabbat,* and the women hand it off to each other, kissing or touching it as they please. In the late 1990s, the HIR hired a female graduate student in Jewish education to work as a congregational intern on a part-time basis. That this intern not only taught but also offered pastoral services and spoke from the pulpit during a *shabbat* service raised eyebrows in other sectors of the Orthodox community. It was, however, consistent with other practices that had become accepted at the HIR over recent years.

Political Action

The most idiosyncratic aspect of Avi Weiss's rabbinate is his political activism. Weiss was a leader in the movement to free Soviet Jews and became a close confidant of Avital Sharansky in her efforts to obtain release of her husband, Anatoly (now known as Natan), from Soviet prisons. When Sharansky was finally freed, the Hebrew Institute of Riverdale was the site of his first public appearance in the United States, a gesture of gratitude for Weiss's tireless efforts on his behalf.

In a similarly single-minded way, Weiss has spearheaded the effort to rally Jewish community support for Jonathan Pollard, an American Jew in the employ of the American military who was convicted of passing classified information to the state of Israel. Weiss traveled to Buenos Aires after the bombing of the Israeli embassy there in 1997 to demand more aggressive investigation of that terrorist act. He showed up at rallies and speeches when David Duke and then Pat Buchanan ran for the presidency, each time using signs to bring media attention to the bigoted stands of the respective candidates. He has likewise protested at rallies for Louis Farrakhan.

Weiss is fairly hawkish on the issue of the Middle East peace process, hesitant to trade land for peace or to make significant concessions to the Palestinian Authority, led by Yasser Arafat. But as outspoken as Weiss is on an issue like the security and peace of the state of Israel, he has not shut his community off from other opinions. He is proud of the fact that on the issue of Israeli-Arab relations, he has provided forums for leading doves like Leonard Fein and Balfour Brickner to speak to his community. Even one of his assistant rabbis was surprised when Weiss encouraged him to be more outspoken about his political views within the community, views that were both more dovish and more universalistic than Weiss's.

In 1985, when President Ronald Reagan traveled to a military cemetery in Bitburg, Germany, to lay a wreath, Weiss showed up at the nearby concentration camp of Bergen-Belsen with a handful of his supporters. His point was that Reagan should not be bestowing honor on the perpetrators of the Holocaust. Better that the American president honor the memory of the innocent victims. Similarly, Weiss and some of his followers organized a protest in Geneva, Switzerland, in 1988 when the United Nations extended an invitation to Yasser Arafat to travel to New York to address that international body. Weiss objected to such an unwarranted honor being accorded to a man that many consider a terrorist.

Among his most highly publicized acts was to travel to Auschwitz in 1989 to protest the erecting of a convent and large cross at the site of the former concentration camp. It drew the ire of Cardinal Glemp of Poland and unmasked the continued antisemitism of the Polish Catholic Church. Nine years later, as the U.S. Holocaust Memorial Museum and the government of Poland were negotiating about the future status of the Auschwitz site, Weiss mounted a national campaign accusing the museum of betraying the memory of the victims of the Holocaust in its dealings with the Polish leadership.

Through all of these activities, Weiss has had little patience for the vast network of Jewish organizations whose mandate it is to defend the interests of the Jewish people. His sharp criticism of the establishment leadership of the Jewish community has garnered him both much publicity and much disdain. Of course, Weiss also has legions of admirers. Nor would anyone doubt Weiss's passion or commitment. He has continually been willing to put his liberty and even his safety on the line for what he perceives to be the best interests of the Jewish people.

Support for Avi Weiss's political activity is organized through an organization he created called the Coalition for Jewish Concerns (AMCHA). Its more than twenty thousand members receive news updates and copies of Weiss's speeches and columns in return for annual dues. The organization is run by a paid administrator out of the offices of the Hebrew Institute. Though AMCHA carries its own legal identity, it pays no rent for the space it uses at the HIR, a fact that reflects the support of the congregation for the advocacy work of its rabbi, if not sympathy for every position he stakes out.

Though a handful of HIR members have been drawn to the congregation by Weiss's high public profile and most of those who have traveled with Weiss around the world have been members of the *shul,* political activism would rank low on the scale of qualities that attract people to the HIR. Weiss himself guesses that his activism has kept more people away than it has drawn. Leaders of the congregation would concur, noting that should Weiss retire from the pulpit, that aspect of his rabbinate would be the least likely to remain a feature of the HIR.

Many observers acknowledge that Weiss's activism has acquired for the HIR the reputation as a "maverick" congregation. Many people have avoided the Hebrew Institute, thinking it was organized around Weiss's activism. Only after an initial visit do they recognize that most of the finest qualities of the community have nothing to do with politics. Indeed, to observe Weiss in the disparate settings is to see two different men. For all of the aggressiveness, verve, and audacity that characterize Weiss in public demonstrations, he is virtually the opposite in congregational contexts, where he is soft-spoken, gentle, and eager to solicit opposing views.

If there is a way to understand the seeming paradox between the public Avi Weiss and his synagogue personality, one must revisit the theme of *ahavat Yisrael,* love of the Jewish people. Because Weiss sees all Jews as part of his family, when a Jew is in danger, there is no limit to what he feels must be done to come to that Jew's assistance. He is quick to remind his critics that two of the greatest achievements of the postwar Jewish community— advocacy for Soviet Jews and the rescue of Ethiopian Jewry—were causes that got pushed onto the community's agenda by students and activists who were outsiders to the established leadership of the community.

Not only does Weiss not apologize for his activism, but he brings the themes of his latest cause into the worship services at the HIR. Whether inviting guest speakers, promoting a rally, or using the opportunities during the service itself to draw connections between a piece of liturgy and the cause at hand, Weiss makes the point that his advocacy work is not a side hobby; it is part of his theology. He wants people to pay more attention to what he does than to what he says. If congregants don't mount the barricades with him, they at least get the message. And he certainly earns their respect and admiration for acting on the courage of his convictions.

○

Lamppost Activism

After three years as associate rabbi, I found it hard to avoid the clutter in the *bayit.* I decided to bring some order to the chaos. In every corner, from the basement up to the second floor, there were cartons and cartons of flyers for events that had already taken place. Rabbi Weiss was single-handedly supporting the printing industry by ordering thousands of extra flyers in the belief that they would be posted on every pole and distributed to every house in Riverdale. Indeed, that often happened. I personally became intimately aware of every lamppost and tree up and down Henry Hudson Parkway.

It was at the HIR that I learned about the importance of activism. Too many Jews are guilty of burying their heads in the sand. Too often we are timid about making our voices heard during times of adversity. Rabbi Weiss taught me how to stand proud and make my voice heard. I remember so clearly our demonstrations in Manhattan in front of the United Nations and the Russian compound in Riverdale on behalf of Soviet Jewry. I remember our rallies on behalf of Israel during politically difficult times or after a terrorist attack. I recall the stands that we took together when a political leader made disparaging remarks about Jews or Israel. One of our greatest moments was that magnificent evening when Natan Sharansky spoke at the Hebrew Institute. It was his debut speech in America. Every one of us was exhilarated by his remarks and by being part of this memorable moment in history. We were euphoric because it was our Rabbi Weiss who kept Natan Sharansky's plight in the eyes and ears of the world.

Among our many demonstrations, none was more powerful than our trip to Bergen-Belsen. We went there to protest President Reagan's planned trip to the Bitburg Cemetery to lay a wreath in the place where German SS soldiers were buried as a symbol of "reconciliation." Our message was clear: honoring the perpetrators of murder can only dishonor their victims. It is impossible to express the intensity of emotions I felt, but suffice it to say that the memory of that experience is forever in my heart.

[Recalled by Rabbi Ronald Schwarzberg, HIR assistant rabbi, 1981–1986.]

○

Everything But a Band on Yom Kippur

It was at the Hebrew Institute of Riverdale that I learned that a synagogue could, and must, have a mission. I came to understand that a *beit knesset* (synagogue) needs to be more than simply a *m'kom tefillah,* a place of prayer. It had to set as a goal the actualizing of the core values of Judaism as understood by the unique perspective of the leadership and congregants. At first I thought it cute that our stationery established a theme ("Torah, Outreach, Activism, Israel"); later I came to realize how important it is to frame everything that a synagogue does in its perception of the central message of our faith and peoplehood.

To this day, I am uncomfortable sitting on the *bima* of my own synagogue, and I blame Avi Weiss. I would much rather circulate around the sanctuary, finding someone who might appreciate a moment to hear the Torah read with the rabbi at his side or helping carry the song of the *baal tefillah* (the prayer leader) to the yonder reaches of the room. In Riverdale, one of my self-appointed jobs was to position myself near the back corner of the *kehillah* (congregation) during *Kedushah* (an important prayer in the *Amidah*) to pick up the *niggunim* (melodies) that Eli Kranzler or Rabbi Weiss would be singing.

I can still feel the energy in the room at the open service on the High Holydays, my need, literally, to climb across the chairs in the packed social hall to make my way to the front to help things work. I recall the time that in horror, I opened the *Jewish Week* to find that I had been misquoted in my description of the Yom Kippur service; I tried desperately to have the paper print a retraction, clarifying that we would not have a band and refreshments that afternoon! What we did have was an uplifting, sensitive, joyful, emotional experience, connecting with Jews who otherwise had too little contact with us, the synagogue, and G-d. Year after year, it was perfectly clear just how significant this hour was in people's lives.

[Recalled by Rabbi Chaim Marder, HIR assistant rabbi, 1988–1990.]

The HIR Program

The Hebrew Institute has a wide array of programs for its members. The synagogue's motto is "Torah, Outreach, Activism, Israel," and most of the programming fits in at least one of these categories.

The most energy revolves around *shabbat* services. In addition to the increasingly popular Friday evening service featuring the Carlebach melodies and the main *shabbat* morning service, the HIR also sponsors a weekly teen *minyan,* a weekly learner's service conducted in English for people unfamiliar with the service, and the monthly women's prayer group. Many people return to *shul* on *shabbat* afternoon for study sessions conducted by one of the rabbis and for *mincha* and *maariv,* the afternoon and evening services that conclude the sabbath. In the spring and summer months, the congregation sponsors "*Perek* in the Park," offering study of *Pirkei Avot* (Ethics of Our Ancestors) in a nearby public park.

The congregation's adult education program is organized under the rubric of an Academy of Judaic Studies, also known as the Midrashia. Although most of the courses offered by the rabbinic staff take place on Monday nights, during most of the year there are courses available four nights a week in addition to Sunday mornings. Topics include studies of rabbinic texts, Bible, philosophy, theology, Hebrew, and Jewish meditation. The recently developed *kollel,* designed to train modern Orthodox rabbis, features one-on-one text study (*hevruta*) in which some members of the congregation participate as well. Several times a year, the congregation hosts a scholar in residence who will offer talks over the course of a *shabbat.* A significant number of members are also organized into *havurah* study groups of seven to ten families that meet in each other's homes for a lay-run program of study.

The vast majority of the children of members attend Jewish day school or *yeshivot* in the greater New York area. As a result, most of the youth education done by the synagogue is outreach to unaffiliated Jews in the area. This not only includes the Jewish Youth Encounter Program described earlier but also a Judaic enrichment program for children in kindergarten, first, and second grade on Wednesday afternoons. The HIR actually provides bus pickup from a local public school, bringing the children to the synagogue for Bible stories and exposure to the Jewish heritage. The program is free to any and all who want to participate.

An extremely effective program that integrates the children of members with the many unaffiliated young people in the JYEP program is the big brother and big sister program. As noted earlier, beginning in the fourth or fifth grade, students are matched up with older teens who serve as tutors, friends, and mentors. The regular meetings might have the big brother or sister tutor Hebrew, help prepare for bar or bat mitzvah, or serve as a sounding board for the many issues that growing up presents. The big brothers and sisters receive a modest fee in return for their time, but far more important is that they feel good about serving as a role model and friend to a younger Jew who might not otherwise receive much in the way of positive Jewish influences.

Rabbinic Style

The Hebrew Institute under Avi Weiss has never shied away from charting its own course. The existence of several other vibrant Orthodox congregations in Riverdale allow the HIR to be idiosyncratic; people have choices. If, at times, this has earned the reputation of being a maverick congregation, the leadership seems to wear that label comfortably. In fact, one senses pride among members that people who once criticized the Hebrew Institute for one thing or another can now be seen paying occasional visits. Some former detractors have become members. It is hard to argue with success.

The elements of the HIR's success flow from Weiss's personal priorities. The rabbi is undeniably a powerful personality, and most of the members of the Hebrew Institute are avowedly his *hasidim*, his followers. Because so much of the congregation's character and program flow from Weiss's philosophy, it would be hard to be a member without being committed to the man in a deep and personal way. The commitment is reciprocal; most member families can recount stories of the rabbi's making extraordinary efforts to be with them at times of personal crisis.

Avi Weiss is well aware of the atmosphere that he has created at the HIR, and he has done it with great deliberateness. His earliest memories of synagogues were not very positive. Although his father was a rabbi at a small, private synagogue in Sheepshead Bay, Brooklyn, young Avi frequented many other *shuls* and found most of them cold and off-putting. The sight of Jews being refused entry by uniformed guards when they showed up on the High Holydays without tickets is seared in his memory. It helps explain his insistence on free outreach High Holyday services and Pesach *seders* even as such practices fly in the face of conventional synagogue economics.

Weiss was also shaped by his first two congregations. Upon ordination, he took a pulpit on the outskirts of St. Louis. Although it was nominally an Orthodox synagogue, many of the members were nonobservant, and there was not even a *mechitzah* in the sanctuary. Weiss enjoys recounting the odd practice at that congregation that would have men insert styrofoam partitions on rivets between the seats when women came to sit next to them!

From St. Louis Weiss went to a congregation in Monsey, New York, a solidly Orthodox community. As he reflects on the two experiences, Weiss most values what he learned in St. Louis. Despite the lack of observance within the congregation, he couldn't help being impressed at how serious his members were about Judaism and Jewish learning. He became convinced that the encounter between people with different outlooks and religious ideas is the key to spiritual growth, something that was not as possible in the environment of Monsey, where people were much more similar to one another.

Given the high percentage of observant Jews in Riverside, Weiss could have easily created an environment reminiscent of the *shtetls*, or small

Jewish villages, of Eastern Europe, but he opted for a much more open model wherein the Hebrew Institute would be home for any Jew seeking spiritual connection. Calling the synagogue building the *bayit,* Hebrew for "house" or "home," underscores this interest in providing a welcome to all.

One gets the feeling that the Hebrew Institute is Avi Weiss's private *shul* and that everyone, from the rabbi to the average member, likes it that way. For all of the participation of members in services, classes, action projects, and the like, there have never been a large number of people involved in the governance of the institution. Weiss has tended to work with a handful of close confidants who see themselves as privileged to offer counsel and provide support to Weiss's visionary leadership. Certainly most of the presidents of the congregation would thus describe their role. It is not so much a matter that the board was weak or fickle as much as it was that the lay leadership wanted to support its rabbi. It is ironic that as far as Avi Weiss has traveled from the days of his *yeshiva* upbringing, he has put into place a synagogue model that is closer to the private *shul* of his father than to the more standard lay governance model of most American synagogues.

At a board meeting early in his tenure, Weiss proposed a new program that met with some resistance because of cost. Despite his youth and his untested standing in the new congregation, he resolutely stated: "A synagogue is not a business." Soon enough, the congregation echoed Weiss's sentiments. Although most HIR leaders acknowledge the inadequate administrative structure, the need for capital improvements, and the below-average dues structure as congregational weaknesses, none of these things seems to impede the congregation's ability to reach out and touch thousands of Jews on a regular basis.

To many observers, Weiss is a paradox. His political activism; his support for the policies of Likud-led Israeli governments, particularly on the peace process; and his willingness to take on the Jewish organizational establishment, claiming that it is betraying Jewish interests, have led many to brand him a right-wing ideologue. At the same time, he is in the forefront of the attempt to open up Orthodoxy to more tolerant and liberal views regarding the role of women in religious realms and interaction with the non-Jewish community. Not only has he offered his pulpit to leaders whose views are anathema to him, but a succession of assistant rabbis working under Weiss will attest to the fact that Weiss not only doesn't try to censor their views when they disagree with him but actually encourages them to speak the truth as they see it. Notwithstanding the passion of his convictions, over time Weiss has come to believe that fair-minded people will have different opinions that must be heard. Weiss will admit to some degree of self-righteousness on issues that he has felt deeply about. As he has grown older, he has been increasingly willing to admit that he may not always be right.

One anecdote highlights the tension between the prophetic, judgmental Avi Weiss and the pastoral, accepting Avi Weiss. During a *shabbat* morning service, Weiss is all charm and hugs to those who enter the sanctuary. And yet when he ascends the *bima* to offer a *d'var torah* or takes the liberty to raise an issue of particular concern, the people seated before him can easily feel the sting of his rhetoric. Such was the case at a service that followed the riots that erupted in a black neighborhood in Los Angeles after the policemen who had attacked Rodney King were acquitted. Weiss raised the issue and elicited from members their feelings about the chaos and the human and material toll of the riots. But when it came time to make his point in summary, he told his congregants that to characterize any one group (in this case, African Americans) as "them" and assign collective responsibility to that group would be a violation of Torah-sanctioned behavior. A people that has been subjected to bigotry can ill afford to succumb to bigotry itself. It was a timely and powerful teaching to those present.

On another occasion, Weiss did not hesitate to act on his stated outrage at men in the Orthodox community who will not provide their wives with proper religious divorce documentation (*get*). According to *halacha,* because only a man can initiate a *get,* a women without such papers is unable to remarry. The Orthodox community has attempted to put pressure on such husbands when they can be identified. On one occasion when Weiss spotted one such husband in his congregation, he walked over and told him that he was not welcome in the *shul.* This from a rabbi who is as likely to hug a strange newcomer as say a perfunctory "hello."

——————————————— o ———————————————

A Racist Love?

In the course of a public dialogue, I remarked that I feel greater pain when coming across the name of a Jewish victim of a plane crash than that of a non-Jewish victim. During a question-and-answer session, I was accused of having made a racist comment. The questioner protested that one should feel equal pain for all human beings.

Was he right? Is it racist for Jews to love other Jews more than non-Jews? . . .

The distinction becomes clear when comparing love of family to love of non-family. I love my spouse, children, grandchildren, parents and siblings in a way I don't love others. My connection is emotional, the love for them more intense. . . .

Am Yisrael (the people of Israel) is my family. Not my inner family, but my family nonetheless, my larger family. . . .

This does not mean that we do not feel the suffering and joy of non-Jews. Of course we do. Jews together with non-Jews are part of the even larger community of humankind, but the ties of kinship and custom, of shared values, experiences and traditions are not nearly as closely meshed. To believe that there is no difference is ultimately to deny human nature.

For this reason, I become very concerned when people say: "You know, rabbi, I love everyone." I respond: "It is fine to love everyone, but tell me do you love your father, your mother, your child?" Saying you love everyone is a dangerous self-delusion. It is easy to love everyone; it is far more difficult to love someone. . . .

It is the great and abiding love and concern that our synagogue displays for our fellow Jews that has brought us also to initiate activities that have a much larger focus, like food drives for the hungry, clothing collections for the homeless and an ongoing program for the mentally retarded in which half of whom we serve are not Jewish.

People often ask me why I do what I do. Why do I run to Buenos Aires after a terrorist attack? Why do I travel to Oslo to protest Arafat's peace prize? Why go here, why go there?

It is because I love my people. That is the basis of my activism. My people are my family. As I love my inner family, unconditionally, as I react to their pain as if it were mine, so do I relate to my larger family, *am Yisrael*. For me the questions is not, why go to the end of the world to help another Jew, but rather, how can one not go to the end of the world to help another Jew?

Yes, I feel the pain of Jewish victims of plane crashes more than non-Jewish victims. That's not racism. It is part of the human condition. To feel for all, yet to feel for family more.

[Excerpt from Rabbi Avi Weiss, "A Racist Love," *New York Jewish Week*, Nov. 4, 1994.]

Beyond the HIR

In recent years, Avi Weiss has given increasing attention to training other rabbis to carry his vision of open Orthodoxy to other communities around the country. The half-dozen rabbis who have worked with him on the rabbinic staff of the Hebrew Institute credit him for being primary influences on their rabbinate in far greater measure than their seminary training. As these rabbis move on to congregations around the country, they carry with them models of congregational programs and leadership that they are eager to replicate.

Two more formal institutional attempts to spread the ideas and practice of open Orthodoxy have been the creation of Torat Miriam and MeORoT, the Modern Orthodox Rabbinic Training Fellowship. Torat Miriam, a program launched in 1997, is designed to train women in homiletics, teaching, and *halachic* decision making. In many quarters of the Orthodox world, exposure to such subjects for women would be unheard of, and press reports of the new program raised speculation that women would soon be serving in quasi-rabbinic capacities in Orthodox synagogues in the near future. For the ten women in the inaugural class of Torat Miriam, the program is an opportunity to expand the skills that they seek to apply in Jewish day schools, synagogues, and Jewish communal institutions.

MeORoT is a program for rabbinical students, primarily from Yeshivah University, who are mentored by Rabbis Avi Weiss and Saul Berman for a period of a year and exposed to a range of issues and perspectives that may not be part of their formal rabbinical training program. Since its founding in 1996, about a dozen students have participated in the program each year.

The program of study includes lectures and discussion around such issues as pluralism, the religious meaning of the state of Israel, Jewish-Gentile relations, the limits of rabbinic authority, the status of women, outreach, and activism. The speakers are luminaries from the Orthodox world who have also been active in the broader Jewish community, including Rabbi Irving Greenberg, Rabbi Haskel Lookstein, Rabbi Shlomo Riskin, Menachem Elon, Rabbi Emanuel Rackman, Rabbi Haym Sloveitchik, Barry Shrage, and Richard Joel.

The hope is that this program and exposure to the successful models of the Hebrew Institute of Riverdale will complement the formal course of study for the rabbinate and help a larger number of rabbis than might ever work directly with Avi Weiss think about ways to create institutions that model the HIR's effectiveness. For Orthodox-trained rabbis whose seminary education is so focused on the interpretation and application of *halacha,* to spend time with some of the more progressive thinkers in the Orthodox world is a true eye-opener. One rabbi remarked that the experience helped him realize that an understanding of the human condition was at least as important as the precepts of the Jewish legal tradition. It gave him the permission to consider that the needs of an individual may supersede the promulgation of a code of law. To a non-Orthodox person, this insight might be obvious; to an Orthodox Jew about to serve as a rabbi to a community, it is a revelation.

○

It is too soon to say how much of the synagogue model created by Avi Weiss will survive him. Some aspects of his program are much more deeply rooted in the community than others. Nor is the model without some internal contradictions. While the expansion of outreach efforts could never have been sustained without the outside funding that has made it possible to hire professionals to run the programs, the consequence of professionalization has been that fewer members of the Hebrew Institute have to interact with outside populations like the aged, infirm, or disabled. Clearly, when the programs were created, the transformative *mitzvah* opportunities for members were as much an intended consequence as the service to the specific populations. Much less of that happens today.

It is also unclear how much the Hebrew Institute model might influence other Orthodox synagogues. The prevailing trend in Orthodoxy today is rightward. The openness of the HIR—to the nonobservant, to women, to cooperation with liberal denominations in the Jewish world—runs counter to that rightward drift. It may well be that recent initiatives to bolster the forces of open Orthodoxy and to influence new rabbis in that direction will succeed and the approach represented by the Hebrew Institute will gain strength among the Orthodox. It is just as likely that there will be some coalescence between the progressive leaders and institutions in the Orthodox world and the right-wing break off from the Conservative movement now organized under the banner of the Union for Traditional Judaism. If this were to happen, it would be easy for the rest of the Orthodox world to dismiss the adherents of open Orthodoxy.

But whatever the ultimate alignment in the Jewish world, nothing can take away the fact that Avi Weiss and the Hebrew Institute of Riverdale represent a model for a synagogue-community that is worthy of emulation. Whether one is more traditional in practice than the norm at the HIR or more liberal, one cannot spend any amount of time within the orbit of the Hebrew Institute and fail to be impressed with the intensity of commitment among the members and the sheer love of Judaism and the Jewish people that pervades the community.

9

PHILLIP'S PATH

MY INTRODUCTION TO FORMAL JUDAISM took place in a cathedral-type Conservative synagogue in the Bronx complete with wooden pews, choir loft, and organ. The cantor and rabbi dressed in robes with priestly hats and neatly folded satin *tallitot* (prayer shawls). The cantor performed and was critiqued as though he were giving a concert. The rabbi was watched to see if he followed the rules of *shabbat* and *kashrut*. He in turn made superficial attempts to lecture the congregation on how to "become more Jewish."

The neighborhood, a postwar planned housing development for working-class people, with around a thousand apartment units, was carefully segregated. Approximately 15 percent of the residents were Jews by birth, and 75 percent were Irish Catholics. The community had a second, better-established Conservative synagogue and a vibrant Young Israel (a type of Orthodox congregation), which felt as foreign to me as the Catholic churches in the neighborhood.

I knew all four of my grandparents as I grew up. My father's parents spoke Yiddish and accented English. They emigrated from Austria before World War II. We never discussed their religious beliefs or life experiences in Europe. They were simple, family-oriented people. Grandpa was a quiet, well-groomed man and a good provider. Grandma had a commanding, strong, style. She was clearly a leading force in the home and protective of the whole family. Their home was basically kosher (although I had no idea what that really was all about), and my grandfather attended

---

Phillip Schneider is a speech pathologist in private practice and an associate professor of communication disorders at Queens College, City University of New York. He and his wife, Jean, have raised two sons, Uri and Elan.

a local traditional synagogue on major holidays. I am not sure if he maintained any other rituals.

My mother's parents lived in a rural-suburban area in northern Westchester County. Grandpa emigrated from Russian Poland and had many colorful stories to share about his life as a Jew growing up. He spoke of socialism, activism, struggling to earn a living in the "old country," acquiring a professional education, and then confronting antisemitism in New York in the early 1900s. Being Jewish was a central theme in Grandpa's life, although it was not expressed in religious or spiritual terms. He helped found and maintain a Conservative-type synagogue in Yorktown Heights, New York, and wrote about his experiences as a Jew in its newsletter.

Grandma was born and raised in Philadelphia and had an excellent command of English as well as Yiddish. She seemed culturally connected to being a Jew. I had a warm, close relationship with these grandparents and saw their country home as my physical, emotional, and spiritual retreat from the city. With them I developed a love for the outdoors. I believe that their interests contributed to my early spiritual roots and Jewish identity. For Grandma, dietary considerations revolved around healthy eating and fell loosely within the framework of Jewish dietary laws. They had a commitment to *tzedakah* (charitable giving), Jewish organizational work, and Zionism.

My parents became members of the local Conservative synagogue when they needed to send me to Hebrew school so that I could become a bar mitzvah. We never attended synagogue as a family but found ways to mark the major Jewish holidays. Chanukah meant candles, gifts, and latkes. Passover included a brief *seder,* with the *seder* plate objects and special foods. Rosh Hashanah and Yom Kippur meant meals with grandparents, dressing fancy, and gathering in front of the synagogue to greet the other Jews as they filtered in and out of the synagogue, though we never ventured inside. We did not discuss religion, and my parents did not seem to believe in God one way or another.

Attending Hebrew school, two afternoons after school and Sunday morning, was a rather unpleasant and unruly experience. I was introduced to the holidays and basic Hebrew language skills. I acquired the ability to sound out Hebrew print, which was referred to as reading. I attended mandatory *shabbat* morning youth services, which served to ingrain the traditional *shabbat* melodies in my right brain. The meaning of these "songs" never became clear to me.

My bar mitzvah was a stressful, unpleasant event. I was to share my day in synagogue with another bar mitzvah boy, whom I perceived as better than me at everything. I performed the Haftarah and then stood as the rabbi used me for a stage prop to address the audience. I remember his hand on my shoulder as though I knew him or he knew me. Since I enjoyed acting, I knew I could handle this, although I knew this was supposed to feel like something more. My extended family came from all over to sit and observe this show. Following the synagogue event, the entire group, including about a dozen schoolmates and friends, proceeded to drive to a restaurant where we had a nonkosher meal accompanied by accordion music.

The following summer, I spent my first two weeks in a kosher Boy Scout sleep-away camp. Early one morning, someone woke me and asked if I had been "bar-mitzvahed." Once having established that I was a bona fide member of the tribe, I was told that I was needed for a *minyan* because someone had to say *Kaddish*. These were unfamiliar words to me. I can remember feeling good about being needed as a Jewish man. I followed them to a clearing in a pine forest with a sweet smell in the air, dark evergreens all around, and blue sky with white puffy clouds above. The seats were made of logs, as was the ark. I hummed the familiar melodies, soaked in the beauty of nature with all my senses, and felt a powerful connection to the earth, sky, God, and the world of Jews. It was a sense of peacefully being at one. This was my place.

I don't recall other strong Jewish moments until I traveled to Surprise Lake Camp a few summers later to bring my sister's trunk to camp. I was about to turn sixteen. As we drove up a densely wooded road into the camp, I fell in love. I wanted to stay in this place. We met the director and asked if he could use me on staff. He said he needed someone to sort mail, do laundry, and answer the phone. I jumped at the opportunity and went back to the city to pack and return to camp. I spent the next four summers working there as the pioneering counselor. This camp was devoted to serving city children who were generally of limited economic means. Its mission was to introduce them to Jewish ritual and culture, Zionism, teamwork, and the outdoors. It certainly succeeded for me. I became familiar with *kashrut, shabbat,* Israeli songs and folk dances, and Zionism. I remember feeling peaceful strolling around on a quiet *shabbat* afternoon and enjoying the services outdoors. Prayer rituals in the presence of nature always felt important to me.

During these summers, I met and fell in love with my wife of twenty-seven years, made my two closest male friends (one now lives as a secular Zionist in Israel), and made a lifelong friend of an Israeli *kibbutznik.* I developed a deep love of Israel's mission and the idea that one day I would live in Israel. With my paycheck from this camp job, I bought High

Holyday seats in the synagogue so that my father and I could attend together for the first time. Having my own seat for the first time helped me feel that I belonged.

College days at the City College of New York were occupied with issues of civil rights and activism related to the Vietnam War. When I was drafted, I decided it was time to go to Israel. But then the lottery kicked in, and fate intervened: I did not have to go into the killing fields or leave home. Immediately after college, I married Jean, and we set up home in the neighborhood where I grew up. There were almost no Jews of our age. We became members of the same Conservative synagogue I had attended as a youth. We wanted some Jewish connection and felt an obligation to support this shrinking institution. Jean made it clear from day one that our home would be kosher even though we had limited technical knowledge of how to do it. Without hesitation, I went along to please her. However, we continued to consume all types of food outside our home.

After eight years of marriage, our first child arrived. Almost without words between us, we looked to find a Hebrew name for him. He would only have one name—no secular and Jewish separateness. Unfortunately, we lost Jean's father while she was pregnant. His name was Phil, same as mine, and his Jewish name was Fivel. Jean researched this name and found that Jews began to use it during the Hellenistic period, a version of the name Phoebes, the god of light. So we named our son Uri, "my light," and I thought in my mind that he would become a "light unto the nations." We learned about the rituals of *brit milah* (ritual circumcision) and *pidyon haben* (redemption of the firstborn) so that we could bring our son into the Jewish tradition in the proper way. It all felt foreign but somehow right.

This was the catalyst for our journey toward more connection. We wanted to find a Jewish community for ourselves and for our son. After two years of house-hunting, I ran into two sisters who had been classmates of mine in Hebrew school. They told me that they had come to lead observant lifestyles as part of an exciting Jewish community in the Bronx. They invited us to share a *shabbat* experience in their home, and we felt like we had found new family members.

I had always thought of Jewish observance as something negative, something that took away from a full and joyous life. But as I participated with these two families, I observed tremendous joy revolving around family togetherness, shared rituals, and the meaningfulness derived from feeling connected to a community and the world of Jews, past, present, and future. Still, I was resistant to making ritual commitments, and traditional prayer still did not have meaning for me.

It seemed that these families had something that we were seeking. As if by fate, after two fruitless years of searching for a house, we found one that met our needs in this very neighborhood. We became members of the local Young Israel that our friends attended. Going to this *shul* was an intense and strange experience for me. Men separate from women, *tallitot* that were large and woolen instead of small, neatly folded satin scarves. A service entirely in rapid Hebrew with everyone able to follow and do all the rituals with no prompting from a rabbi or cantor. Simultaneously, I felt both like a stranger in a strange land and like I had come home to my roots. Jean began to learn more about *kashrut, shabbat,* and *chaggim* (the festivals). She drank in as much *yiddishkeit* as she could, sensing this unmet need since childhood. Our second son arrived. He was named after my maternal grandmother, Eta Leah, the one who connected me to the earth, Zionism, *tzedakah,* and Jewish identity. Elan's name is an anagram of Lena, the name by which my grandmother was known.

When it came time to find a preschool for our sons, we were introduced to the Orthodox day school in the Riverdale section of the Bronx. I had lived in the Bronx all of my life and had never heard of or seen this rather affluent area. I was scared. Would my children learn to become religious bigots? Would they become self-righteous and arrogant, feeling that they knew the "right" way and that less observant and less knowledgeable people were bad or inferior to them? This was particularly scary because I feared they would find out that I was one of the "other" people. Being a nonbelieving, nonobservant Jew who could not easily define what being Jewish was all about and raising children to be observant believers seemed potentially problematic. But with Jean's strong support, we took the risk. I began to see that my boys were getting something that was lacking in my life and that it was their development that really counted. They were happy in that school and proud of their *kippot* (skullcaps). They loved the rituals, began to learn Hebrew, made friends, and seemed to get a lot from their Jewish connection.

Jean was still looking to learn and grow. Our friends told her about a "special" rabbi, and so Jean went to a class taught by Rabbi Avi Weiss at the Hebrew Institute of Riverdale. This encounter was the next step on our path to a fuller Jewish life. Jean was totally taken and urged me to go to a class. She said this was a rabbi I could truly relate to. She was right.

I went to a class to argue with him. The theme was the Jews as the "chosen people," a topic that had always angered me. I had always been against the concept of organized religions because it seemed to separate people, to contribute to hatred, prejudice, and mass violence. After all, if each group believed that it alone was chosen, that would justify its setting itself apart from the rest of humanity, and that struck me as the explanation for the many rivalries between religions and nations in the world. This had always troubled me and was one of the reasons for my intellectual resistance to a religious lifestyle. So I went and listened to Rabbi Weiss, and I was won over by his warm, caring, humanistic style and by his way of interpreting and explaining a Jew's role in the world. The message seemed to be one of loving all people and relating to other Jews as one would to one's close-knit family. He was as open to me, a nonbelieving Jew on a journey, as he was to anyone else. I did not feel judged. The door was open with love, acceptance, support, and respect for who I was and for everyone else. That was the recipe.

Rabbi Weiss was a warm, approachable, unpretentious man and a great teacher who inspired me with his strength. He demonstrated the ability to have an impact on the world while remaining lovingly connected to a wide range of people on an individual basis. I wanted my children to be exposed to this kind of religious leader. Here was a man who could inspire us by his actions while educating us with his words. I recognized him as the first hero in my life. I could see him up close as he responded to all kinds of people from all kinds of life circumstances.

He supported each person on their journey with love and without judgment. He seemed to draw so much strength from his religious beliefs and rituals. He is still my hero, after learning from his example for the past fifteen years. We do not speak often now, but I feel his support and his guidance, and his image comes to mind when I have to deal with difficult decisions.

We began to commute the seven miles by car for *shabbat* morning services and holidays. The HIR community welcomed us with meals, friendship, and acceptance. While I was hunting for parking spots on *shabbat,* the rabbi would on occasion pass me as he scurried to *shul.* He always stopped for a warm greeting and one of his loving hugs. This allayed my concern that I would be judged for being different, a nonbeliever, and not yet *shomer shabbat* (observant of all *shabbat* laws).

One *shabbat* morning, as I rushed the boys into our car for the ride to Riverdale, Elan, age four, said, "Abba, isn't today *shabbat?* So why are we going in the car?" I answered that the synagogue was seven miles away. He said we could go to the one a few blocks away with our neighborhood friends. This dialogue sank deep into my soul. I told him that the rabbi at that synagogue did not help me grow and that I really needed to hear Rabbi Weiss speak because I learned so much from him. That conversation marked my decision to sell my house and move to within walking distance of the Hebrew Institute of Riverdale. We never regretted the decision.

In Riverdale, Jean became progressively more learned about the laws of Judaism, and she enjoyed her growing participation in Jewish life. We did not discuss theology, and I noticed that others did not either. I started to realize that although there were hundreds of people praying together in our *shul,* they didn't all have the same beliefs, feelings, backgrounds, or lifestyle commitments. I also became comfortable separating ritualistic behaviors from spirituality and religiosity. One was the surface action, and the other was the soulful, spiritual core. For some people, these seemed to go together, while others seemed to have more of one or the other. The *shul* drew so many people from so many points on the Jewish spectrum that I continued to grow not only in comfort but also in interest because of the close connection to people who were at different points in their own spiritual journeys. This was a unique environment where I could wrestle with deep, honest questions and also be exposed to ideas and behaviors that had previously seemed foreign to me. The message of love was always the key for this unique *shul,* which seemed to nurture growth in people in so many ways. This was not a *shul* that had hired a rabbi; it was a rabbi who had built a *shul* around the most meaningful aspects of Jewish law, ritual, spirituality, outreach, and Zionism.

It did not matter to me whether I was ready for a *halachically* committed lifestyle or not because I learned so much from the rabbi's example of how to treat people. I felt lucky to be able to expose my sons to his model of *menschlikeit* (being a person of good character). It seemed that he was always there, for individuals and for Jews all over the world. The rabbi's life provided constant lessons for elevating our own actions through Jewish values, words, and behavior. His sensitive interactions with the elderly, with children, and with people with disabilities combined remarkably well with his strength when speaking to authority. He could share in celebration with energetic joy, listen quietly as people shared their pain, provide a hug or just be at your side when you needed support. He gave our family a warm sense of support while serving as a catalyst for our growth on all levels. There is a sense that he is a unique member of our family and truly knows and cares about each of us.

I still march to my own beat with regard to my spirituality. Sometimes I go to *shul;* at other times it feels more honest and meaningful to me to wander in the woods along the Hudson River. I still feel my deepest connection to spirituality in the midst of trees, sky, and water. That is where I feel a deep sense of oneness. Standing in the *shul* on a sunny Saturday morning looking at the sky through a window often makes me feel like I want to be elsewhere.

As my journey continues, my sons have become strongly identified as Orthodox Jews. My older son has just completed a year of *yeshiva* study in Israel and intends to return for further learning in the near future. My younger son attends an Orthodox high school and aspires to *yeshiva* study in Israel when he graduates. The son who returned from Israel brought me a gift: a line-for-line translation of daily prayers. Now I am beginning to understand the meaning of the prayers, and this is helping me connect those prayers to my inner emotional and spiritual life. Prayer is beginning to take on a level of meaning, and I have begun to put on *tefillin* and to feel honest, grateful, and at peace when I do it. I feel connected to the universe and to a set of guidelines for how to handle day-to-day life decisions.

My journey seems to get richer with each passing year. I now look forward to *shabbat* as a time of reflection, and the time I spend in *shul* is spent connecting to the meaning of the prayers and the weekly *parsha* (biblical reading) to my personal and work life. Last winter, I went to Jerusalem to visit my son in Yeshivat Hakotel and spent the first few days engaged in my own learning in that setting. I was surprised to find that I loved it and am looking forward to a return trip to spend some time learning in the Aish Hatorah program. I have started a weekly walk and talk with the local Chabad (a sect of Hasidic Judaism) rabbi as another means of deepening my insights. On my spiritual journey, the future possibilities seem limitless.

PART FOUR

BUILDING COMMUNITY THROUGH EMPOWERMENT IN A RECONSTRUCTIONIST CONGREGATION

ELAINE'S PATH

I WAS BORN AND RAISED in Queens, New York, the unexpected sixth child of Eastern European immigrants who arrived in the United States nearly a century ago. My father left Russian Poland in 1904 to escape conscription into the Russian army to fight in the Russo-Japanese war. Born in a *shtetl* near Kelz, he vividly recalled suffering pogroms at the hands of the local peasants and Cossacks. One of my earliest memories of my father was hearing him describe how his mother had sold her pearls to buy potatoes for her five children. When my father and his brother Morris left for London, my grandmother gave each of them a pair of brass candlesticks, dating back to about 1850. Those candlesticks, one of them tilted like the Tower of Pisa, were used every *shabbat* for as long as I can remember. It was my job to polish them on Friday afternoons for lighting that evening. The candlesticks are now in my possession and are being passed on to our eldest granddaughter.

My mother was from a small agricultural village in Hungary where her father worked on a plum farm. According to a cousin of mine, my grandmother was murdered when my mother was only four weeks old. Some drunken local peasants, the story goes, threw her into a vat of boiling *lekvar*, the prune filling used in Danish and other pastries. My grandmother, Yetta Raizel, died of third-degree burns several days or weeks later. My mother was then adopted by a local man and his wife, who had just delivered a stillborn, so that my mother could be nursed. This was back in 1885, before commercial formulas were available.

Elaine Weiner is a psychotherapist in private practice in the Washington, D.C., area. She and her husband, Bert, have three grown children and seven grandchildren. Elaine considers herself blessed to be able to integrate her work and her spiritual journey by helping her clients find their own path to God.

My mother's education was limited to three years at a local school run by Austrian nuns. Judaic knowledge was at best spotty, fraught with superstition and on-the spot, made-up *halacha*. For example, she claimed that dairy wasn't considered kosher at Passover. It wasn't until I was grown that I realized that she couldn't afford dairy and meat dishes and silverware for Passover, hence that "ruling" about dairy products.

Our home was Orthodox, although my parents worked on Saturdays. There was strict *kashrut,* both in and out of the home, and my mother had little tolerance for Jews who kept kosher homes but ate out at the local Chinese restaurant. I loved the Jewish holidays, especially Passover, despite the strenuous work involved sterilizing the refrigerator, stove, oven, and cabinets and boiling pots and pans.

When I was nine years old, we moved into a two-family house next door to an Orthodox synagogue called Beth-El. Life became more restrictive there because our windows looked out onto the windows of the *shul,* so that during warm weather, when we all had our windows open (there was no air conditioning in those days), we could hear the men *davening* next door, and they could hear us flushing the toilet.

Despite some of the restrictions, I actually liked living next door to Beth-El. Something within me was drawn to the synagogue, even though girls were not particularly welcome in Hebrew school. Since I was the youngest in my family, it was not considered necessary or even desirable to provide me with a Hebrew education. Because I had a very strong personal relationship with God, I fought to get into Hebrew school, thinking that it would enhance my strong religious inclinations. I was fascinated by the mystery of the strange sounds and movements of the praying men. I wanted a Hebrew education, and I fantasized of becoming a rabbi.

Since I was the only girl in the class (and sometimes in the whole school), I was the perennial Queen Esther at the Purim festivals, usually a head taller than my consorts. I loved everything about Judaism in those days and accepted everything without question. Every morning, I would say my prayers in Hebrew, experiencing a very personal connection to God, similar to the way I felt as a two-year-old when I would sit on the grass in a park, watching ants carrying crumbs up and down separate blades of grass. I would silently order the ants to move in a particular direction, and when they often obeyed my silent commands, I knew that I was connected to something very large that I didn't understand.

My disillusionment came at about age thirteen when I entered puberty and suddenly was rejected by my own religion. I wasn't permitted to stand on the *bima,* touch the Torah, or sing in the choir that the *chazan* had put together, all because I was preparing for my menses. I left Hebrew school feeling bitter and discouraged, ambivalent about my spirituality and ashamed of being a girl. There was a huge hole in my soul, one that would take many years of wandering in my own desert to fill.

At the age of seventeen, I entered nursing school (not my first choice of career, but my desire to go to medical school was rejected out of hand because "nice Jewish girls don't become doctors; they marry them"). It was there at Bellevue that I became an atheist. If there was a God, how could He allow such misery to befall human beings? I encountered death for the first time. I administered last rites to Catholics who had not been attended by a priest on their deathbeds, held an infant in my arms while she died from smoke inhalation, and treated young children from the slums for rat bites on their toes. My alienation was reinforced upon learning that my mother's entire family was wiped out in the Holocaust. I became impatient with my mother's obsessive collecting of newspaper photographs of emaciated corpses heaped up like so much firewood. She kept a scrapbook of those pictures, hoping always to be able to identify at least one member of her large family. The only information she had was that her village had been occupied by the Nazis, who rounded all the Jews up on Shavuot and marched them to someplace unknown before exterminating them all. "How could there be a God?" I raged, not realizing at the time that I was probably going through my own form of grieving.

Even though I dated several non-Jewish boys, I was convinced that I would only marry another Jew, which surprised me. I did, and he was as alienated from Judaism as I was. We were married in a synagogue, and our three children received the rites of passage in Judaism, but we never felt very Jewish, nor, for that matter, were we very connected to our faith. We were secular Jews.

It wasn't until I went back to work after having my children that I began to circle back to religion, or, as I prefer to call it, spirituality. I was hired to develop a community mental health program for alcoholics in 1965. Psychiatry wasn't doing a very good job in treating alcoholism effectively, and since I didn't know anything about alcoholism or its treatment, I embarked on a learning adventure by attending Alcoholics Anonymous meetings to find out what worked. It was there that I began my spiritual *teshuvah* (journey back). The twelve-step program moved me greatly, and as I began to incorporate the program into my daily life, I began to feel a resurgence of my childhood love of God.

After several years, I was assigned to develop a drug treatment program for adolescents. Again, since I knew very little about drugs, I sought to observe clients who seemed to be recovering successfully. I learned that they had become involved in spiritual paths that included such practices as meditation, yoga, organic gardening, and breathing exercises. Always the seeker, I was initiated first into Transcendental Meditation (TM) and then other philosophical and religious systems. The more deeply I delved into these various systems, the hungrier I became for Judaism, a hunger that was not being satisfied in the Reform temple to which we belonged. We were active in our synagogue, serving as youth group leaders and taking adult education courses in Judaism but somehow never feeling emotionally "fed."

The rabbi was a brilliant man who had great difficulty relating to children and, for that matter, to many adults. When our older daughter eloped on the eve of Rosh Hashanah, at the age of eighteen, with a non-Jewish marine who had a big cross tattooed on his arm, we were devastated. What made it even worse was that she called us to give us the news as we were preparing to leave for services. The rabbi's sermon that evening was on the evils of intermarriage; it didn't help. It also didn't help to learn that his own son had intermarried and subsequently committed suicide, ostensibly unable to face his father's disapproval. We felt alienated, guilty, angry, and depressed. When we dropped our membership, after having been active members for more than ten years, not one person contacted us to learn the reasons for our departure.

Feeling rejected, hurt, and invalidated by my own religion, I began to explore other spiritual and religious systems. TM became my entry point to Eastern religions. It was through meditation that I first began to reexperience what I knew as a child—that I was connected in some mysterious way to an energy, a presence, something that could not be perceived with human senses but that was nonetheless very real. Sitting on the floor of a mansion at 3:00 A.M., meditating with Swami Muktananda followers (many of them Jews), some small voice within me kept urging me on to continue my journey "home."

I danced with the Sufis, beginning to see through what is known as the veil of illusion, or *maya*. I studied Hinduism and modern physics to learn about unified field theory. Each foray into a spiritual system led me to the next one. It is as if doors kept opening and I kept walking through them. I was learning to say yes to whatever the universe served up for me. From Buddhism I learned to be mindful—without judgment—of myself, of all of my actions, and by extension, of others. Sufism, Buddhism, Hinduism, Christian metaphysics, the *I Ching*, tai chi, and rebirthing were all part of my circuitous journey. It was largely through my breathing practices that I began to have some experiences that can only be described as direct, nonintellectual experiences of God. When I learned that the Hebrew word for breath, *neshima,* also meant soul or spirit, I felt an irresistible pull toward Judaism, intuitively knowing that I was looking to return to my starting point.

One day, I had a revelation: I made a connection between the unified field of Maharishi Mahesh Yogi, the Tao of physics, and the *Sh'ma*: "The Lord, Our God, the Lord is One." I realized that it wasn't just monotheism that the prayer was referring to: "God is One" meant to me that God is all there is, that there is nothing that is not God. Everything clicked in that moment. I realized that I had come home, back to Judaism, but with a very different awareness. The Kabbalah spoke to me in a very personal way even though much of it was obscure. It was my grounding in all of the other paths that finally made Judaism comprehensible to me in an emotionally fulfilling way. I then knew what I was looking for in Judaism and narrowed my search.

One small group of meditators had formed a Jewish congregation that studied and compared Judaism with the Maharishi's teachings. I was very impressed with the rabbi and later learned that he was a Reconstructionist. Since I had never heard about Reconstructionism, it made no impression on me. After that group fell apart, I learned that another rabbi whom I liked and admired had also been a Reconstructionist. Unfortunately, he moved to another state. I continued my *shul* shopping, trying out various Reform and Conservative congregations, never feeling quite right about any of them.

Then I saw an ad in the *Washington Jewish Week* announcing Reconstructionist *shabbat* services that were being held at a Lutheran church. Curious, I attended services alone, since my husband had long before given up on the search with me. From the first moment that I entered the sanctuary, I had the distinct feeling that I had finally found what I had been searching for for nearly half a century.

Warmth, intelligence, and acceptance. The warmth came from the people present at the service. The intelligence was from the rabbi, who, through interactive dialogue about the Torah portion being read that day, allowed for a variety of points of view and interpretations. This expanded my understanding of and appreciation for Reconstructionism. I found the approach very refreshing and intellectually stimulating as well as spiritually fulfilling. I spoke with members of the congregation at the luncheon that followed the services and found many stories that were similar to mine. In fact, I recognized a few of the congregants who had been on a parallel journey with me. It was at Adat Shalom Reconstructionist Congregation that I came to make the connections between my very long, arduous journey through other religions and Judaism.

At Adat Shalom, I am accepted, honored for who I am, even though I don't keep kosher, which was usually one of the first questions I was asked in some of the Conservative congregations that I visited. Reconstructionism, for me, has substance and heart; it's not just for show. I am learning the significance of ritual, not to be blindly followed but with deep spiritual meaning and import. I feel more Jewish now than I ever have; how ironic that the Orthodox Jews in our neighborhood don't even consider me Jewish in light of our having been members of a Reform congregation and now, heaven forbid, a Reconstructionist one!

My only regret is that my children, who all went to Hebrew school in a large, cold, Reform temple, could not have experienced what I now know to be possible—that Judaism can be warm, loving, exciting, spiritually fulfilling, relevant, and nourishing. I can only hope that some day they, too, will feel pulled back to their roots. I have some anger at the way Judaism was taught to me, to my husband, to my children, and now to my grandchildren, all of whom were turned off and turned away from an incredibly rich, exciting history and tradition.

There is a Hasidic saying that every human being is connected to God by a rope. If the rope breaks and is later repaired with a knot, that person is tied even closer to God than he or she would have been had the rope remained intact. I certainly feel that way now. I also feel a deep well of gratitude toward my many spiritual teachers, of all persuasions, who led me through many doors and opened my eyes to what has always been true, that "my mind is part of God's. I am very holy" (Foundation for Inner Peace, *A Course in Miracles* (Workbook for Students), 1992, p. 53).

ADAT SHALOM RECONSTRUCTIONIST CONGREGATION BETHESDA, MARYLAND

I HAVE ALWAYS BEEN STRUCK by how many Jews feel themselves marginalized. In my parents' generation, the marginalization was relative to non-Jewish society. It had to do with concerns about antisemitism, the fate of the Jewish people around the world in the wake of the Holocaust, and concerns about acceptance in America. Members of my own generation seem totally at ease with non-Jewish society, but they express a sense of marginalization from the Jewish community itself.

Elaine Weiner recounts several of the ways that Jews have been driven away from the Jewish community. She was marginalized as a female in an Orthodox environment that did not give her the support to pursue her deep religious feelings, by a rabbi who was insensitive to the pain of parents whose daughter had just eloped with a non-Jew, and by a community that is suspicious of, if not antagonistic to, a person who explores a wide range of contemporary spiritual practice. Elaine was precisely the kind of Jew whom I hoped would find a home at Adat Shalom.[1]

Founding

Most congregations begin when families in a given geographical area meet for worship, education, and fellowship until such time as they can afford to hire a rabbi and, eventually, build a building. Adat Shalom's origins were far more deliberate, and its success owes to a series of fortunate coincidences.

The conversations that led to the formation of Adat Shalom began in my office in the spring of 1987. At that time, I was serving as the executive director of the Jewish Community Council of Greater Washington, D.C. Gathered in my office were Lillian Kaplan, the lay president of the Federation of Reconstructionist Congregations and Havurot; Rabbi Mordecai Liebling, the executive director of that national umbrella organization; and George Driesen, a member of the board of governors of the Reconstructionist Rabbinical College. Lillian happened to be a resident of Silver Spring, a suburb of Washington located in Montgomery County, Maryland. A woman in her sixties, she was also the central personality in a Reconstructionist *havurah* of her contemporaries that had been meeting in each other's homes for some twenty years. The subject of the meeting was the possibility of "seeding" a new Reconstructionist congregation in lower Montgomery County, an area of significant Jewish density and favorable demographics.

The Reconstructionist movement is the youngest and smallest of the four denominations in American Jewish life. Its emergence as a fourth denomination dates from the opening of its seminary, the Reconstructionist Rabbinical College (RRC), in 1968. Compared to the Reform and Conservative movements, each boasting about eight hundred affiliated congregations, and the Orthodox community, which, though far smaller, has more than two thousand congregations, the Reconstructionist movement had fewer than one hundred affiliates in 1987. At the same time, movement leaders were actively thinking about how to market a philosophy that they felt would resonate with the contemporary American Jewish community.

What emerged from the meeting was an agreement to organize High Holyday services in lower Montgomery County, targeting the unaffiliated. The services would be sponsored by the national Federation of Reconstructionist Congregations and Havurot. The national office agreed to provide the prayer books and a small budget for publicity, as well as stipends for the rabbi and cantor, so that our advertised ticket price could be lower than that charged by most congregations in the area running overflow High Holyday services. I agreed to serve as the rabbi and to find some people who would help organize the effort.

It was far from clear that this experiment would work, no less produce a new congregation. My interest was driven by two factors, one idealistic, the other more selfish. First, I had long argued in national Reconstructionist forums that a more deliberate strategy of seeding new congregations should be undertaken. The lack of qualified rabbis to lead such services hampered the implementation of this strategy. Here was a chance to put my time where my mouth had been. Second, though my family had joined a warm and thriving Conservative congregation when we moved to the Washington area, we did not feel it lived up to what a congregation could be. My wife was tiring of kicking me in the shins during services to stifle my complaining, and my shins could hardly take another High Holyday season. The outreach services were worth a try.

During the summer of 1987, we invited to our home three couples, all close friends, to plan the services and to parcel out responsibilities for the High Holydays. We advertised in the community Jewish newspaper and in the secular press. Lillian Kaplan wrote a letter to a mailing list of friends of the Reconstructionist movement in the area, inviting "those who are unaffiliated or who have become disaffected by the conventional approach to Jewish life."

The services were held in the fall of 1987 in a small auditorium in the Jewish Community Services building, which housed a variety of Jewish organizations. About one hundred people attended the services, which I led with Jonathan Kligler, at the time a rabbinical student at RRC, who served as cantor. A handful of the attendees were familiar to me; the majority were new faces, young and unaffiliated Jews who were willing to try something a bit different.

Capitalizing on the high energy and spirit of the High Holydays, we invited everyone to my home for a break-the-fast meal after Yom Kippur. It was the first opportunity to have people meet one another and for those of us who organized the service to assess whether there was sufficient interest among the attendees to continue to meet after the holidays. The excitement about that idea expressed that night led to the immediate scheduling of an organizational meeting the following month.

About fifty people came together for that first organizational meeting in November 1987 to discuss what might come next. The more modest proposal was to create a monthly study group or an informal *havurah* that would meet without any plan to professionalize the undertaking. The bolder approach, which generated the most excitement, was to form a new congregation. I was asked whether I would be willing to serve as the part-time rabbi of the group in return for some modest compensation. I agreed. The lawyers in the group filed the papers of incorporation, and three committees were formed: a program committee would plan upcoming events for the group, a mission committee would work on a charter document that would set forth what was unique about this new congregation, and an organizing committee would explore issues like marketing, membership, and dues to make the congregation viable.

A *havdalah* program and Chanukah party in the fall had swelled our ranks to the point that we had close to two hundred families on our mailing list. Neil and Lisa Makstein, one of the couples who helped organize the High Holyday outreach service, were elected co-presidents at a meeting in December, and the new congregation, which adopted the name Adat Shalom (community of peace/wholeness), began to invite households to pay dues and join the fledgling group. By January 1988, we had found a beautiful Williamsburg-style church, Potomac Presbyterian Church on River Road in Potomac, Maryland, that was willing to rent us space for services.

A *Shabbat*-Centered Community

I was given a free hand to create the *shabbat* service. Early on, I advocated the idea that our main service be on *shabbat* morning and be accompanied by a full lunch to encourage community interaction. The idea was met with raised eyebrows and skepticism: "People are busy on Saturday morning." "Children have sports." "No one will stick around for lunch." "Why not make the main service on Friday nights?" I pressed my case and overcame the objections. We agreed to meet on two *shabbat* mornings per month and to refrain from any other programming. In my view, if we were going to be a Jewishly serious congregation, the primary communal gathering had to be for worship and study. The energy and camaraderie that had been generated in the early months needed to be channeled into *shabbat* services and not some ancillary community functions.

It worked. Nearly everyone came. In fact, during our first few years, we consistently saw 70 to 80 percent of our membership at each *shabbat* service. Responsibility for the lunch was shared by member families on a rotating basis, and people lingered until two in the afternoon, forging bonds of friendship that would create the strong community spirit that continues to characterize Adat Shalom today. Within a few months of the inception of our congregation, we began to schedule potluck *shabbat* dinners in people's homes, holiday workshops, and special events, but our *shabbat* morning service remained the focal point of communal energy.

The initial membership was an interesting mix of people: about 60 percent young couples who were just starting families, 30 percent singles, and 10 percent empty nesters. We quickly learned that families with children already enrolled in Hebrew schools and with bar or bat mitzvah dates scheduled on the synagogue calendar, even three and four years in advance, were not interested in joining a new synagogue. The few children we had in our first couple of years met in a separate classroom during our *shabbat* service and were taught by one of our members on a volunteer basis.

Even more interesting were the kind of people that we attracted. Reconstructionism, as a separate stream in Jewish life, was less than a generation old, so very few people came to Adat Shalom because they had been raised in the movement. Many were attracted by our style of worship and the character of our community, both of which stood in fairly stark contrast to what was available in other synagogues in the greater Washington area. Our early advertising let people know that we intended to be different from other local congregations, and many came to check us out. Those who decided to stay generally fell into one of three categories: the disaffected, the seekers, and the "unchurched."

The disaffected were Jews who were raised in Orthodox, Conservative, and Reform synagogues and grew up swearing that they would never join the kind of synagogue that they experienced in childhood. Depending on their respective upbringings, they were looking to avoid aspects of synagogue life that turned them off as youths. The seekers were Jews who had done a good bit of religious exploration on their own—Eastern religions, meditation groups, yoga disciplines, ashrams, and so on. They were open to reentering a Jewish context only if it provided the spiritual fulfillment that they had found elsewhere. The unchurched were Jews who had had little in the way of a Jewish upbringing. As adults, they were looking for a context of meaning that was accessible despite their minimal Jewish background.

Although the heterogeneous mix of Adat Shalom members presented many challenges, we always viewed it as a particular strength of the community. Not only were we willing to accommodate the needs of each part of our newfound constituency, but we believed that the diversity enriched our practice of Judaism. We allowed members who had been spiritual seekers to introduce meditative and spiritual practices learned in other religious contexts to our services. Feminists raised the community's consciousness about how to make the tradition more gender-neutral. Gays and lesbians helped make us aware of how the Jewish community had marginalized homosexual Jews who wanted to explore their Jewish identities. Singles and empty nesters made us realize that rather than being shunted into affinity groups, they longed to be included in the mix of ages and life stages of the synagogue at large. Members who had attended *yeshiva* in their youth and others with extensive Jewish backgrounds were enlisted to serve as cantors, Torah and Haftarah readers, and *gabbaim* (organizers of the Torah service during worship) and to train other members who wanted to learn those skills.

A regular offering of the congregation was the availability of settings in which members could increase their skills in reading or speaking Hebrew, chanting a Haftarah selection, reading Torah, or serving as a cantor. The system that took root supported two of the central values of Adat Shalom —members volunteering to train other members in synagogue skills and a continuously expanding pool of members leading parts of the service on a rotating basis.

This method took programmatic shape several years later in the Ben/Bat Torah program. Conceived as an adult bar and bat mitzvah program with higher standards, the name was borrowed from Mordecai Kaplan, the founder of Reconstructionist Judaism, who felt that young men and women at age twelve or thirteen were not emotionally or intellectually ready for bar or bat mitzvah. He advocated a new rite of passage called ben or bat Torah for sixteen- or seventeen-year-olds before they left home.

Though we intended our Ben/Bat Torah program as a successor to bar or bat mitzvah, it quickly became popular with adult members who wanted to grow Jewishly and needed some kind of road map. The nine-step program consisted of formal Judaica classes, reading books from a prepared bibliography, Hebrew competency, service to the community by serving on a committee or chairing a project, developing the ability to read Torah or Haftarah, a social action undertaking or project, providing personal support to members of the community, and delivering a talk of Jewish content at a service. Each of the areas was overseen by a member of the congregation who taught and then "certified" the candidates' satisfactory completion of the level. By publicly recognizing graduates of the *aleph, bet,* and *gimmel* levels of the program during *shabbat* services (completing three categories qualified a candidate for the next level), we made the community aware of the aspects of Jewish life we found admirable. To paraphrase a verse in the Book of Zechariah, "Not by wealth or by power, but through Jewish learning and growing" did we honor our members.

Most unique about the program was that enrollees ran the gamut from the most advanced and the least initiated in terms of Jewish background. We wanted to create an environment in which lack of Jewish background would not stigmatize any person. The goal was for each person to grow in Jewish knowledge and commitment relative to his or her starting point.

○

Touching

Not everyone likes to be touched at Adat Shalom. But most people do. Notwithstanding the fact that it makes a few people uncomfortable, for what I wanted to create, as the rabbi, at Adat Shalom, linking arms in song and prayer was as important a ritual act as closing one's eyes for the *Sh'ma* or kissing the Torah as it came through the congregation. Ritual can affect behavior. Never have I found this more true than with our ritual of touching.

I usually invite people to join arms for the singing of "Oseh Shalom" after the *shacharit Amidah* (the morning standing silent prayer). Since a lot of people usually gather in the back during the few minutes of silent prayer, once the singing starts, twenty to thirty people start to walk down the aisle to take seats. It's a great moment because as people look for open rows, others reach out to them to join arms during the singing of the prayer. We also end the service with arms linked, singing *"Mah yafeh hayom, shabbat shalom"* ("How beautiful is this day, a sabbath of peace"). We have a luncheon every week after services, catered by members on a rotating basis. I often think that the extensive hugging, which continues through our eating time together, has been conditioned by what happens during the services.

Some years ago, I introduced the custom of singing Debbie Friedman's *misheberach* healing prayer at services. I would invite all those who wanted the prayer said for themselves or for a loved one to stand in front of the *bima*. People then had the option of saying the name of the person for whom the prayer was intended. For a few weeks after we started this custom, maybe half a dozen people would come forward. Then one week, the people lined up in front of the *bima* spontaneously put their arms around one another as we started to sing the prayer. From that week on, the numbers of people who went to the front of the sanctuary for the prayer grew to thirty or more. I think that people need the touching as much as they need the prayer. Indeed, I realized that touching is an integral part of the prayer.

One *shabbat* morning, one of our veteran members named Dale returned to services after having missed a few weeks due to chemotherapy treatments. She was losing her hair and looked terrible. We were linking arms for "Oseh Shalom." There was no one close to Dale, and it occurred to me how often we treat sick people as lepers, shunning them just as they need the most support. As we sang, my heart was crying for the pain that she was going through, knowing that she wouldn't have much time left. I left the *bima*, approached her, and held her as we sang. For the next several months that Dale attended services, until she died, she never again stood alone.

[Author's reminiscence.]

○

One Relationship at a Time

Adat Shalom's Torah School for children started around the kitchen tables of member families. It made up in spirit what it lacked in facilities and budget. Among its innovative features was a program called *Chaverim ba'Telefon,* "friends on the phone." Adat Shalom's director of education, Elissa Kaplan, wanted to pair adult congregants who had some knowledge of Hebrew with students grades three and above, to encourage and supplement their study of the language. All the adult tutors were, like myself (the coordinator of the program), volunteers. Each adult was paired with one student. Congregants who were recruited were given the Hebrew exercise book for the class level of their assigned "pupils" and assured that they need make contact—phone contact only—no more than once a week and that the time spent reviewing that week's lesson need last no more than ten minutes.

There were glitches, of course. Busy, beleaguered families often did not urge their children to make these contacts a priority, and some tutors felt neglected. Many mentors worried that their knowledge of Hebrew was inadequate or too rusty to be of any use. Commitments—to one student and one school year—often did not last.

Nevertheless, a miracle happened. Children in the Washington area, in single-parent homes or without grandparents, cousins, aunts, or uncles, had "family" to talk to every week, family they saw each *shabbat.* Aging couples, with children and grandchildren far away, who were living lives that they struggled in vain to share, were connected, each week, to children who knew them personally and needed them. Single men and women, some young, some old, some straight, some gay, with no offspring of their own, learned what it felt like to be important to the young, one child at a time. Ten minutes on the phone turned into ice-cream outings and *shabbat* afternoons at tutors' homes and quasi-therapeutic conversations that stretched to an hour or two as children opened up about school, loneliness, and other personal frustrations. Perhaps most important of all, families got the much needed relief that comes in not being all alone in trying to inculcate a certain set of values and a course of action with their resistant, equally isolated children. Calls of gratitude, for the connection and reinforcement of priorities, poured in.

Yes, the students' Hebrew got better. More important, they even began to compete on the intensity of their mentor relationships: whose mentor called the most, who stayed on the phone the longest, whose "friend on the phone" invited them out and where, and so on.

It was classic Adat Shalom: building community, one relationship at a time.

[Recollection of Nancy Hoffman, who chaired the *Chaverim ba'Telefon* program.]

A Synagogue with Principles

From the very first organizing meeting, I was very clear about the fact that I was interested in working with a new congregation only if the people who were part of it were willing to be serious about their Judaism and to take some risks. Very few people knew much about Reconstructionist Judaism. In my previous congregation, I had encountered many who assumed that, as the newest American Jewish denomination, it must be less observant than Reform Judaism. Indeed, some shared that view in our first organizing meeting for Adat Shalom. It was a view that I quickly and clearly corrected. My own understanding of Reconstructionist Judaism was that it was maximalist, progressive Judaism. By maximalist I meant that it was not a place for people who wanted a quick and convenient way to be affiliated with a synagogue. By progressive I meant that we would look to experience the richness of the Jewish tradition but would not shrink from challenging it and changing it where necessary.

I proposed to drive this point home through a communal statement of principles. I had undertaken a similar project in my first congregation, with very positive results. It forced both the leadership and the membership of the community to struggle with what it meant to be a religious/spiritual community. Most important to me was that it would be drafted by members and then presented to the community as a whole for feedback, discussion, and eventual ratification. It would be a vehicle to shape the communal culture.

Therefore, at our initial organizing meeting, we set up a mission committee to work on drafting the document. I worked closely with the committee, teaching some basic Reconstructionist theory and sharing my ideas of what that theory might look like on a congregational level. The formulation, however, came from the lay members of the committee. An initial draft was dubbed "Adat Shalom Initial Statement of Principles." It read in part:

Adat Shalom Reconstructionist Congregation is dedicated to the moral and spiritual fulfillment of its members and to Jewish continuity. We affirm the idea that Judaism is the evolving religious civilization of the

Jewish people. Through this congregation we will explore, enjoy, evaluate, and participate in revitalizing and reconstructing Judaism in all its aspects. We are determined to make the process of reconstructing Jewish civilization a responsible, communal undertaking.

Drawing on the richness of historical Judaism, we seek meaningful ways to express our Jewishness and to enrich our lives. In this search, people take precedence over doctrine and communities over institutions. We insist that the essential guidelines of our faith be judged by the standards of morality and justice that members of the congregation feel to be relevant to their lives.

We strive to be a community where members at all levels of observance and commitment to Judaism are welcomed and encouraged to freely express themselves. This freedom of expression encompasses differences of opinion. We view ideological diversity or uncertainty as a challenge to be faced; we seek a more reliable basis for Jewish unity and the future of Judaism than a uniformity of belief and practice.

We are Jews who stand in a relationship of combined affection and challenge to the norms of our tradition. We are Jews in search of contemporary, reasoned, and still evolving ways of thinking about our Judaism. We are, in short, *baalei she'ela,* Jews with questions.

The statement went on to address specific issues like worship, religious practice, our relationship to Israel and world Jewry, social and community responsibility, and gender equality. As important as the particular way each issue was framed in the document was the process by which the document came about. We used it as a model for many other issues and decisions that the congregation would confront, and it reflected my understanding of Reconstructionist decision making. As the rabbi, my responsibility was to raise and frame the issues and then serve as teacher and resource for the members who were drafting the document. The very fact that the drafting, feedback, and ratification process was entirely in the hands of the membership signaled that the locus of authority in the congregation would be the laity. The empowerment that resulted from this method had the effect of getting the members to take their responsibility extremely seriously.

We used the Initial Statement of Principles not only to clarify and articulate the aspirations that we held in common for our congregation but also for membership recruitment. We were well aware that the document was as likely to scare people away as it was to attract new members, but that was just fine with those of us in positions of leadership. At regular "meet the rabbi" sessions, organized by the membership committee for prospective members of the congregation, I would point out that there were many congregations in the area where people could pay their dues in return for the usual range of services provided by the synagogue. We expected more. We wanted people to read our statement of principles and, by virtue of joining the congregation, implicitly endorse its objectives. We wanted them to commit to attend services and serve on committees. We also expected every member to take responsibility to host two *shabbat* luncheons per year as a way to support our postservice lunch and fellowship time.

Innumerable discussions were held at board and committee meetings about the wisdom of this strategy. Some people argued that it was coercive. Some felt that it unduly scared away potential members. Still others felt that we had to be receptive to new members who might join with a lower level of commitment to the synagogue and the concomitant responsibilities of membership and who might move toward increased commitment over time. Indeed, as the congregation grew, some inevitable laws of organizational dynamics took hold. The percentage of members who regularly attended services began to decline, and more people joined without agreeing to take an active part in the committee work that helped run the congregation. Although our percentages of involved members continued to be much higher than in other congregations, a good deal of time was spent discussing the advisability of setting participation requirements for being a member in good standing. No such proposal ever passed the board, but the discussion itself contributed to the culture of participation as an expected, though unenforceable, standard of membership.

One example of how the congregation's statement of principles helped in a major decision began in 1992, when the congregation launched a yearlong process to determine if we should seek to buy land, conduct a capital campaign, and erect a building. At the time, commitment to building our own synagogue was far from a foregone conclusion in the community. The community was torn between two competing pressures. On the one hand, we had already outgrown our second rented church space and were having a hard time finding a new facility to accommodate our growing programmatic needs and the number of people who attended on *shabbat* morning. A building seemed to be the logical next step. On the other hand, we knew that building would put increased pressure on us to engage in aggressive recruitment of members to help shoulder the financial burden. There was also concern that families would join Adat Shalom solely to be able to drop off their children for religious education in our recently started Torah school.

Ultimately, the solution was driven by the commitment to participatory community articulated in the statement of principles. Recognizing that part of what made Adat Shalom unique was the high level of attendance and participation, the board endorsed a "qualitative growth policy." We would not cap membership, but we would not fall into the trap of seeing every prospective member with dollar signs in our eyes. We would redouble our efforts to educate prospective members about our expectations of them should they choose to join. If that meant that it would take twice as long to reach the membership level that could support a building campaign, we were willing to wait. We were not willing to sacrifice the quality of our community for the sake of a building.

The resolution supporting the congregation's intention to launch a building campaign was endorsed by 85 percent of those voting. What swayed many toward support was our stated commitment to launch an internal building campaign simultaneously with an external building campaign. The latter would build the physical structure that would eventually house our congregation; the former would ensure that the community that moved into the building would be as committed to prayer, study, and communal participation as the first hundred households that made up the congregation.

The congregation has upheld this principle of qualitative membership through the Community Life Committee and its program of new member coffees. Every new member is invited to gatherings of five to eight new member families during their first year of membership. Part of the gathering is social, so that new friendships might be formed. But the meetings also have a very specific agenda. They provide the opportunity to convey a set of communal norms and expectations regarding participation, attendance, and taking Judaism seriously. We encourage people to join committees. We find out about people's talents and skills and seek early opportunities to enlist them in some way in a community project or program through inventories of skills circulated to committee chairs. Obviously, not every new member jumps in with both feet. Some get involved more slowly than others, and some people become nominal members despite our efforts. But we have succeeded in creating a communal consciousness that to be a member of Adat Shalom suggests a willingness to be drawn into higher levels of Jewish involvement.

Retreats and Communal Guidelines

Among the most original ways that Adat Shalom reinforced its primary commitments to community, empowerment, and engaged Judaism were its programs of retreats and the resulting development of communal guidelines on key aspects of Jewish life. Long before I became interested in becoming a rabbi, I aspired to be a camp director. My love for sports and the outdoors drew me to camps as a youngster, and I found it to be the ideal environment in which one could integrate Judaism into everyday life. Six months after Adat Shalom had gotten off the ground and it was clear that it would be a viable congregation, I proposed that we plan an annual weekend retreat at a camp away from the city.

We put the same emphasis on promoting the retreat that we had on the launch of our *shabbat* morning services. It was going to be a community "happening." You had to be there. In the spring of 1989, sixty people attended the first of what would become annual retreats attracting more than three hundred. In the early years, attendance ranged from 70 to 80 percent of the membership. As the congregation grew in size, participation dropped to around 50 percent of the community, but there are few members who have not been to at least one retreat, and virtually all hail it as a transformative experience.

Several things were programmed into the retreats that were critical to the Adat Shalom community. The *shabbat* morning service was always the highlight. The style of our services back home was never suited for the rented church and theater space available to us. At our retreats, first in the Catoctin Mountains and then, as we outgrew one facility, in the foothills of the Shenandoahs, our outdoor *shabbat* services became unforgettable experiences. We experimented grandly with instruments and music, dance and movement, meditative practices and improvisational prayer. Some practices, introduced at retreats, made their way back into our regular *shabbat* services. But even when an experiment was not so well received, it sent a message that it was OK to take risks, to push the envelope on what would enhance our sense of the transcendent aspects of life and the universe.

A second goal of the retreats was to forge closer bonds for the community. We were already doing much during the year to help integrate new members into the community. The retreats' extended duration, with meals, talent shows, sports, hikes, and late-night campfires, allowed many new bonds of friendship to be formed. Though friendship is impossible to quantify, I have always felt that one indicator of the strength of a community is how often people are in each other's homes. Adat Shalom has sponsored Friday night services only monthly because on most other Fridays, *shabbat* dinners and programs (sometimes as many as five on one night) are being held at members' homes, coordinated by the congregation.

The most memorable aspects of the retreats were the themes and how we developed them. In articles and in national forums of the Reconstructionist movement, I had been the primary advocate for a process of decision making around *halachic* (Jewish law) and communal norms. I believed that what set Reconstructionist Judaism apart from the other denominations was the belief that synagogues could create their own process of setting guidelines for the norms of Jewish life. Orthodox Judaism left such matters to a handful of great Torah sages in each generation. Conservative Judaism vested a national committee of rabbis with that authority. The Reform movement advocates a system of personal autonomy in which every Jew decides what to do individually.

I had already used a method of congregational study, deliberation, debate, feedback, and ratification at my first congregation and met with some success. In fact, I used those early experiences to develop a model that I then came to advocate for the rest of the Reconstructionist movement. I now sought to use the Adat Shalom retreats as the setting to test the limits of the process.

The model was as follows. I would propose a topic to the board as the theme for the retreat. My intent was to find some aspect of Jewish life that had a direct bearing on our personal and communal practice of Judaism. I would then begin to assemble a sourcebook with biblical, rabbinic, and contemporary views on the topic. On occasion, when the material was voluminous, we would start the study of the material in adult education sessions prior to the retreat.

At the retreat, three sessions were devoted to the topic. I would lead the sessions through an examination of traditional sources and then facilitate discussions on the extent to which the traditional *halachic* standards had relevance to our own lives. By the Sunday session of the retreat, participants would work on personal and communal contracts in which they would try to articulate what of the traditional norm they would seek to integrate into their personal life and what standard they would like to see for the Adat Shalom community.

The voluntary sharing of these contracts and divergent aspirations for the community led to some very heated exchanges. The process itself threatened a good many participants. Raised in the liberal tradition of America, the implication that what was being done would take final form in some communal guidelines seemed to be a violation of their own autonomy. "No community is going to tell me how to practice Judaism!" and "If I wanted this, I would have joined an Orthodox synagogue!" were but two of the more strident reactions. But most stayed to slug it out. Being part of the process implied that you accepted the notion I was advocating—that there is no meaning to communal Judaism unless there are standards that show that we stand for something. Furthermore, people wanted to confront the Jewish tradition with fellow members who were neither bent on rejecting the entire system nor willing to follow it blindly. We were all fellow travelers on a narrow ridge, and we needed each other's insight, criticism, and support.

The theme of the first year was *shabbat*. It was the first and last time that I determined the theme without much discussion or debate. It was, however, a great place to start, as *shabbat* had quickly become the focal point for the Adat Shalom community and many members were struggling with ways to increase their personal observance along with their newfound practice of coming to services on *shabbat* morning. The personal contract form that I developed for the final session of that retreat included a list of dos and don'ts that individuals and families had to create for themselves and then commit to follow for a minimum of three months. The list of possibilities went far beyond the strictures of traditional Judaism. We took the time to establish the spirit of the laws of *shabbat,* which we felt was our starting point rather than the letter of the traditional *halacha.* Thus a family might choose to abstain from shopping but to visit a museum instead, even though the use of a car was a violation of traditional Jewish observance.

In subsequent years, we tackled other key issues that affected Jewish communal life: *tzedakah* (the uses and sharing of our wealth), *gemilut chasadim* (ways to extend acts of lovingkindness to other members of our community), *tikkun olam* (how we might address the injustices of our society and our world), *avodah* (how we engage in service to the community), Israel and the Jewish people (our relationship and how we express it), and "eco-*kashrut*" (what might guide our consumption patterns in an ecologically threatened world).

The theme never ended with the conclusion of the retreat. We would collect everyone's ideas for communal standards, and then I would recruit several volunteers to express those ideas on paper to serve as guidelines for the entire community. At the High Holydays later that year, I would devote a sermon to summarizing what we had studied and learned at the spring retreat and announced that a committee was currently working on drafting guidelines, which would be published after review and ratification by the membership. This would always elicit several new volunteers, and the committee commenced its work.

The committee process was a delicate balancing act. We wanted to say something about the given issue of Jewish life but not be so overly directive as to exclude other valid points of view. I adopted a similar relationship to the drafting committees as I did with the Adat Shalom statement of principles. Although I would look at the drafts and offer comments, the language came from the members. Each draft circulated to the entire membership for comment. Feedback was incorporated into the guidelines and then brought to the board for endorsement and to an annual congregational meeting for ratification. The guidelines are on display at our services, and some of the language from each of them has found its way into revised versions of our statement of principles. Similar to the principles, we have no way of checking compliance with the ratified guidelines. They serve as educational tools for the congregation and are a source of great pride to the membership.

The process of creating each set of guidelines did more than raise the knowledge of Judaism and of its texts among our members. It also raised consciousness about the way we might live our lives more in keeping with the spirit of the Jewish tradition. And many people became more observant as a result. Having been brought into the process of shaping the standards that might guide Jewish life, members became far more invested in how their personal or family practice might be a part of that vision of Jewish life.

In addition to the impact on the thinking and practice of members, the dedicated attention to a theme gave the congregation the impetus to look at the congregation's program profile to see if we were living up to the aspirations articulated in the guidelines. The *tzedakah* guidelines spawned a *tzedakah* collective. The *gemilut chasadim* guidelines brought about committees that gave attention to the way we supported each other when a death occurred and during other times of personal crisis. We made great strides in making people feel comfortable in asking for what they needed in terms of personal support. In turn, the community responded by creating an elaborate personal support network that was quick to respond when a member of the community was in need.

The *tikkun olam* guidelines launched an annual High Holyday appeal for activism using pledge cards listing an array of activities. It led to an explosion in social action projects in the congregation, from low-income housing projects to volunteering in shelters to monthly work at a food bank. Members of Adat Shalom formed the leadership of a countywide living wage campaign designed to raise the salaries of county-contracted blue-collar employees. A delegation from the community traveled to South Carolina with me to help rebuild a black church that was burned to the ground in an arson fire in 1995. We adopted the Jewish community of Briansk in Russia, sending vast amounts of goods and religious articles as a way to sustain its residents, both physically and spiritually. The congregation has also reached out to provide assistance to refugee families in our area, first to some Jewish families from the former Soviet Union.

More recently, the congregation adopted an Albanian family that escaped from the Serbian invasion of Kosovo in 1999.

As with all lay-led congregational undertakings, some projects continue to thrive while others lose energy over time. Yet there is little doubt in the community that we have encountered major aspects of the Jewish tradition and shaped them in ways that have had a major impact on the lives of the members of the community.

○

Growing in Faith

For a long time, I avoided joining Adat Shalom, even though every time I attended, I was more and more taken with the spirituality of the services, the intelligence of the interactive Torah dialogue, and the warmth of the people. Perhaps part of the hesitation to join came from my belief that Judaism is an all-or-nothing religion, that no longer living the experience of my childhood's Orthodox Judaism made me a bad Jew. Listening to Rabbi Sid and reading more about Reconstructionism slowly eroded that myth. I gradually came to realize that to be a good Jew, I did not need to discard anything. I did not have to be anyone other than who I was, and I only needed to honor the past and stay open to what might lie ahead.

Adat Shalom is not a community where everyone has the same notion of God or the same life experiences. It is a place that, more than anything else, encourages people to tell their stories, learn from each other and from our tradition's history and texts. Week after week, I am amazed at the sharing among members that takes place during a *shabbat* service. Sometimes it is a profound insight about the week's Torah portion. Sometimes it is a parent invoking cherished memories of a deceased relative while conferring that name on his or her new baby as part of a covenant ceremony. And sometimes it is a member of the community announcing that he or she has just become engaged, and the congregation breaks into spontaneous applause. It is impossible not to be drawn into this eclectic and caring community.

I am now astounded at my own level of involvement in Adat Shalom. In my leadership role on the board and executive committee, I have come to appreciate how well a community can negotiate the different views and desires of so diverse a membership. Since I am an organizational consultant by training, I know how hard it is to achieve such a dynamic. The congregation's ability to create consensus guidelines on the topics of *shabbat, tzedakah, gemilut chasadim,* and *avodah* is just the most notable example of the community's commitment to healthy group process.

Most important, I have come to feel joy, pride, and hope for my culture and tradition that comes in large part from permission to change with the times and to accommodate my own growth. I feel that Adat Shalom affirms and accepts me as the kind of Jew I am now—and will have room for me when I am different.

[Susana Isaacson's recollection.]

○

Spirituality Without God?

The most distinctive characteristic of the Adat Shalom service is the intense level of participation of the congregants. As time went on, I came to appreciate the attributes of egalitarianism and inclusivity that were valued and practiced by everyone. Here was a heterogeneous mix of cosmopolitan Jews that included families with children of assorted ages, interfaith and interracial families, young singles, older singles, older couples, gays and lesbians. These people had so much to offer each other, and they valued each other's special characteristics and distinctiveness. They also valued each other's contributions to the services. I was enchanted by the various members' ability to share their life events in a very personal way with the entire congregation and the ways in which Rabbi Sid Schwarz encouraged this abundant sharing and participation. I was spiritually moved at Adat Shalom services in a way that I had not felt in my former synagogue or any other synagogue I had ever attended.

Seeking to understand more about why I was so spiritually moved by the services, I took Rabbi Sid's spirituality class. On the first evening of class, the rabbi really got my attention when he said, "We won't use the word *God* in here because for most Jews, the minute they hear the G-word, they go brain-dead." I thought "Wow, that's not what I expected at all!" A Jewish spirituality course in which the word *God* is not used seemed a rather astonishing concept. Sid created an environment in which each of us could explore and define our own spirituality and then share it with others. I never quite understood why it was that despite not believing in God, I had such deep feelings of spirituality. The class helped me understand that God can be experienced by richly inhabiting the living world and fully expressing the longings of the human spirit.

[Sheila Feldman's recollection.]

The Worship Experience

From the very inception of the congregation, *shabbat* morning services have represented the essence of Adat Shalom. To some extent, our decision to hold Torah School, our religious education program for children, concurrent with *shabbat* services helped support the phenomenon of making our services the occasion that brings the bulk of our membership into contact with one another. But our services predated our school by several years. We were clear when founding the congregation that only if the adults would take their own Judaism seriously would the institution have any chance to get the children to take Judaism seriously. Although *shabbat* morning school has presented some real logistical challenges as we have grown, we wanted to avoid the ironic spectacle of other synagogues, which buzz with activity on Sunday morning but are almost empty of members on *shabbat.*

As the founding rabbi, I had considerable freedom in designing the service. The initial members joined because they enjoyed the High Holyday services that I created and led. They were happy to let me follow my instincts as we began our communal experiment. For my part, I sought to have our services both shape and reflect the core principles that I articulated at our first High Holyday services and in the organizing meetings that followed—community, study, and spirituality. In fact, these three principles were organically related. Innovations that I introduced at services that were designed to advance one of the principles invariably advanced the other two as well.

The first challenge to have services serve the goal of creating community was to get everyone into the room. Serving lunch had the requisite effect. People genuinely enjoyed being with one another, and the meal provided an additional context in which people could enjoy the fellowship of the community. But the lunch was always thought of as a bonus. The main focus was creating a service that blended the best elements of camp- and *havurah*-style prayer experiences.

What that meant was designing a service in which many voices might be heard. Some of that was choreographed in advance, and much of the rest was spontaneous, but all of it was deliberately crafted. Because the style of worship familiar to most American Jews does not allow for the sharing of what is in people's souls, the space for such sharing had to be carved out. It was soon clear to anyone who attended even one of our services that the spiritual high moments were more likely to come from the person in the next seat than from the "clergy team" of the morning.

For example, during the time that a rabbi more typically delivers a sermon, I led a Torah dialogue. In a style common to *havurah* worship, I would frame a question that emerged from the assigned biblical portion of the week and then open it up for comment. I would encourage people to make their comment to the rest of the congregation instead of to me and then have people respond to each other's observations. Sometimes a comment would mirror the observation of a traditional rabbinic commentator, and I was sure to point out the parallel. After twenty to thirty minutes of dialogue and discussion, I would try to bring together the various strands of the conversation and offer my own insights.

The Torah dialogue format lends itself well to small groups; astonishingly, we have succeeded at engaging in such dialogue with two hundred people or more. Only on the High Holydays do I deliver a straight sermon, which gives me the opportunity to develop some big themes in a setting that would have made dialogues unwieldy. But the dialogue experience on *shabbat* mornings really allows our community to "wrestle" with tradition, and comments are as likely to criticize the teachings of the text as to reinforce them. The fact that time constraints often force us to close the dialogue with hands waving in the air, seeking the opportunity to comment, leaves the impression that Torah study is a deep well to be pursued at greater length and that we are only skimming the surface.

My desire to send the message that I did not own the *bima* led to a program of talks by members called the *d'var chinuch* (words of teaching). Every few weeks, a member of the congregation prepares and delivers a seven- to ten-minute talk right before the Torah dialogue. In the first two years of the program, the presentation was on a passage from *Pirke Avot*, the *Ethics of Our Ancestors*. Each member who volunteered would prepare the talk using a rotating library of commentaries. I would review the talk in advance and make a few suggestions. As an outgrowth of a class that I was teaching on Jewish spirituality, these presentations soon focused on one prayer that a member found especially meaningful. The speaker would relate that prayer to something in his or her personal life, thereby sharing a bit of the person's own spiritual journey while opening up new layers of meaning in the prayer. The presentations ranged from poignant to profound.

Seeing so many congregants, some with little to no Jewish background, ascending the *bima* and offering Jewish "words of instruction" was most empowering. By the third year of the congregation, so many members wanted to participate in the service that we began a "second *shabbat*" program on the second Saturday of each month. The service was entirely lay-led, with members taking responsibility for leading the Torah dialogue and serving as cantor. Even as the congregation grew and had the resources to staff every *shabbat* service, we retained the second *shabbat* tradition out of a commitment to lay-led worship and study. Even that service now draws fifty to seventy-five people on a regular basis.

We have used the same model regarding music in our *shabbat* services. Our first cantors were all volunteers. In our third year, one of our lay cantors, Anita Schubert, asked for her position to become professionalized. The board agreed under two provisos: we would call the position "music director" and not cantor, and Anita would do no more than two-thirds of our regular *shabbat* services so that others could also serve as cantor. The main reason for creating the paid position was to train members in cantorial and synagogue skills and to coordinate their integration into our regular program of services.

Over the years, as new members offered their musical skills, we would seek ways to work them into our services. People who could play musical instruments would prepare a presentation we called *zemirot ameinu* ("songs of our people") in which they would introduce a piece of music from some period of Jewish civilization and then play it during services. As we developed a repertoire of songs that we felt enhanced our services, we created song sheets and had members who played guitar lead the congregation in some singing toward the end of the service even though the songs were not from the liturgical canon.

The melodies of our services were chosen for their singability. We always reserve a couple of pieces of liturgy for the designated cantor of the day to offer as a cantorial solo, but the rest of our service is sung by the entire congregation, aided by a prayer book that transliterates all of the songs so that participants with limited Hebrew skills can join in.

Another objective of our services is to create an environment in which people feel comfortable sharing their most personal stories with the community. This evolved naturally when I encouraged parents, naming a newborn child as part of our *shabbat* morning Torah service, to share the name legacy of their new child. One or sometimes both parents would share a story of a beloved parent or grandparent and indicate the attributes of that person that they hoped their child would emulate. Similarly, the presentation of a *tallit* (prayer shawl) by parents to a young bar or bat mitzvah is accompanied by personal words from the parents to their child. Such presentations reveal much, not only about the dynamics of the family on the *bima* but also about the universal struggles of child rearing, attitudes toward Jewish identity, and the tensions around the growing independence of adolescents from their parents. Even those who don't know the families involved in these ceremonies are touched by the sharing of the intimately personal in a sacred context.

Our services evolved over time, and I did not shy away from introducing new elements, even when the innovation raised some eyebrows. After a congregational trip to Israel during which we visited Reform congregation Kol Haneshama in Jerusalem, I was taken with the effective use of liturgy as meditative chant by Rabbi Levi Weiman Kelman. Upon our return, we introduced following the Torah services several simple one-line pieces of liturgy that would be sung repetitively and then be followed by a period of silence, perhaps a minute in length. The cantor and I would lead this piece seated on the *bima* with eyes closed to encourage a meditative mood. It was atypical, and some members found it awkward, but we persisted, and it became another unique feature of our service that some congregants say increased their sense of spirituality.

I once remarked at a meeting with prospective new members, "If you are the kind of person who gets upset when *Adon Olam* is sung to a different melody than the standard, you will not be happy at Adat Shalom." It was intended to signal that we were committed to innovation in an attempt to blend traditional elements of the service with new approaches that might touch people's souls. But this has its pitfalls. One person may experience an innovation as a deeply spiritual moment, and the next person may simply think it's hokey. But I never let that dissuade me. I relished religious committee discussions in which I would play the role of the "radical" and the committee would argue for a more conventional approach to the service. As is so often the case, the most traditional members often gravitate to the religious committee, and I felt that my job was to speak for the many people who were coming to Adat Shalom with very little of that traditional baggage.

Because of the high degree of lay involvement in our services, there is tremendous variety from week to week in the style and content of the services. The constant is the openness of our sacred space to people's struggles with the tradition and with their notion of God. The sharing of these struggles in the public domain of our services has been a critical element in forging strong bonds in our community and a sense of spirituality.

○

Beyond Responsive Readings

About twenty years ago, I published an article in *The Reconstructionist* titled "Beyond Responsive Readings." I observed that the Jewish community is in a lot of trouble if the only innovation to Jewish worship services that one hundred years of liberal Judaism had produced was English responsive readings! A friend of mine cynically dubbed the responsive reading "ping-pong prayer."

At the time, I was already in my first pulpit and was experimenting liberally with what could happen in the context of a worship service. I developed a course at the Reconstructionist Rabbinical College in which we explored alternative forms of prayer. When we founded Adat Shalom, I continued to explore the terrain of prayer technology, as I was increasingly convinced that a certain eclecticism was needed to create the most spiritually satisfying service possible.

Is there a place in a Reconstructionist service for traditional *davening?* Yes. Instrumental interludes? Yes. Hoe-down sing-alongs? Yes. Cantorial solos? Yes. Meditative chants? Yes. Hebrew prayers to American melodies? Yes. Singable English words to Hebrew prayers? Yes. Clapping to spirited melodies? Yes. Drums and tambourines? Yes. Silence? Yes. Yiddish? Yes. Ladino? Yes. English? Yes.

I think that you get my point. Part of what makes Adat Shalom's service unique is how eclectic it is. We happen to be most fortunate that our cantor, Rachel Epstein, continues to stretch her own repertoire to allow for all prayer modes. Most trained cantors have one style and that's it, love it or leave it. What's more, our *bima* remains open to congregational members who may introduce any form of prayer that they are talented enough to present.

Of course, every worshiper has his or her own preferences. What one member may love, another member may find problematic. Nor is it always easy to blend a variety of styles into one service. Personally, I would prefer to be part of a service that took some risks than I would want to sit through a service that was fully predictable and of one style. In fact, I can hardly wait to lead a service in our new sanctuary, where the seating pattern will allow for dance and movement in a service, a natural way to express the feelings of joy and celebration that are evoked by our liturgy.

As with so many issues that we have dealt with as our community grows, negotiating different preferences will take patience and open-mindedness. The upcoming workshop that I will be leading on "styles of worship" is meant to take us a bit closer to that spirit. Let's realize that some of the most powerful prayer moments may not be found on a page in our prayer books.

[Author, *Adat Shalom* newsletter, June 1999.]

○

Leadership Transition

There have been many moments at Adat Shalom of what I would call revelation—revelation not necessarily about God but about the importance of community.

Our annual retreat is one of the highlights of the Adat Shalom year. It is as much about our being together as a community as it is about the topic chosen for that particular year. Several hundred members gather for a weekend each spring to pray, study, think about communal values, sing and dance, make each other laugh, and get to know one another. We experiment with prayer liturgy, music, and movement. There is room for quiet meditation and for high-spirited singing and dancing. Singing the prayer *Esah einai* ("I lift my eyes up to the mountains . . .") during our outdoor service in the foothills of the Shenandoah is awe inspiring.

Several years ago, our founding rabbi, Sid Schwarz, announced that he would be stepping down as our rabbi to concentrate on his other activities and to allow us to hire a full-time rabbi, which we really needed at that point in our development. Sid had given so much of himself in the shaping of Adat Shalom that many of us could not imagine our synagogue without him at the helm. Still, we felt fortunate that the student rabbi who worked with Sid, Fred Dobb, and who had already begun to win our hearts, would be taking over.

At our *shabbat* morning service at the retreat, we created a transition ritual during the Torah service: as we returned the Torah to the ark, Sid carried the Torah through the congregation. When he finished his recessional, he handed the Torah to Fred, for a second circuit through the congregation. All the while, I led the congregation in a musical setting of the priestly benediction.

As the Torah passed by each time, the congregants, standing in respect, were raising the corners of their *tallitot* with tears streaming down their faces. It was painful to say goodbye to such a beloved leader and scary to welcome a new one, not knowing him fully. This powerful, ritualized moment helped us focus on the significance of this transition.

For me, and I think for others, the moment helped us gain some understanding that our strength was in our community and not in any one person, regardless of his or her dynamism or talent. We saw that our tears were not just tears of sorrow but also tears of joy—for what we had created together and the challenges that still lay ahead.

[Rachel Epstein's recollection. Rachel was one of the early members of Adat Shalom and since 1995 has served as its music director.]

Eight years after I helped found Adat Shalom, I made the decision to step down as its rabbi. I started working with the congregation in the same year that I founded the Washington Institute for Jewish Leadership and Values, an educational foundation promoting *tikkun olam,* social justice, and civic engagement grounded in Torah and Jewish values. My intention to spend two to three years to help launch the synagogue stretched into eight for no other reason than that it had become a labor of love. Still there was no mistaking the fact that a congregation that had exceeded two hundred households with plans to build a permanent home required full-time attention. I was doing all of the synagogue work in between my other full-time responsibilities with my institute. Even though the leaders of Adat Shalom had made every accommodation to allow me to juggle the twin responsibilities, there were only so many hours in a day.

My successor was Fred Dobb, who served for one year as a student rabbi with me and then continued for a year as interim rabbi during his last year of rabbinical school. The congregation is well enough into his tenure to realize that the fears around the loss of the founding rabbi were unwarranted. Fred and I have a close relationship, and the mentoring that began when he was a student continues, though to a more limited extent. But Fred clearly has his own style, and the congregation continues to thrive under his leadership. In somewhat unorthodox fashion, but with broad consensual agreement, I continue to lead a limited number of services each year, give a sermon on the High Holydays, and teach periodically.

What has been most interesting for me to observe as I take on a participant role in the community is how deeply a unique organizational culture has taken root. For eight years, I had a high degree of success having members buy into my programs and ideas. But one is often left to wonder how much of that is a phenomenon of a strong-willed leader being able to noodge/inspire/lobby to get his way. Now that I don't hear myself talking quite so much, I am overjoyed at finding many of our founding principles articulated and put into practice by members who joined the congregation after I stepped down as rabbi. A communal culture has taken root, and I am not the only one who is filled with pride that we have succeeded at creating a very different kind of synagogue.

The experience has reinforced my belief that it is possible to raise the level of Jewish observance, commitment, and identity in the context of a liberal approach to Judaism. It requires a strong community where personal relationships reinforce the values of the community. And it requires the creation of sacred contexts in which people can begin to understand and articulate their own search for meaning and spirituality, framing that journey in the language and ritual of Judaism.

I 2

NANCY'S PATH

MORDECAI KAPLAN WOULD HAVE SMILED. The founder of Judaism's Reconstructionist movement, he argued for a Jewish "religious civiliza-tion," embracing all Jews. He envisioned an experience of Jewish practice and thought so compelling that alienated Jews would be inspired to dis-cover the treasures that Kaplan knew had been there all along. The con-nection to our tradition and history and the excitement and challenge of reexamining them through today's eyes, Kaplan believed, would bring to-gether Jews of every background and forge a new kind of community, as strong and vibrant as our best memories of the *shtetl.*

I knew nothing about Mordecai Kaplan or his Reconstructionism when I found Adat Shalom. But after some twenty years of apathy and inaction, I was yearning to be engaged in a Jewish enterprise that com-pelled belonging. All that Rabbi Kaplan envisioned was there, in those rented rooms of a colonial Presbyterian church; I was hooked and have remained so ever since.

In fact, my continuing love affair with Judaism, inside and outside my Adat Shalom community, is still so shocking to me that I am loath to an-alyze it, afraid that it will vanish if I scrutinize it too closely. I am also anx-ious about dwelling on why I waited so long to return. Any way I turn it, the fable is titled "Sleeping Jewess"; I am not proud of my inaction.

But the straight facts about getting to Adat Shalom are simple. I found our community eight years ago, several years after trying, unsuccessfully,

Nancy Hoffman (formerly Alper) writes and does research for Jewish organiza-tions, drawing on both her legal background and her knowledge of Judaism. It is her hope to inspire other Jews to support their community and experience the wonders that she has found reexamining Judaism.

to get back to Judaism through another synagogue. I attended a *shabbat* morning service there at the behest of an equally frustrated Israeli friend, with whom I had spent many hours discussing what we wanted, and were not getting, from our congregation. Through Hebrew classes, board meetings, and *sukkah* building, we would grouse: Where is the excitement of study and debate that can take us to the edge of our knowledge, the warm familiarity of committed community, the articulation of a tradition that demands our consideration? Where might we find a place that would transform the mindless shuffle to and from occasional ritualized boredom into a Jewish place so compelling that our spiritual lives would depend on our being there?

Perhaps thirty or forty were in attendance my first *shabbat* morning at Adat Shalom. I remember the shock of seeing congregants jockeying to be chosen to stand up and ponder Rabbi Sid Schwarz's questions about the *parsha* (weekly Bible reading). Here was a rabbi without a single canned answer, just a couple of scholarly annotations on the subject, but overflowing with food for thought. I exited in a daze, shaping answers to the questions that he had posed and marveling at how much these people seemed to care. Never once had I opened the novel I had hidden inside the prayer book, my boredom-saving companion on many a *shul*-shopping venture.

Later, at the *oneg* (after-service refreshments), I was approached and welcomed repeatedly. There was simply no way to shrink into the background, merely to observe. Yes, the group was small, but it was determinedly inclusive, cajoling and demanding participation. I was pulled up and into the Israeli dancing they were doing. I was approached by the rabbi's wife, Sandy Perlstein: "I heard you singing during services," she said. "What a lovely voice you have. We really need a choir. Would you like to start one?" Start a choir? Were these people crazy? But I was hooked.

Next *shabbat*, I surmounted the collective resistance of my husband and daughter to get us back there together and argued with them all the way home, justifying a switch to Adat Shalom. My daughter cherished her kindergarten religious school teacher, and at that time, Adat Shalom had no school at all. As pioneers, we would clearly be essential to the building of this community—an exciting, heady experience for us adults, but more burdensome, I knew, for my daughter. Indeed, my biggest leap of faith was made, even then, on behalf of her, hoping that being cherished by people who knew her would outweigh the limitations of what would be, for years, a one-room schoolhouse. I prevailed. And along the way, I decided, feeling that eerie unreality that always accompanies major shifts in behavior before belief, that the Judaism I barely knew would be essential to my life from then on.

I had traveled twelve hundred miles as well as twenty years to get to Adat Shalom. My formative definitions of Judaism in particular and religion in general were shaped growing up in Dallas, Texas, in the 1950s and 1960s. Our large Reform congregation was booming along with the city, so it abandoned the bulky brick Knights of Columbus–looking temple where I was consecrated for a stretch of flat, virtually empty prairie land and an equally flat, austere new temple to the north.

My father dubbed the sprawling new structure "the pajama factory"; to me, it was merely unfriendly, with its endless corridors of cold, gray stone. The hallways were devoid of any hint of old world Jewry, of Brooklyn, of Jerusalem. It was as rigorously utilitarian and bare as the Reform Judaism of the time. The centerpiece of the main sanctuary was the soaring padded doors to the ark, encased in something akin to gold lamé with the stone tablets of the Ten Commandments, the Hebrew etched in gold, perched higher still. Levi Olan, our temple's tiny senior rabbi with the huge booming voice, thundered away from that high place, like Moses himself, although he could barely be seen over the lectern on the *bima*.

I was not, of course, privy to Judaism before the Jewish "Reformation." But implicit was the message that the "Reformers" had roto-rootered the faith, distilling it down to its essence, a rational code of behavior; its ancient and fierce God reduced to a shadowy, antiquated backdrop; its irrelevancies of language, custom, and debate flushed out and away.

My mother's Judaism was like the temple's. "No Hebrew or Yiddishisms allowed" was a commandment she rigorously enforced, echoed by her mother, who lived with us. Grandma sneeringly labeled a quite presentable acquaintance of mine "the *oi-yoi-yoi* girl" for her colorfully ethnic expressions and actively discouraged our friendship. In public, we lowered our voices for all matters Jewish, and the greatest compliment was "passing" for Gentile.

My father's Judaism was reduced in a different way. He was proud of the accomplishments of the Jewish people—and slept through High Holyday services. God and religion were for frilly dilettantes with nothing better to do. Work—acquitting yourself with dignity and skill as a professional in the larger, non-Jewish world—that was what mattered.

Moving to the East Coast exposed me to a cornucopia of other strains of Jewish minimalism, just as unsatisfying as my experience of Judaism, Dallas-style, and alien to boot. There were the "gastronomic Jews," for example, their identities engorged on heavy *shtetl* dishes. *Knishes, kugel, kreplach, schmaltz*—I earnestly memorized the names and ingredients as if I were suddenly privy to a secret code. My very different "roots" had slow-cooked all day with ham hocks, green beans, and new potatoes and overheated our un-airconditioned kitchen with frying chicken and bitter, dark brown gravy made from the huge iron skillet's burnt floury bits.

I was less prepared for the "intellectual Jews," whose Judaism was measured by their IQ and whose families of ambitious academicians, writers, and scientists had never entered a synagogue. Like them, my parents took our perfect report cards for granted, receiving them without the slightest fanfare. But ours was not a world of Jewish overachievers, nor was academic success the linchpin of our Jewishness. Other exotic political and cultural breeds I encountered included union organizers, socialists, Zionists, and Yiddishists. At home, we listened to the music of Jews, all right, but it was the melodies of Irving Berlin and Benny Goodman, not the cantorial Jan Pearce, that inspired my mother and father to foxtrot across the living room. I was dazzled by and envious of the vitality of these East Coast, cradle-to-grave identities and the sofa-cushioned comfort and security they seemed to provide. But in the garb of these Jews, I would have felt like an impostor, and too scantily clad for the journey I was after.

There had to be some path to Judaism as a *religious faith,* if I could only find it. And that presented a problem. The idea of faith that made up my childhood assumptions was pure fundamentalist Christianity. Once, when no one else was home, I timidly followed the television evangelist's exhortation to press my hand against his on the screen, to be "saved" through the divinely transmitted intensity of his belief in Christ as the son of God and our personal savior. Nothing happened—how could it when it required belief in something that my Jewish world considered so absurd?

What did happen? My conviction grew that this sort of ecstatic, creedal realization, there for the taking in an instant by other people, was unavailable to me and that there was no other way toward faith. It was cold comfort to be too rational or intelligent to receive, so achingly easily, through the simple touching of hands, a conviction that brought instant connection and great joy.

I have heard many Jews complain about the mindless, heartless lock step of their childhood's Jewish education and ritual observance. Though I respect the fact that they have struggled mightily to surmount these bad associations in order to resurface as Jews, I have often wished I could have returned to Judaism dragging such "baggage"—like the Hebrew and cantorial music I never learned, the bat mitzvah I never had, or the *shabbat* candles I never saw my mother light.

Still, the sterility of Reform Judaism falls short of explaining why I waited so long to look elsewhere. And now I understand that what I was given as a child was pretty miraculous in its own way. Miracle number one: my mother was the lone practicing Jew in her immediate family. The others, cynics all, reviled faith and accorded Judaism special ridicule. Her beloved father had abandoned his Baptist upbringing dramatically by eloping, via horse and buggy, with a Jewess. The event was astounding enough to warrant an article in the local paper.

In spite of my grandmother's omnipresent role in the household as resident sneerer, Mama persevered in her Judaism. Our recitation each night of the *Sh'ma,* in Hebrew and English, and our God-blessing of everyone in our mercifully small extended family were integral, along with toothbrushing, to the bedtime drill. Everything a woman could do in those days in such a community she did. My mother taught religious school for years, ran the sisterhood, and gave tours of the temple to Dallas church groups eager to see the room where they suspected we sacrificed livestock. To the very last breath of her life, terrified of dying and worn down by years of illness, she clutched at a God and a faith that would cushion her passing.

Miracle number two: my father grew up in Comanche, Texas, a tiny cowboy town one hundred miles west of Fort Worth, romping with his younger brother on the endless prairie where a *minyan* was not even a possibility. Brand-new immigrants, his parents bought and successfully ran the dry goods store there, the only Jews Comanche would ever know. His pride in the Jewish people was contained and sustained by his great love for his father, an uneducated Polish runaway who became the revered chairman of Comanche's school board, and by his gentle, scholarly *zeyde* (grandfather), who brought him to Fort Worth in the summertime to teach him Hebrew. His parents, preoccupied with running the store, had no time for Jewish education, practiced no rituals, celebrated few if any Jewish holidays. Never, until adulthood, did Dad see the inside of a synagogue.

Yet it never occurred to him to abandon his Jewish identity or to become anything else in a place where it clearly would have been expedient to do so. His outstanding law school grades and achievements meant nothing against his Jewishness. Big-city Texas law firms would not even interview Jewish students. My father remained, in the grand Jewish tradition, the stalwart patriarch of our family, whether conducting our

Passover *seder* or faithfully saying *Kaddish* for the father and grandfather he loved.

Miracles number three, four, etc.: our Sunday school teachers—isolated Jewish intellectuals, scientists, professors, doctors—resisted being swallowed up by the larger culture and tried to give us reasons to do likewise. It was their seriousness—in fact, their very presence in those classrooms—that I felt most profoundly, watching them pore over our textbooks, wanting so much to get through to this rowdy group of affluent kids.

And that tiny rabbi, raging from on high against America's nightmare, the jungle war in Vietnam—I can still remember my father's anger at his effrontery. He spoke to a largely unsympathetic audience, but he broke through, if just for a moment, that thick wall of congregational comfort and complacency.

There was an intense young rabbi who recognized and awarded my studiousness by seeing to it that I got a scholarship to study *kavanah* (intentional Jewish prayer) on a beautiful estate outside of Boston, with the cream of the Reform rabbinate. Late into the night we studied a popular nineteenth-century text on the subject and pondered issues of motivation and faith. I was seventeen. I had completed my freshman year of college. I can still call up the face of the Yemenite Israeli rabbi who was struggling against the burdens of discrimination in Israel. And I will never forget the dashing Israeli folk dancer who encouraged me to nurture my independence and carry my Jewishness with pride.

"My children, give me an opening—no bigger than the eye of a needle, and I will widen it into an opening through which wagons and carriages will pass," beseeches a paraphrase of Shir Hashirim Rabbah, a *midrash* (explanatory story) on the Song of Songs. My "eye," I think, had been opened long ago, just waiting for me to use it. Yet even my daughter Alexandra, age six, "saw" before I did. One snowy night, she stared into our winter fire and stated that she had seen God there. Taking up sketch pad and pencil, she then drew, with unusual clarity and delicacy, an elegant woman in long, flowing robes. The timing was perfect. We had taken her to a Purim celebration at some arbitrarily chosen synagogue, and I remember feeling tired of being surrounded by strangers and disgusted that the "best costume" award had gone to Raggedy Ann.

Alexandra was not the cause of my "awakening," however, though the beginning did come with having a child. Taking responsibility for her meant taking responsibility for my own life in a profoundly different way. Suddenly, by giving birth, the most ordinary of experiences, I had become

part of a four-thousand-year-old living chain of life givers and life nur-
turers. In my half-sleeping state, they would return to me again and again,
Jewish mothers in coarse, dark robes folding in around the babies they
cradled and nursed, their backs hunched and alert for blows or rain or
cold. In my mind, they stretched across continents and straddled centuries, crooning the lullabies of their time and place.

During those reveries, I learned that I would die; I would age as she grew
up and always be reminded of it by her blossoming. The experience of
knowing, for the first time, that I was only a tiny link in this seemingly in-
destructible chain, doing nothing more than what hundreds and thousands of women had done before me in endless extremes beyond my
comprehension, was at once terrifying and comforting. And I learned that
if catastrophe required it, I would die for her. Night after night, in my
dreams, I planned our escape from some conjured Holocaust, mapping the
route through our neighborhood, calculating who would risk their lives to
help us and what drugs I could give her to keep her from crying out.

During those early months of Alexandra's life, if I did not find God, I
at least found a sense of connection—to my people, to my history, and to
a sense of life's profoundly etched cycles. I am sure that my ancestors
learned all of these truths, which I had stubbornly refused to know,
through their mothers' milk. Where else could the Bible's and Jewish history's searing confrontations with God have come from?

But old habits—and thinking—die hard. After some ten years in avid
pursuit of what was excised from the Judaism I learned as a child, I am
still capable of feeling suddenly self-conscious and awkward with how I
practice Judaism now. And for me, it is definitely "practicing." I get on
the bike over and over again, often racing down that hill, the wind blow-
ing through my hair, but just as often falling over, veering into the ditch,
or choosing—despairing, fatigued—not to get on at all. That is why I
have been heartened rather than discouraged by the Jewish notion that
understanding and living this religion is not an overnight phenomenon.
The very eclecticism of Judaism that I used to find so perplexing and
alienating is, I now know, waiting there for me between the moments of
clarity and inspiration. The intellectual excitement of study, the beauty
and security of ritual, enough *mitzvot* (commanded actions) to keep me
busy and questioning myself for a lifetime, and the reassurance of the
community—all of these reward me for my efforts.

There has been nothing in Judaism, as Edmond Fleg put it, "demanding of me the abdication of [my] mind."[1] Rather, it is a refocusing, away
from my particular insecurities and distractions, my idolatries, for which
I must marshal the same concentration and analysis that I have given to

literature and law over the years. I explore and slowly add ritual or observance that can, if I let it, comfort and cajole me along with this changing of mental scene.

But all of this for what purpose? To return, again, and more often, to knowing that my partnership with God, each moment of God-on-earth-through-me, cannot exist without my being there. Being there, Judaism has taught and reassured me, includes all my wanderings, alone, distracted, and lost. It embraces all my doubts, confusion, pain, tantrums, even despair. All, except apathy and smugness, because sin, as I have learned, is merely missing the mark—infinitely correctable, says Judaism, by simply attempting sincerely, again and again, to get it right.

I recall that the Jewish philosopher Spinoza attributed man's frailties to the failure of imagination. Coming back so late to Judaism, in such a state of ignorance, I could not possibly have developed even the most tentative beginnings of imagining these thoughts without Reconstructionism as lived through Adat Shalom and as articulated by Rabbi Sid Schwarz. Nor could I have begun and sustained the actions I have taken to center my life Jewishly.

Reconstructionism, like me, has moved from more secular, rational beginnings to an active, God-grappling spirituality. I like that. And Reconstructionism assures me that never again will I be shut out of the decision-making process, whether it pertains to the articulation of the divine, the interpretation of text, or the origins of ritual. At its core is a reverence for tradition, in observance and scholarship. Again and again, we revisit it, keeping it fresh, part of the congregation's consciousness.

In my experience of Reconstructionism, great integrity is brought to this balancing act, of holding onto the past while redigesting it in and for the present. I cherish this the most. Our rabbi has reminded us often that this push for relevance is not an invitation for cursory study or casual observance. Rather, we are enjoined to work harder and learn more if we as individuals and as a group are to be the bearers and re-creators of our religious life. For me, the wonder of my responsibility has not faded. Like a small child, I hold a tiny, glass-domed snow scene, peering inside, turning it upside down, watching the flakes fall, looking again. It is a faraway world, unreachable; yet it is there for the holding, the size of my hand.

As a forum for Sid's articulation of Reconstructionism's vision, Adat Shalom is like a huge sieve, stretching across Washington's metro area, attracting, winnowing out, and collecting Jews from so many pasts, eager to search for new meaning from Judaism and ready to commit to the community. We are united by that excitement and reinforced by our collective journey. Perhaps that is why I have never felt shut out or put down by anyone with greater knowledge or a different point of view. In Washington, bright, articulate Jewish people are easy to find. People who find their home in Adat Shalom are not. Those who do are ready to put huge chunks of themselves and of their time into constructing individual spiritual lives within a community they build themselves. There is about the place much of the fervor and enthusiasm of a barn raising, which somehow sustains itself through the considerable *schlepping,* sawing, and hammering required.

I cannot imagine even putting my toe in the waters of finding faith without this congregation—I need the inspiration of Rabbi Sid's clarity of vision and others who are doing their own seeking. Precisely because Judaism is a way of life, a process of becoming better, it needs the reinforcement of useful work and dialogue with others who are similarly directed. The instant, easy, sound-bite belief has always been unavailable to me, and now I would not have it any other way. Reciting the *Sh'ma* in the dark without my new support system would mean as little to me as it did in childhood; and because this is still all so new, I especially need Adat Shalom.

Study is easy and thrilling, long years of work and academic habits coming together for this wonderful purpose. I am lucky to be coming back, if it had to take so long, during an era of Jewish renewal. So many Jews—not just Reconstructionists—are putting their minds and hearts to spreading before us the underappreciated and long-forgotten wisdom and tradition of our people, glittering and fresh.

My daughter, whose childhood was spent at Adat Shalom as a pioneer student, has been cherished by the educators, congregants, and other children of the community. This is a gift, rare in such a big metropolis, on which the foundation of her Jewish womanhood has been firmly established. Her bat mitzvah was a shining hour, not simply because of the amount of material she mastered and the poise with which she presented it but because of the community's celebration of her achievement.

Now I am at another threshold of truth—like motherhood—facing tardily the circumstances of my life. I have chosen to end my marriage. I am crashing, woefully unprepared, into being fifty, and suddenly I find myself living with an alien being, a child-woman who only looks like my daughter. It is a scary, overwhelming time. I wish that I could attest to the unfailing resoluteness of my path. Instead, once again, I am faced with the fragility of what I have been laboring toward these past ten years and how easily I lose my way. Kaplan's all-embracing Jewish civilization, however, is piled with treasures. I may have lost the will to study and meditate daily with the wisdom of my people, but I am learning to appreciate my community in a new partnership—if I just show up, it supports me, and I am grateful, once again, to be part of this circle of faith.

Even now, from where I have been in recent years with Judaism, I need little imagination to thrill to words such as these, which would have once seemed useless or out of my reach. Here Elizabeth Barrett Browning is describing Moses' encounter with the burning bush: "The earth is crammed with heaven and every bush afire with God."[2]

What a journey, to get there, even for a second.

PART FIVE

DANCING IN THE AISLES AT A CONSERVATIVE SYNAGOGUE

MARK'S PATH

I GREW UP in the 1960s in New Rochelle, New York—home of TV's Rob and Laura Petrie on the *Dick Van Dyke Show*. My father wasn't quite as funny as Rob; my mother wasn't quite as high-strung as Laura. But add a couple of *mezuzot* on the doorposts, and everything else—right down to the ottoman—looked pretty much the same as it did on TV.

I can't say that I ever really thought much about being Jewish in those days. It's not that I had anything against being Jewish. It's just that it was, as we used to say, irrelevant. Let's be fair—we had our share of distractions back then. Between Vietcong land mines, LSD, and that ottoman, everybody seemed to be tripping on something. Judaism just wasn't one of them.

Still, we knew that we were Jewish. We belonged to the Reform "temple." My mother lit candles on Friday night, and my father drove us to religious school on Saturday morning. Ah, religious school. What better way to pass a Saturday morning than to butch-stick your hair, slip on a pair of your itchiest wool pants, and go off to sit in a classroom for a couple of hours to study "customs and ceremonies" (which no one observed), "Bible stories" (which no one believed), and "Jewish history" (which no one cared about, since it was studying a time when people observed customs you didn't observe and believed stories you didn't believe). Then, around 11:00 A.M., you'd get marched into the chapel for "services," where you'd sing some German-style hymns like "Open the Gates of

---

Mark Sameth is now the rabbi of Pleasantville Community Synagogue in Pleasantville, New York. A former country and western songwriter, his songs have been recorded by Loretta Lynn, Ed Bruce, Dickie Lee, and others. He wrote this article while a rabbinical student at Hebrew Union College-Jewish Institute of Religion. The names of his childhood friends have been changed in the article.

Righteousness" and watch a group of boys (usually at least three, some-times as many as five) get "bar-mitzvahed."

Eventually, my own bar mitzvah came around, which, once it was hap-pening to me, ended up seeming (in spite of my general lack of interest and the fact that I had to share it with four other boys) like a pretty big deal. I don't remember it as being what you would call a "religious" ex-perience. But on the other hand it wasn't every day that you got to dance with Penny Weiss, either.

After my bar mitzvah, my parents and I came to an agreement regard-ing my advanced Jewish studies: I would go on to confirmation class, but I didn't actually have to get confirmed. "What would I be confirming?" I remember asking.

Looking back now, I don't think that I was the only one in my class who might have been confused about that question. In our temple's 1970 yearbook—*Our Heritage: A Break with the Past*—my classmates were indeed breaking with the past. Forget the hairstyles. More startling are the quotations my classmates had chosen to appear under their pic-tures: Nadine Cohen quoted Matthew 6:21, Dina Atlas chose John 4:18, Miriam Kushner gave us Hebrews 11:1, and Linda Leiner checked in with Corinthians 5:7. OK, so they pulled their quotes out of *Bartlett's*. Still, there was no one around to suggest that it was inappropriate for Jewish kids to be quoting the New Testament on the occasion of their confirmation!

It was the year after Woodstock. I was sixteen. To be honest, I'm sure I didn't even notice it. And had I noticed it, I'm sure I wouldn't have cared. I had more important things on my mind—like stopping the war, playing in my band, and figuring out how I was going to get to see my girlfriend now that her father had totally disrupted my life by moving the family to Boston. He had quit his pulpit in order to take what he considered to be a better job at the national office. I was hardly the one to talk him out of it. What did I know about the United Church of Christ?

I really don't think it was until college that I ever once thought seriously about being Jewish. But when I arrived at this small midwestern liberal arts school, there were people there—unbelievable as it seemed at the time—who had never met a Jew. A friend of mine told me that a fresh-man from Alabama had actually asked if she'd be kind enough to show him her horns.

I didn't feel threatened. It was just . . . weird. There was a whole mul-ticultural thing going on then on campus. I got caught up in it myself, wondering if I, too, had a heritage. "Pseudo-German-Protestant" some-how didn't feel fully authentic. I started hanging out with a group of Jewish students (there was no Hillel) and tried to learn something—anything —about Judaism.

It was a scattershot effort on my part. I bought a few books: *I and Thou,* by Martin Buber, and something on *Mishneh Torah,* a code of Jewish law written by eleventh-century Jewish philosopher Maimonides, of all things. I went to a lecture off campus by Rabbi Shmutkin, a Lubavitcher (Hasidic sect) who used to come down from Milwaukee. Finally, one weekend, as the joke went, I "made *aliyah*" (literally, went to a higher place): I went up to Milwaukee to "spend a real *shabbos*" with the rabbi and his family. It was . . . interesting. But let's say it just didn't work for me—women in wigs, exotically modest marital practices, I mean, come on.

Nonetheless, I was still committed to finding my "roots." At some point, I decided that I'd try Israel. Working on a *kibbutz* seemed to be the way to go for young Jewish American students. And so in September 1973, I flew over and got placed on a small, poor, Polish *kibbutz* just outside of Petach Tikva. Just weeks after I got there, the Yom Kippur war broke out.

Four months later, I came back—a Zionist. I kept *shabbat* that semester, started going out with Jewish women, and that spring ended up moving back to New York, where I studied with a Reform rabbi for a little while. It was interesting but not compelling. Maybe I was looking for something that didn't exist. Anyway, I got into the music business, went to temple on the High Holydays, and was basically happy not to think about being Jewish again for the next fourteen years.

In 1989, I turned thirty-five. I'm not sure why—maybe it was the shock of reaching "middle age" so soon—but I decided that I needed to do some serious exploration that year. I started making a list of the many books I'd somehow never read in college, and I began reading them. One of the books on the list was the Torah. The Bible was supposedly the best-read book in the world. People—lots of people—had died fighting over it. All I knew were the Bible stories they taught us as kids, like the one about Abraham smashing the idols (which, it turned out, wasn't even in the Bible). And I still had, I suppose, this residual interest in Judaism.

I knew enough to know that I couldn't just read the Torah cover to cover. I had to study it with someone. But with whom? I wanted to study in a traditional way, but I needed to think about the text critically as well.

My resolution to the dilemma felt, at the time, like a compromise. But in retrospect, it turned out to be one of the most exciting ways imaginable to encounter the text. Monday nights, I studied with Rabbi Bennie Krasnianski, a young, amiable Lubavitcher Hasid who came to Manhattan from Brooklyn a few times a week, trying to convert Jews to Judaism.

Wednesday nights, I went to the "Y" to study with Rabbi Alan Miller, a brilliant, if combustible, teacher who held the pulpit Mordecai Kaplan had established at the Reconstructionist Society for the Advancement of Judaism on the Upper West Side of Manhattan.

Rabbi Krasnianski was a fundamentalist. Rabbi Miller was an agnostic. Rabbi Krasnianski believed that every word of the Torah came directly from God. Rabbi Miller was not even sure that God existed. Rabbi Krasnianski (under the spell of his *rebbe,* Rabbi Menachem Mendel Schneerson) believed that civilization was inherently unstable and that we needed to ground ourselves in the text. Rabbi Miller (under the spell of Jacques Derrida) believed that the text was inherently unstable and that we needed to ground ourselves in civilization. For a few months, it was as if I was engaging them in a dialogue of sorts. Rabbi Krasnianski would make a statement, and I would throw back some outrageous thing I'd learned in Rabbi Miller's class. Rabbi Miller would make a statement, and I would throw back some outrageous thing that I'd learned in Rabbi Krasnianski's class. "But isn't it true that Wellhausen (a nineteenth-century German biblical scholar) said . . ." "But isn't it true that the Alter Rebbe (a Hasidic master) explained . . ."

It was exhilarating but exhausting. After a while, I longed to find one rabbi who could put it all together for me. Someone who had the warmth and love of my Lubavitcher teacher but the critical mind and intellectual scope of my Reconstructionist guide. I couldn't bear to make the choice between heart and mind and didn't understand how a true religion could ask you to make such a choice.

Fortunately, one night, someone mentioned that there was a teacher that I would probably enjoy studying with very much. His name was Rabbi Marshall Meyer, and he had just a few years earlier taken over the pulpit of a dying synagogue on the Upper West Side—Congregation B'nai Jeshurun. Marshall (as he liked to be called) was teaching a course on Wednesday nights that was open to the public. It was focused on a book called *The Prophets,* written by his teacher, Rabbi Abraham Joshua Heschel.

And so one Wednesday night, I walked into his class. There were a dozen or so students seated around a bunch of pushed-together, broken-down tables. I sat off to the side and listened as Marshall taught and engaged the class in discussion. My interest in these studies was no longer academic—if it had ever really been. I was struggling with issues of theodicy, of authority, of belief. With Rabbis Krasnianski and Miller, I had been studying with two men who had read more than I would probably read in my entire life, and yet they saw the world in profoundly different and irreconcilable ways. How was one to evaluate their claims? How could one know what was "true"? Where was the system that could encompass all the contradictions and messiness of life? In Marshall's class that night, I began to ask my questions. And Marshall responded passionately: "We can't contain the perfect, infinite God in our imperfect, finite theology!"

Now *this* was different. Here was a rabbi who had all the fire of a fundamentalist preacher, but listen to what he was saying! Against Rabbi Krasnianski, Marshall was arguing that not every word of the Torah could be considered holy. Against Rabbi Miller, Marshall was arguing that the Torah—that life—is not fundamentally meaningless. Marshall was arguing, in Heschel's words, that there is "meaning beyond the mystery." I didn't know yet how I felt about these issues. But Marshall was playing both ends against my confused middle. When class ended, he called me over and kissed me. Kissed me! Like a *chasidishe rebbe*! Marshall welcomed me into his world, a world where the struggle was not so much about finding the answers as about finding the questions.

I loved Marshall's class and began attending regularly. But I had also set that year as my year for studying the Torah, and Marshall only taught the weekly Torah portion during services at B'nai Jeshurun on Saturday mornings. I really was not looking for a synagogue (I still considered myself an agnostic), but I began going Saturday mornings to hear Marshall.

The synagogue itself was beautiful: a bell-shaped sanctuary in ornate Moorish style. But as striking as the sanctuary was, the people were equally striking. In one row sat an old Jew in his suit and tie, a survivor from Eastern Europe, passing out cough drops. In the row in front of him were twenty-somethings in jeans and sneakers. Across the aisle, a gay couple held hands. And on the *bima*, next to Marshall, was his Argentinean student and now co-rabbi, young Roly Matalon, who wore his hair down to his shoulders.

The service itself was alien to me. It was mostly in Hebrew (which I did not know), but the music was very appealing. There didn't seem to be a cantor. Instead, a young man sat off to the side at a keyboard and accompanied the rabbis. Ari Priven, it turned out, was more than just a keyboard player. When he sang, I was struck by the subtlety and sensitivity of his voice. He was a cantor, but unlike any I'd ever heard. He could do all of the operatic turns beautifully, but it was the lightness of his touch, the almost conversational singing style, the honesty and immediacy that one usually associates with the best folk or pop singers, that really drew me in.

I was grateful for the music, because while the service was going on, I was spending most of my time reading articles in the Plaut edition of the

Torah. At a couple of points in the service, the congregation would rise, face east, and pray something called the *Amidah*, which, I learned, was the "standing prayer." I had never heard of it, but from the ritualized body movements that everyone seemed to know, I judged it to be a very well known prayer, probably an old one. After the first *Amidah,* at around 10:30, came the Torah service. The Torah scroll was removed from the ark and paraded around the sanctuary, and people would lean over and kiss it. Kiss it! (I made a mental note that kissing somehow played an important role in Judaism.)

As the Torah made its way back up to the *bima,* I looked forward to the rabbi's sermon. It's the reason I was there. Except there wasn't any sermon. Rather, Marshall would talk a bit about the portion of the week, raise some maddening questions, and then engage in what seemed like a spontaneous dialogue with Roly. He would press Roly hard to deal with the questions he raised—sometimes, I thought, too hard. But it was because of Marshall's respect for Roly that he kept pressing him to dig deep and to grapple. And Roly's ability to respond often left me gape-mouthed. After a while, Marshall and Roly would pass out wireless microphones, and they would engage the congregants in the discussion. Here were writers, artists, psychotherapists, and professors, each offering a different take on the text. I had come to study with Marshall, but I had found a whole community of people from whom I could learn.

Downstairs, at the *kiddush* (refreshments), I met some of the members who knew Marshall, and they began filling me in on his life. He had been Heschel's personal secretary for a number of years before moving to Buenos Aires, where he had established a rabbinical seminary. He had become very politically active during the years of the junta. He used to visit the political prisoners—Jew and non-Jew alike—in their prison cells. Jacobo Timmerman had dedicated his book *Prisoner Without a Name, Cell Without a Number* to Marshall. The rabbi had railed against the secret police, even as he knew that they were sitting in his synagogue. Death threats against him became routine. He was, in short, everything that he appeared to be: larger than life, playing it for real, *"tuchas ofen tisch"* (the anatomically more colorful Yiddish equivalent of "nose to the grindstone").

Social action was at the center of Marshall's rabbinate. But for Marshall, social action meant bringing your full, authentic being to bear; it was about making the people "out there" (on the street) comfortable while making the people "in here" (in the synagogue) uncomfortable. A few months after I met him, I did something that never in a million years could I have seen myself doing—I affiliated with a synagogue.

Had I not met Marshall, I really wonder whether I would have found my way back to Judaism. Marshall made it possible for me to see the Jewish path that lay before me. But Marshall knew that in addition to the communal path, each person has a personal path to follow. And for me, that personal path had to do with resolving, somehow, the issue of my agnosticism.

I'm not sure why I was so vexed by this question of belief in God. I had always found life inherently meaningful; I was comfortable with the fact that certain things were simply unknowable. I didn't *need* there to be a God. Belief in God would throw open more questions than it would answer. But I was stuck on it. And I needed to approach it in my own way—which meant, at the time, rationally. I was tremendously moved by Heschel's notion of radical amazement. But I had this need to know, if it could be known—were we here accidentally? Was the universe the result of a simple quantum wave fluctuation, or had it been created on purpose?

I began reading a lot of books on science—mostly cosmology (Hawking and Gribbin and Rees), quantum physics (Zukov), and chaos theory (Prigogine and Gleick). By the end of my studies, to my astonishment, I could no longer call myself an agnostic. The evidence was overwhelming that the universe had been created with intention, therefore by some Being whose qualities encompassed intention. In other words, there was a God.

Which made being a Jew that much more interesting.

CONGREGATION
B'NAI JESHURUN
NEW YORK

MARK SAMETH'S PATH typifies many of his generation. Growing up in an upper-middle-class suburb, Mark left his Reform temple with few feelings for Judaism and no impression that the religion of his youth might provide a source of spiritual sustenance as he matured and starting asking some of life's big questions. Fortunately, he was later in the right place at the right time to hear about the renaissance taking place at Congregation B'nai Jeshurun on the Upper West Side under the dynamic leadership of Rabbi Marshall Meyer.[1]

The American Jewish community is full of precious jewels that no one has ever heard of. Communities of Jews that take their Judaism seriously and care for one another. Rabbis whose intelligence and caring inspire Jews to deepen their connections to their heritage and to the community. B'nai Jeshurun is a big diamond. It is as close to a phenomenon as happens in the Jewish world. Located in the midst of one of the most heavily populated Jewish areas in North America and at the hub of the Jewish and national media, B'nai Jeshurun is the most storied and talked-about Jewish congregation in America. A pilgrimage to B'nai Jeshurun's *shabbat* service is now a required stop on any Jewish tour of New York. To the extent that there is growing energy around transforming the American synagogue today, in large measure it can be attributed to the desire to replicate B'nai Jeshurun's miracle.

○

B'nai Jeshurun was founded in 1825, making it the oldest Ashkenazic congregation and the third oldest Conservative congregation in the

United States. Ironically, today it represents the cutting edge in American synagogue life. The story of B'nai Jeshurun's transformation and how it became one of the most successful synagogues in the country is instructive to anyone interested in the possibilities of religious fellowship in America.

B'nai Jeshurun (BJ) had several homes in its history. Established in the heart of lower Manhattan, its first home was on Lafayette Street. As New York's Jews moved uptown, so did BJ. In 1850, the congregation built a new synagogue on Greene Street. A mere fifteen years later, BJ moved to Thirty-Fourth Street, just west of Broadway, currently the site of Macy's. In 1883, the congregation opened the doors of a new building at Madison Avenue and Sixty-Fifth Street. At that site, two of the most eminent rabbis of American Jewry served the congregation. Rabbi Stephen Wise, who would later go on to found the Jewish Institute of Religion, the Free Synagogue, and the American Jewish Congress, began his rabbinate at B'nai Jeshurun in 1893 and served for seven years. Judah Magnes, later to become the first president of the Hebrew University in Jerusalem, also served the congregation briefly following Wise's tenure.

By the early twentieth century, Jewish New Yorkers were moving even farther uptown, and B'nai Jeshurun again followed, establishing the home that still exists on West Eighty-Eighth Street. From 1919 to 1960, the congregation was served by another icon of American Jewry, Rabbi Israel Goldstein. One of the leading congregations in New York, B'nai Jeshurun reached a membership of approximately eight hundred households in the 1960s. Membership began to decline in the 1970s during the tenure of Rabbi William Berkowitz, and by the time he left in 1984, the congregation had lost most of its members and services were attended primarily by a handful of elderly loyalists.

B'nai Jeshurun's Renaissance

B'nai Jeshurun's renaissance began in the spring of 1984 with a trip to Buenos Aires. Judith Stern Peck and Stephen Peck were prominent members of the New York Jewish community, active in a wide array of organizations, who had recently taken up residence in Manhattan. Stephen Peck was the chairman of the board of the Jewish Theological Seminary (JTS), the central institution of Conservative Judaism. The Pecks decided to join B'nai Jeshurun.

The Pecks were going to Buenos Aires to visit the rabbinical seminary there, which was associated with JTS. The Seminario Rabinico Latino-Americano, as it was known, was founded in 1962 by Rabbi Marshall

Meyer, an American rabbi who had moved to Argentina in 1959. The Pecks also visited Comunidad (Congregation) Bet-El, also founded and led by Meyer, which had become the largest synagogue in Buenos Aires.

Marshall Meyer achieved significant prominence in Argentina, not only as a rabbi who created and led several key institutions in the community but also as a political activist who often put himself at risk to oppose the military dictatorship in the country and who worked to help establish the democratic government of Raul Alfonsin in 1983. The Pecks were sufficiently impressed with what they saw in Buenos Aires that when a year later, Judith heard that Marshall might be interested in coming to New York, she approached the board of B'nai Jeshurun with the proposal to hire this dynamic rabbi.

Meyer assumed the pulpit of BJ in August 1985. He inherited a congregation with a notable history but little else. The building was in disrepair. The membership was about thirty-five households, an all-time low. There was no office. There was little in the way of an organizational infrastructure. During his first year, Marshall Meyer, with help from Judith Peck, who had by that time joined the board, organized parlor meetings and focus groups to set out a vision for the congregation. A relevant Judaism, they felt, had to put emphasis on social action, a strong community, and spirituality. Marshall had used this vision with great success in South America, and he readily attributed it to his late teacher, Rabbi Abraham Joshua Heschel.

That first year, Marshall Meyer breathed significant new life into BJ. The renewed vigor was most notable at services. Meyer, a great lover of music himself, possessed a powerful and pleasing voice. The music he introduced, coupled with the integration of Torah study and progressive political and social action, soon had the Upper West Side abuzz. B'nai Jeshurun was making a comeback. And many Jews came to witness it for themselves.

By Rosh Hashanah in the fall of 1986, only a year after he arrived, Marshall Meyer had begun to reshape the institution. Rolando Matalon had been a student of Meyer's in Argentina. The young man came to New York in 1982 to finish his studies at the Jewish Theological Seminary. After Meyer's arrival, Matalon not only attended services at BJ but also led services on occasions when Rabbi Meyer had to be away. Upon Matalon's ordination, Meyer arranged for a half-time rabbinical position for the young rabbi at BJ. Within a short time, Roly, as he came to be called by virtually everyone in the BJ community, was fully part of the synagogue's rabbinical leadership.

Roly was hardly a carbon copy of his mentor. Marshall was physically large; Roly was slight. Marshall spoke with a commanding voice; Roly was soft-spoken. Marshall could be intimidating to congregants; Roly was extremely approachable. And yet week after week, Marshall and Roly would stand, side by side, in front of the congregation and jointly lead the service. Their relationship signaled a rabbinical partnership in which each rabbi complemented the other. During the *shabbat* morning Torah study, Marshall and Roly would commence the examination of the weekly biblical selection in dialogue with each other, with Marshall probing and challenging and Roly responding. It was a private conversation in front of several hundred sets of eyes. After the rabbinical exchange, members were invited to join in the conversation.

A wide array of committees and programs emerged. A shelter and a luncheon program for the homeless were established. A religious school for children was launched cooperatively with a neighboring synagogue, Ansche Chesed. Adult education programs were sponsored. Key committees began to attend to the day-to-day issues of congregational management, from finance to membership.

Consistent with Marshall Meyer's commitment to social justice, BJ became a place where Jews could confront the most controversial issues of the moment. Under Rabbi Meyer's guidance, BJ sponsored a variety of forums on the Israeli-Palestinian conflict and the prospects for peace in the Middle East. The congregation heard perspectives on human rights problems around the world, something that Meyer had experienced firsthand during his time in Argentina. As scores of churches and a handful of synagogues provided sanctuary to refugees from oppressive regimes in Central America, BJ wrestled with its own responsibility to provide aid to that cause. Similarly, Meyer felt that the congregation had to confront the problems of poverty and homelessness, so much a part of the urban setting in which BJ found itself. As a result of Meyer's prodding, the congregation began a shelter and food program for the homeless, despite the fact that the building that housed the synagogue was in need of massive restoration work. It was a reflection of the reinvigorated congregation's priorities.

○

Social Justice—Hands On

Volunteering is what we do. We come, we pray and then we roll our sleeves up and get involved. Along the way we put our prayers into action. Along the way we make friends, build a community and take part in the world.

THE BJ SHELTER

What it is: A respite from the streets, a hot meal, a friendly conversation and a warm bed for eight guests a night, five nights per week, screened and sent by a program of the Partnership for the Homeless. Solely staffed by volunteers from BJ, St. Pauls/St. Andrews Church, New York Cares, and the neighborhood.

What's it like: Quiet (if you don't mind the TV). Relaxed. No one pushes anything. People eat. People talk if they want to. Someone asks to play chess. Sometimes dinner's there. Sometimes you shop. Overnight it's just about sleep. "I was getting increasingly depressed about the homeless situation and wanted to both learn more and do something about it. I also wanted to meet more people so that when I came to services it felt more like home. This gave me the chance."

What's needed: Two groups of volunteers per night, four to set up, serve dinner, and provide friendly conversation, and two people to sleep over.

THE BJ LUNCH PROGRAM

What it is: A lunch with a heart. Preparing sandwiches and snacks for 250 or more every Wednesday.

What it's like: Warm, friendly, hands-on, inter-generational. Truly like a big family talking around the table. "I like going from morning *minyan* to here. It's like an extension of the prayer service."

What's needed: People to separate cheese slices, bag muffins, slice loaves, and make up vats of tuna surprise.

THE BJ/ST. LUKE'S HOSPITAL AIDS BRUNCH

What it is: Shared food and shared talk with hospitalized patients, bringing the outside world in.

What it's like: Varies. Sometimes people want to talk; sometimes they don't; but they always appreciate the company and the food, especially the sweet stuff. Some volunteers stay in the lounge with the ambulatory patients. Others deliver brunch on carts to patient rooms. "I was very wary and went with a lot of trepidation. I didn't know what I would find there. But you realize you bring joy to a lot of people. They are thrilled to have company and food they enjoy. Most of them don't have visitors."

What's needed: Up to ten volunteers per brunch to assemble and serve the donated food, talk, share, and just be there. Also needed are entertainers. Laughter and song never hurt.

[*The BJ Volunteer Catalog, 1995.*]

o

Rabbinic Leadership

Marshall Meyer was at the center of every one of the new program initiatives. In fact, one of the attractions of assuming the pulpit of B'nai Jeshurun for Meyer was the congregation's lack of infrastructure—a clean slate. Meyer was a dominating presence who much preferred to galvanize a community through his words and deeds than to spend time behind closed doors working with a committee. Now in the hub of the largest concentration of Jews in the country, he took Manhattan by storm. In the first two years of his tenure, membership grew from thirty-five to two hundred fifty households. By 1993, the year Marshall Meyer passed away, the congregation had grown to nine hundred households, fairly evenly divided between families and singles.

Anyone associated with the rejuvenated B'nai Jeshurun's revival would readily admit that Marshall Meyer was the single greatest factor behind the revival. Many describe Marshall as larger than life. He was passionate. He was charismatic. He lived his life in superlatives. It was impossible to be neutral about him. There were some people who could not relate to such a forceful rabbinic figure, but they were far outnumbered by the many who gravitated to his strong leadership. Meyer assumed prerogatives that would be unheard of in most other congregations. When he brought in Roly Matalon, it was clear that those prerogatives were not about personal ego (though one cannot totally dismiss that) but rather about the way Marshall believed that synagogues needed to function.

Whether the issue was the creation of a men's club and sisterhood (typical of most congregations but never established at the "new" B'nai Jeshurun), who could ascend the *bima* for an honor (Meyer allowed non-Jewish parents of a bar or bat mitzvah to do so), acceptance of gay and lesbian Jews who came to the congregation, or the hiring of new staff, the rabbis of BJ shaped the decision. In most synagogues, boards of directors and committees would have a much stronger hand in setting policy. However, Marshall Meyer felt that as the rabbi, he had to set the tone for congregational priorities. On one occasion, he protested that the salary of one of the members of the maintenance staff was unconscionably low. The matter was taken up, and the salary was increased. Such interventions set the tone in acknowledging that social justice was not only high-minded rhetoric about abuses across the globe; it started at home.

One of the oddest things about the new B'nai Jeshurun is that in the short time since its renaissance under Marshall Meyer, the synagogue, a phenomenon in the heart of North America's largest Jewish community, has come to be led by clergy from Argentina. Roly Matalon, the man

Meyer named co-rabbi in 1986, had of course studied at Meyer's seminary in Buenos Aires. In 1989, Meyer invited Ari Priven to come from Argentina to serve as cantor for the High Holydays; within a year, Priven had moved to New York to become the full-time music director. During the 1990s, two additional musicians were brought from Argentina to lead overflow High Holyday services. When Meyer passed away, Matalon was asked to nominate a new rabbi candidate, subject to board and congregational approval. His choice was Marcelo Bronstein, also a former student of Meyer's and the youth director at Bet-El in Buenos Aires for ten years. Bronstein also happened to be Roly's best friend and a fellow Argentinian. Thus by the mid-1990s, BJ's two rabbis and music director were all from Argentina.

Several things are significant about the Argentinean axis at B'nai Jeshurun. First, it reflects the power of the rabbinic office at BJ. Though the caliber of the board improved significantly under Meyer's tenure, it was clear that the rabbi was running the show. But issues of authority and hierarchy never became a major source of dispute or tension. This deference to rabbinical leadership continued after Meyer's death, even though Roly Matalon was not quite the forceful personality that Meyer was. Thus strong rabbinical leadership, regarded by some as idiosyncratic during Meyer's tenure, had become an institutional value that was seen to have positive merit.

As might be expected in any voluntary association, there were some raised eyebrows and voices of criticism after BJ hired its third full-time Argentinean, Rabbi Marcelo Bronstein. Yet part of the magic of the new BJ was its style of worship, and it was no coincidence that first Marshall Meyer and then Roly Matalon wanted to preserve a clergy "team" all of whom were on the same wavelength. The ties between the religious professionals at BJ were closer than the casual observer might know. Matalon, Priven, and Bronstein had all been members of Marshall Meyer's synagogue, Bet-El, in Buenos Aires. All had gone to the Ramah camp that Meyer started in Argentina. Matalon and Bronstein attended the seminary that Meyer had founded in Argentina before finishing their rabbinical studies in New York. Matalon and Bronstein were also best friends.

○

Religious Synergy

The gates are closing, and it's the end of Yom Kippur services in 1997. The emotions of my first *yamim noraim* (High Holydays) at B'nai Jeshurun are running high and the *shofar* has just sounded. Immediately the music of the *havdalah niggun* (melody for the closing prayer of the day) begins to fill the sanctuary, enveloping the close to two thousand people in the space. As I look up in the darkness, with only the light of the *havdalah* (prayer marking the movement from sacred time to normal weekday time) candle blazing, several hundred children dressed in white begin to come down the aisles carrying electric candles until they are all inside the room. The entire congregation sings the blessings marking the end of the holiday, and I can barely get the words out with the tears streaming down my face.

My experience during Yom Kippur was not an isolated one during my time at BJ. Every *shabbat* two thousand Jews from all walks of life come and worship in the two *kabbalat shabbat* (service welcoming the sabbath) services, and sometimes six hundred will come on *shabbat* morning. The service is prayerful, spiritual, and joyful. When members dance around the sanctuary during *Lecha Dodi,* when they encircle a couple at their *aufruf* (celebration of forthcoming marriage), or when as many as a one hundred people join in the *aliyah* on *shabbat* to pray for the healing of a loved one or themselves, the service is a striking, emotional one. It's an amazing feeling—leading services in this incredible community—and a privilege too. How often can a rabbi help to create sacred space and also be able to dwell in that space at the same time? The number of people is not what makes my spirit soar, although it doesn't hurt to have twelve hundred people answer when you pray *Barechu et adonai hamevorach.* It is the synergy between the service leaders and the congregation, the energy that flows between us, and exists both in the music and the silence that fills the sanctuary.

When people line up to enter services, or arrive thirty minutes before a service begins in order to find a seat, I am most struck by the deep desire of so many Jews—many of them without the traditional rationale for joining a synagogue—to invest in a spiritual home for themselves. The services alone are not what make BJ a *kehillah kedoshah,* a holy community, but the commitment on the part of the congregation and of its spiritual leaders to praise, thank, question, and wrestle with God does make BJ a vibrant spiritual home for so many Jews.

[Rabbi Yael Ridberg's recollection. Rabbi Ridberg served as the first Rabbi Marshall T. Meyer Rabbinic Fellow from 1996 to 1998.]

Worship Experience

The closeness of the religious leaders gave an extraordinary quality to worship at the synagogue. Even among people originally drawn to B'nai Jeshurun by its social action programs, it soon became clear that the essence of the place was exemplified by its *shabbat* services.

Rabbis Meyer and Matalon would stand close to the congregation, not on a remote, raised *bima*. They would stand side by side, with no hint of senior or junior status. There was no clerical garb. Everyone referred to the rabbis by their first names. Each had a beautiful voice in his own right—Meyer a booming baritone, Matalon an angelic tenor. Ari Priven accompanied the service on an electric keyboard, using both his voice and tempo to engage the worshipers. The melodies were chosen quite deliberately, designed to engage the entire congregation in participatory singing and to deepen the *kavanah* (prayer intention) of worshipers.

The informality lent the service a sense of accessibility that is often hard to find in other synagogues. A student wearing jeans and a T-shirt could slip into a seat next to an older person in a suit and fear no reproach. The raucous clapping to a *niggun* (wordless melody) or the dancing in the aisles to the Friday night singing of "L'cha Dodi" might shock a first time visitor to BJ, but to regulars it flowed naturally from the emphasis on spiritual spontaneity. Decorum took a backseat to expression.

Religious services did undergo some changes as BJ grew. Initially, the Saturday morning service was the larger service, but by the early 1990s, the Friday night service became a happening. As if the attendance at BJ wasn't growing fast enough by word of mouth, an article in the *New York Times* ensured that the revival at BJ would not remain a secret to anyone interested in Jewish life in the New York vicinity. By the late 1990s, BJ had to hold two Friday evening services, one after the other, to accommodate as many as two thousand worshipers. Families gravitated to the early service, and singles were more prevalent in the late service. The lines that formed around the building before the doors opened testified to the appeal of BJ's style of worship.

On Saturday mornings, the crowd was smaller, perhaps four or five hundred people, reflecting perhaps the fact that the service was considerably longer and more demanding than the celebratory and contemplative moods of Friday night worship. Study of the weekly Torah portion formed the central core of this service. As attendance grew, it was harder to include the congregation in the dialogue the rabbis introduced. Either the rabbis would dialogue with each other or one of them would present a *d'var torah* (instructive homily from the assigned biblical reading).

The services at B'nai Jeshurun came to attract everyone, from the person raised with a traditional Jewish background to the uninitiated. BJ prided itself on providing enough traditional content to satisfy the former while remaining accessible to the latter. Many things attracted people to BJ, but none was so compelling as the conduct of religious services.

○

Reflective Retreat

The BJ Meditation, Chanting, and Silent Retreat held between March 29 and April 1, 1998, was the fifth BJ Retreat I attended in as many years and, for me, the most extraordinary one by far. It was much more than a good time; it reached deeply into our souls and offered us transformative, religious experiences.

We were a relatively small group by BJ standards, about forty-five people including our rabbis and cantor, members of the BJ staff, Rabbinic interns, and a retired rabbi from Philadelphia. Three quarters of us were women and we ranged in age. Rabbi Shefa Gold led our retreat at Elat Chayim, the Jewish Retreat Center, structuring most of our waking hours, with morning, afternoon and evening sessions. This retreat, in Roly's words, "was an intensive training; nothing was done by chance. We learned how to prepare, to be intentional, stay focused, be responsible and, moment by moment, be in God's service."

The focus of this retreat was to prepare for Pesach [Passover] by discovering, identifying and naming the *chametz* within us. The *chametz* is that part of us that has soured, that has become puffed-up the way bread rises. Pain, disappointment, and frustration distort us. To protect ourselves, we hide behind masks. The work was to take away the emotional bandages covering us so that we can emerge from under our self-definitions and accouterments becoming freer and truer versions of ourselves. We did an internal Spring cleaning—probing where we usually dare not go, made possible with Shefa's and the group's supportive containment.

Almost everyone made it to the 7 A.M. Shachrit Service. Shefa led us in prayers, focusing on only a few chants so that we could experience their meanings deeply. We felt how repetitive chanting facilitated our silent meditation. By incorporating movements into our chants, we deepened our prayers, and our connection to God. The combination of communal and personal time during the *tefillah* gave a depth and timelessness to the service. Ari commented that he thought 10 minutes had passed only to look at his watch and find out it was an hour later. Our prayers lasted until about 8:30 A.M.—breakfast-time.

Shefa is a very gifted teacher, singer and composer of chants. In chanting, Shefa taught "we use our breath, intention, the power of the sound, melody, harmony, rhythm, the meaning of the words, visualization and movement to move us out of ordinary consciousness. Through the chant, we create awareness, build group energy (and cohesiveness), journey inward, mobilize the will, open the heart, re-member and plant affirmations, inspire ourselves, lift out of normal consciousness, expand the self of Self, become more grounded and prepare for silence."

Shefa invited us to let go while appreciating what a struggle it is to truly quiet the mind in meditation. She spoke about being gentle and patient with ourselves, watching our tendency to be harsh and puni-tive with ourselves as our minds wander. She suggested the use of a sacred word to bring the mind back when one notices it has wandered, or the use of the ever-present breath, as an anchor to keep the mind focused.

We meditated sitting opposite "spirit buddies." With different spirit buddies, we would experience difficult aspects of ourselves. We then shared in a group what we sensed. It was truly exciting when two people confirmed an experience. With our spirit group, of four or five people, we spent an afternoon preparing a ritual, chant or blessing. We privately and as a group explored in as many ways as we could, different texts from *Tanach* (the Bible) relating to water. We were di-vided into ten groups and all the groups took the assignment seriously, developing meaningful and beautiful blessings and rituals. We amazed ourselves that we could come up with ten new ritual experiences of the Divine in a relatively short time.

The most profound experience, and for many people a totally new experience, was our day of silence. Shefa prepared us to feel the pres-ence and the support of the community as we explored our inner land-scape. We all have the experience of silence alone. Being free of cares and responsibilities of our everyday lives and being surrounded by community, while having permission to silently and carefully watch our thoughts, attitudes, habits and impulses, was, for me, an ecstatic and transformative experience. It could be compared to the with-drawal of food on Yom Kippur, which can also bring us to a higher state of consciousness, an opening for a change to occur.

Our twenty-four hours of silence began and ended with rituals. It began with the ten difference rituals around water that we, as groups, created. We concluded our day of communal silence around a large fire into which we individually threw spiritual *chametz* that we were pre-pared to remove from our souls while the community prayed silently for the burners of *chametz*. Shefa instructed us to return to speaking by bestowing blessings upon each other. We were given permission to tell each other all the loving things we so often keep to ourselves. We profoundly touched one another and broke through barriers. This is after all what we so much long for in our lives and attempt to accomplish with our stories, jokes, witticisms, criticisms. . . .

On our last morning, we lovingly nurtured the fragile seeds of change we had planted in our minds through visualizing, chanting and sharing our images with spirit buddies. We ended by publicly, if we wanted to, committing ourselves to some practice flowing from our experience. We had more than a good time; we created openings and purified our souls. A meaning of Pesach and liberation is letting go of the old and rotten that enslave us, making room for new possibilities, new beginnings, and greater personal freedom to sense and serve the Divine.

[Estare Weiser, *Jeshurun Journal*, Summer 1998.]

Leadership Transition

Marshall Meyer's sudden death in December 1993 was, understandably, a great blow to the congregation. Marshall *was* the new B'nai Jeshurun. He had given the institution his personality and had come to embody the institution to such an extent that not everyone was sure BJ could survive the loss.

The fact that BJ not only survived Meyer's death but continued to flourish under the rabbinic leadership of Roly Matalon and Marcelo Bronstein illuminates some critical issues of institutional dynamics. There was no question that as Marshall Meyer's protégé and an already beloved leader, Roly Matalon would take over as rabbi of B'nai Jeshurun. But at age thirty-seven, and with a personal style much different from Meyer's, Roly knew that he would have to make some changes in the way the congregation functioned.

A strategic plan undertaken in collaboration with the United Jewish Appeal-Federation of New York soon after the rabbinic transition at BJ revealed several institutional weaknesses. The congregation attracted a disproportionate number of singles, not surprising given its location. But families had to be better served. Board decisions had to be communicated more effectively to the membership. The office was badly understaffed, leading to significant administrative oversights.

Roly understood that he could not control as much of the organization as Marshall had, given the pace of congregational growth, nor could he make the same kinds of demands as those made by his predecessor. If the congregation was to continue to be as dynamic as it had been under Meyer's tenure, more initiative would have to come from the membership. The congregation had become accustomed to the rabbi's taking the lead on program initiatives even though they eventually involved many congregants. Roly Matalon now sought to encourage some "creative chaos," and an array of new initiatives came about.

The growth in programming took place under some trying circumstances. In May 1991, the ceiling in BJ's main sanctuary collapsed, making that space unusable. A variety of churches and schools in the vicinity had to be used for programming during the five-year renovation. The Church of St. Paul and St. Andrew, located down the street from BJ, became the host of Friday evening and *shabbat* morning worship, and the shelter program started by Marshall Meyer came to be cosponsored by the church as it needed to provide the space for it. BJ continued to sponsor its weekly lunch program for the homeless in its own basement. It also continued its monthly AIDS brunch, which brought food and companionship to AIDS patients at a nearby hospital.

But these signature BJ programs soon became only the tip of the iceberg. As the congregation continued to grow and address its administrative weaknesses, so did the program offerings, and BJ's annual program listings went from a few mimeographed pages to a professionally designed forty-page catalogue. A program of monthly Friday night dinners following services, called *Shabbat be'Yachad* (Sabbath Together), brought together one hundred to one hundred fifty members for food, fellowship, study, and singing in the spirit of *shabbat*. *Havdalah* study groups facilitated Jewish study in small groups of twelve to fifteen on late Saturday afternoon, leading into the ceremony of *havdalah,* which concluded the sabbath. Within a short time, more than twenty-five such groups were meeting approximately once a month.

Several initiatives mobilized BJ members to meet internal needs. The congregation was organized in a way so as to give personal support to members who experienced loss, sickness, or trauma. Members were recruited to help usher at religious services and to help in the reading of Torah and Haftarah. A choir was put together to perform at selected services and in programs outside of the congregation. An arts and culture committee brought together members who wanted to organize dance, choral, and film programs for the congregation.

Some of the most dramatic programmatic growth came in the area of adult education. Study had been a priority since Marshall Meyer came to the congregation in 1985. The expansion of offerings was a response to the growing membership and its ongoing pursuit of this priority. By the late 1990s BJ sponsored some forty to fifty courses in addition to three congregational retreats and several weekend scholar series. The courses took full advantage of the incredible resources in New York City, with instructors coming from many of the major Jewish seminaries and educational institutions across denominational boundaries, including Orthodox scholars and teachers. The courses themselves ranged from introduction to Judaism to Hebrew language courses to advanced courses on Talmud, prayer, and Jewish history. Some four hundred members participated in these courses.

B'nai Jeshurun also expanded its commitment to *tikkun olam* (social justice work), which had been such a high priority for Marshall Meyer. Book, clothing, and toiletry drives were conducted for the homeless. The congregation began to work in conjunction with the Jewish Home and Hospital for the Aged, which B'nai Jeshurun had helped found in 1850. The arrangement had BJ members adopting seniors in the facility and sponsoring a host of religious and holiday programming at the home. In a similar way, BJ members were paired with new Americans in a phone relationship that helped the immigrants, mostly from the former Soviet Union, learn English.

In partnership with the Church of St. Paul and St. Andrew, B'nai Jeshurun adopted a local public school in the neighborhood. Students from low-income families were offered services by volunteers, running the gamut from tutoring to grant writing to arts projects. BJ members also participated in such varied organizations as Jews Against Genocide (in Bosnia), AIDS advocacy and support, Mazon: A Jewish Response to Hunger, and the Worker's Rights Board of New York. Committees were set up to work on environmental and human rights issues around the world and to arrange for programs that forged relationships with other faith communities in the city. As part of its outreach to gays and lesbians, the congregation sponsors an annual Stonewall Shabbat Seder to recount the story of gay liberation.

Despite all this activity, *shabbat* services remained the central activity of the congregation, attracting a very high percentage of the membership. As noted earlier, Friday night services were the most popular. By 1994 it was common for hundreds of people who wanted seats at the Friday night service to form lines around the building before the doors even opened. In order to accommodate the more than one thousand people who wanted to be part of the *kabbalat shabbat* (service welcoming the sabbath), BJ began to sponsor an early and late service. After the congregation moved back into its newly repaired building on 88th Street in December 1996, it continued to sponsor a second *kabbalat shabbat* at the Church of St. Paul and St. Andrew.

The size and programmatic complexity of BJ required a commensurate increase in staff. By 1997, in addition to Rabbis Roly Matalon and

Marcelo Bronstein, BJ also had a full-time rabbinic fellow, three part-time rabbinic interns, a music director, an executive director, a school principal, and a family and youth director. Except for the rabbinic interns, these positions were not atypical for such a large congregation. But the staff does reflect the attention paid by the congregation in the post-Meyer era to creating a more administratively efficient organization.

More unusual was the hiring of a director of programs and the use of volunteers to coordinate the activities necessitated by so large a cadre of members, now in excess of 1,750 households. At a time when many non-profit organizations, including religious institutions, have had great difficulty finding volunteers because so many adults hold full-time jobs, BJ prides itself on inspiring a high level of service to the community on the part of its membership.

When Marshall Meyer passed away in 1993, many BJ congregants wondered whether the revival that took place under his dynamic leadership would continue. They did not realize just how much momentum had been generated in those years. The energy had to be channeled, but a clear mission had been set, and the congregation was well on its way to fulfilling that mission.

Relationship with the Conservative Movement

The post-1985 B'nai Jeshurun has had an interesting relationship with the national Conservative movement of Judaism. As the oldest Conservative congregation in America, in the city with the largest Jewish population outside of Israel, BJ was long a flagship of the United Synagogue of America, the congregational arm of the Conservative movement. The lay and rabbinic leadership identify BJ as a Conservative synagogue consistent with the bylaws of the congregation. The prayer book used is the one issued by the Conservative movement. Even after Marshall Meyer arrived at BJ and began a wholesale reconceptualization of the community, he used Conservative Judaism as the framework for his approach to Jewish life. In an early concept paper, he wrote, "We believe . . . Conservative Judaism has a unique message to impart to all human beings today."

Yet today BJ is not an official member of the United Synagogue of Conservative Judaism (the new name for United Synagogue of America). On the surface, the issue is about dues payments. It is not uncommon for synagogues facing financial crises to seek adjustment of their dues payments to the national body, which are based on membership numbers. BJ was in just such a situation at the time Marshall Meyer first came to New York. Usually, such matters are resolved amicably. In BJ's case, however, not only was there no settlement with regard to dues payments, but the action taken by another arm of the Conservative movement, denying a young gay person a job in a camp sponsored by the movement, led Rabbi Matalon to recommend that BJ not continue to pursue membership in the United Synagogue.

There is a dimension of the affiliation story that goes beyond finances and principles. Many members of B'nai Jeshurun do not consider themselves Conservative Jews. The current rabbinic configuration at BJ includes one graduate of the Conservative movement's Jewish Theological Seminary, one graduate of the Reform movement's Hebrew Union College, and one graduate of the Reconstructionist Rabbinical College. Members of BJ are as likely to hear the institution's approach to Judaism as "progressive Judaism," "liberal Judaism," or even "postdenominational Judaism" as they are to hear it referred to as an expression of "Conservative Judaism."

Contributing to BJ's eclecticism are several practices that are uncommon in most Conservative congregations. The congregation's welcoming of intermarried couples, extending membership rights to the non-Jewish spouse in a household, violates a written policy of the United Synagogue. Similarly, aggressive outreach to the gay and lesbian community, including the willingness of BJ's rabbis to perform commitment ceremonies that create a marriage-like union between same-sex partners, is a rarity in the Conservative movement.

It is ironic that one of the most successful Conservative congregations in the country is decidedly to the left of the national movement on several ideological issues even as the rabbis see themselves as operating within the bounds set by the Committee of Law and Standard of the Rabbinical Assembly (the official rabbinical arm of the Conservative movement).

Many members celebrate the eclecticism of BJ's character, which seems to defy labeling. An articulation of congregational principles drafted by Rabbis Meyer and Matalon in 1993 proclaimed a move away from wholesale identification with Conservative Judaism. In that document, BJ was portrayed as a "bridge between the liberal movements," incorporating "the best of all movements into our spiritual expression." The mere fact that the affiliation issues with the United Synagogue remained unresolved for several years without much concern on the part of the congregation's leadership reveals a certain ambivalence about the community's denominational identity. Thus while the synagogue is officially Conservative, the practices of the community have had a decidedly iconoclastic flavor, and the majority of the members do not much care about its denominational label. That the community has defined its own style and has proved its attractiveness to thousands of Jews who would otherwise know no Jewish home is sufficient to justify its existence with or without "official" movement credentials.

○

"God Has Bigger Plans for Me"

The greater Jewish community has been saying for thousands of years, "We are all Jews." But for too long, Jews who are deaf have felt overlooked by the greater Jewish community.

I stand here tonight, knowing that I am different because I am deaf. I communicate in ASL [American Sign Language], and I identify strongly with deaf culture. But that, in and of itself, is not a reason for me to be separated as a Jew. I am so proud to be a Jew who is deaf. . . .

Alienation and isolation occur too often for the Jew who is deaf. We are left with the belief that we have limited choices. We can form our own social and cultural group, or if our family is Orthodox we can follow their traditions. Or we can convert since other faiths are so welcoming to members of the deaf community.

But I am here to tell you that God has bigger plans for me. I know that there are more choices for Jews who are deaf, and I am determined to share Judaism and all of its richness with my Jewish deaf peers. On behalf of the Jewish deaf community, I am here to tell you that we crave the opportunity to be close to God. We want so much not to spend Friday nights alone. We want to spend *shabbat* together. We do not want to be left out when a major Jewish community event is taking place simply because there are no qualified ASL interpreters hired to make the event accessible to us. Some of us want to become Jewish deaf educators. We want to become an integral part of the greater Jewish community. We do not want to be separated anymore. . . .

We do not need to be taken care of; we want to be equal decision makers and participate fully in every aspect of Jewish life. Jews who are deaf want to have an equivalent experience to their hearing Jewish peers. Clearly we require qualified ASL interpreters who are trained to bridge the gap between our two languages. Interpreters are not here because it looks beautiful; they are here to provide access to those of us who are deaf.

[Presented at BJ *kabbalat shabbat* service Aug. 16, 1996, by Marla Berkowitz, cofounder of MYAJD (the Manhattan Young Adult Jewish Deaf) and of the Jewish Deaf Resource Center. Soon thereafter, ASL interpreting was provided twice per month at *shabbat* services, during the High Holydays as well as at certain other programs.]

_____o_____

Ascending the Ladder

The story of BJ in the last thirteen years is unquestionably one of success. We have been a gateway for thousands of Jews to an inspiring and exciting experience of religious Judaism. However, our tremendous growth, our huge size and our international recognition are such that things can no longer continue the way they are. Far too many people attend BJ without being connected in any meaningful way. We are far from being a community centered around the study and practice of Torah and dedicated to *tikkun olam*.

We desperately need to redefine ourselves. We must all dedicate ourselves to strengthen and nurture our community. We must recapture a sense of shared values and our vision of an active religious community that seeks God, and serves God with love and commitment in order to realize God's will for *tikkun olam*. In order to achieve that, we must be willing to reject a Judaism that remains in the periphery of our lives, a Judaism that is *parve* (Yiddish for neither milk nor meat) and that demands nothing of us. Instead, our experience of Judaism at BJ must be life-changing, engaging, challenging, and must be authentic and true to our values. And it must be lived in community; a community of *kavanah*, of intention, dedication and purpose.

This is not a simple or light task. It will require much of every one of us. It will demand effort of thought and deed as well as discipline. The alternative is stagnation, disillusion, and watering down. The result is a minimalist, superficial Judaism of no substance that already exists in far too many places and has no impact on the lives of individual Jews [or] the life of the Jewish people or of the world at large. I believe that we must begin by taking seriously our commitment to the study of Torah, prayer with *kavanah* and *gemilut chasadim* as the focus of our work as a community. We must be willing to commit to a core of *halachic* behavior as the expression of our communal spiritual and moral values. We must maximize our participation in all programs and volunteer opportunities. We must seek a level of intimacy within our larger community by making an effort to belong to a *havurah*, a fellowship group that meets regularly to study, to celebrate *shabbat* and other holy days, that acts as a support group, and that volunteers in specific areas of our communal work. We must become a community of kindness. We must embrace the sharing of our financial resources and our time and skill resources as an act of love and service of God.

These goals are not only reachable, they are our right. As we approach the summer months and prepare to take a pause and perhaps consider our commitments for next year, I invite you to ask yourself the question: Am I willing to ascend the ladder? If we are all willing to climb, we will have the power to raise our community to spiritual greatness. BJ is already of historic significance. If we become a model community we will have the privilege of sharing our work and influencing other synagogue communities to become vital and relevant. And we may lead in the shift of [a] synagogue paradigm that is a *sine qua non* condition if liberal Judaism is to remain relevant for the next generations of Jews.

[Rabbi Rolando Matalon, *Jeshurun Journal*, Summer 1998.]

Core Principles

Three times since B'nai Jeshurun's "renaissance," attempts have been made to articulate the core Judaic principles driving its rapidly evolving program. Each time, the documents were prepared by the rabbis and put before the congregation.

The first document came out in 1988, three years after Marshall Meyer's assumption of the pulpit, under the heading "A Philosophy for the New Community of B'nai Jeshurun." The document placed the institution of the synagogue in the context of Jewish history, noting that in the modern world, the synagogue has been less than successful in meeting the needs of Jews. Synagogues are, the statement said, "frequently irrelevant," "boring," and "unaesthetic." It went on to envision a synagogue that served as a meeting place, a house of study and prayer, and a refuge for the poor, the hungry, and the needy.

Expressing the greatest hopes and expectations of the newly revived congregation, Meyer wrote: "Congregation B'nai Jeshurun believes that a community synagogue which responds to the authentic questions of life, death, love, anxiety, longing, and the search for meaning can, once again, attract Jews—families and individuals—if it is willing to grapple with the great issues of life and not limit itself to the liturgical experience alone. . . . We do believe that Jews today are in search of some sort of contact with sanctity. We believe, more than ever, in the value of intimacy and loving care to be found within a community structure."

Several other key principles emerged in the first attempt at a comprehensive philosophy of the new B'nai Jeshurun. The synagogue would be an egalitarian, participatory community. It would seek the active participation of all ages and life stages, a particularly important feature given the synagogue's location on the Upper West Side of Manhattan, where there were at least as many elderly and single Jews as there were families with children, a staple of suburban synagogue membership. All musical instruments that might enhance liturgical expression would be encouraged.

The egalitarian commitment of Marshall Meyer for BJ extended to gay and lesbian Jews. The statement expressed openness to Jews of any prior affiliation, as well as to Jews of any race or sexual orientation. Nor did Meyer want to create a hierarchy of wealth in the community, often a feature of synagogue life. Notwithstanding the risks of underfunding an institution that faced a major challenge in rebuilding itself, the statement committed the institution to a self-assessed income-based sliding-scale dues structure, still in place today. Only an honor code ensured that members would actually pay the dues expected for their level of income.

No one familiar with the revived BJ under Marshall Meyer would be surprised at the fact that in Meyer's articulation of the synagogue's philosophy, strong statements were made about the community's commitment to issues. The statement spoke of the centrality of the state of Israel for Jewish identity, the importance of supporting the state financially, the encouragement of regular visits to the state, and even the consideration of *aliyah* (emigration) to Israel. But it did not shrink from speaking about two of the more difficult aspects of Israeli life in the late twentieth century—the search for peace with its neighbors and the attempt to ensure religious pluralism in the Jewish homeland for non-Orthodox forms of Judaism. Both of these issues were a source of concern for American Jews, especially non-Orthodox Jews, and both would be regularly addressed by a variety of programs at BJ.

The commitment to political and social issues in the general community had become one of the most distinctive features of the new BJ. The statement made that range of concerns a clearly articulated value: "In order to be authentic Jews, we must be responsible both as individuals and as a collective to the community at large." This statement pointed to Meyer's deep passion for a range of issues including poverty, homelessness, discrimination, racism, AIDS, war, and any other issue within the purview of Jewish ethical and moral teachings. Following a Talmudic dictum, Meyer stated that the congregation should not limit its focus to Jewish affairs, although Jewish matters could be given first priority.

Four years after the issuing of the initial philosophy of the B'nai Jeshurun community, Rabbis Meyer and Matalon published a column in the synagogue bulletin under the heading "The Coming Years of Congregation B'nai Jeshurun: Who Are We Now? What Are Our Aims for the Year 2000?" The column was organized around three principles from the Jewish tradition: Torah, *avodah* (service of God), and *gemilut chasadim* (deeds of lovingkindness). In certain ways, this statement reflected a maturing of congregational priorities resulting from the interaction between a growing and successful congregation and the principles set forth by the rabbi who had shaped the community's renaissance.

Reading between the lines of the 1993 statement, one can gauge some of the challenges to the rapidly growing congregation. With regard to the size of the membership, the rabbis expressed their commitment to retain the qualities of intimacy and caring even as the membership approached one thousand households. They were resolutely against limiting the growth of the congregation.

Rabbis Meyer and Matalon were forceful about BJ's response to homosexuality and intermarriage, two of the most controversial issues in Jewish life at the end of the twentieth century. "Homosexuality is not immoral," they declared, a debatable position in light of the teachings of rabbinic Judaism. But Meyer and Matalon felt that the issue called for an unequivocal stance, even if at odds with traditional Jewish teaching. Similarly, they felt that nothing would be gained by driving intermarried couples out of the Jewish community. All would continue to be welcome at B'nai Jeshurun.

In the section on Torah, the rabbis stressed the importance of ongoing study with particular emphasis on acquiring competency in Hebrew, a particular failing of American Jewish education. The rabbis had also become more conscious of the need for a more effective way of transmitting the Jewish heritage to children, calling for more parental involvement in the Jewish education of their children. Their desire to make the tradition more relevant led them to acknowledge that "not all of the past is sacred nor [is] all that the present offers to be embraced" as they attempt to balance the twin challenges.

Under the rubric of *avodah,* Meyer and Matalon were particularly focused on ways to enhance the experience of communal prayer. In this regard, they wanted to see more attempts to create liturgical poetry, music, and other aesthetic expressions that might enhance communal worship but would not obliterate the liturgical forms of the past.

Gemilut chasadim was the context in which the rabbis spoke to the need to "sanctify life . . . by eradicating the social ills and injustices that plague the contemporary world." They pledged greater education and action around the local issues of housing, poverty, crime, substance abuse, interfaith and race relations, and AIDS. In a more global vein, they addressed the issue of the environment, raising the notion of a form of "eco-*kashrut*" that would redefine in contemporary ecological terms what Jews should and should not consume. Finally, the statement called for ongoing communal attention to the ways in which the state of Israel could achieve fidelity to the values and visions of the Jewish tradition.

May 1997 saw a third formulation of the congregational principles, this time authored by Rabbis Matalon and Bronstein, titled "Our Mission Is to Inspire and to Require." It was a much briefer statement that restated many of the commitments of the two preceding statements. But the new mission statement was significant in a couple of ways. First, it underscored the point that the current rabbinical team was committed to much the same program that Marshall Meyer had put in place. This testified to his success in having created a unique organizational culture. No matter how the congregational program would evolve, the core beliefs on which Meyer revived BJ would remain fundamental principles.

Second, the new statement outlined greater recognition of B'nai Jeshurun's significance, not only to its own members but also to the Jewish world at large. The last item in the mission statement calls on the congregation to require "the sharing of our mission in order to invigorate the Jewish experience worldwide." BJ had become something of a pilgrimage stop for increasing numbers of Jews, from rabbis to average laypeople, eager to learn how this synagogue had succeeded in attracting so many members in so short a time.

As part of sharing its mission, BJ sought and received funding from Steven Spielberg's Righteous Persons Foundation and the Nathan Cummings Foundation to underwrite a rabbinic fellows program for four years. The program provided the funds to have a senior rabbinical student spend ten hours a week with the rabbinical staff of BJ and then work full-time on staff as a rabbinic fellow in the year following ordination. During that time, the young rabbis not only learned many practical skills about rabbinic functioning in a large congregation but also benefited from being mentored by Rabbis Matalon and Bronstein. The design was intended to equip younger rabbis to understand and potentially replicate aspects of the BJ synagogue model once they moved on to their own congregations. The clergy of BJ also started to think about conducting workshops and seminars for both rabbis and laypeople to share their ideas about how synagogues might transform themselves into more spiritually vibrant institutions.

In 1985, Marshall Meyer approached B'nai Jeshurun as a salvage operation. In the first decade after its rebirth, the congregation dealt with the typical challenges of managing growth, albeit on an unusually intense scale. Now in the second decade since its revival, the leadership of the congregation has begun to recognize the importance of replicating itself elsewhere.

Its work has just begun.

15

TOVA'S PATH

IT'S ABOUT THE LIGHT. And about the terror. Warm golden light from a Chanukah candle. And the pitch-dark black of an eternal abyss. My earliest memories are of both. For a long time, the darkness won. It's only within the past few years, especially at BJ, that I've begun to believe that the light is real.

Let me start at the beginning. I'm the product of a mixed marriage—an Upper East Side mother and a Lower East Side father. The class differences have never abated. Neither has the tension created by the demons each brought to the marriage. My mother, whose mother died at birth, was shaped by her stepmother's manic-depression; my father was shaped by his father's religious fanaticism and alcoholic rage. Whatever innocence they had left was sapped by the Great Depression, which also robbed them of any timely enjoyment of marriage and family life. Theirs was not a background made for emotional, let alone spiritual, connection. Nor was it an environment conducive to seeking help in transcending themselves. That they persevered despite their backgrounds is testimony to courage and imagination.

It didn't help that their second child was a ball of fire born with enough curiosity for four. I was hard-wired with a drive for something for which I had no words and for which they had little capacity. Literally and

Tova Frank (a pseudonym) hopes to give back some of what she has been so generously given by becoming a rabbi and working with Jews, including those in special-needs populations, who are themselves searching and returning. She adores Chinese food, cats, Mordecai Kaplan, and classical music and is finishing her own book, a murder mystery set on Yom Kippur in a seedy synagogue in a gentrifying urban area.

metaphorically, I was a singer in a house where no one else could carry a tune.

Not unsurprisingly, the God of my childhood was the classic, angry biblical model. This was not a God to be close to; this was a God to strenuously avoid. In the dark night of my childish soul, it seemed that the warmth of Chanukah and Passover were *bubba meisas* (fabricated stories) against a bleak judgmental reality. In my concept of the Jewish calendar, we lurched from Yom Kippur to Yom Kippur, and it was only a matter of time before we would be hanged, drowned, burned, stoned, strangled, starved, swallowed, struck with plague, or simply run through.

It's hard to say exactly where this Dickensian theology had its origin. I know today that kids shape God in the image of their parents, but Khrushchev-era parents had too much outside help to claim the credit alone. Trust in a beneficent Higher Power does not bloom naturally in kids caught between Cold War saber rattling and excessive responsibility for Israel's continued existence. Not only was my generation made the guardians of the new state of Israel; its fate and ours were literally intertwined. That might have been a formidable weapon for keeping order in the classroom, but the precariousness of the state's existence was a dark cloak draped over my *talmud torah* (Hebrew school) days. It was also a ridiculously heavy burden for kids already traumatized by cowering under public school desks during weekly nuclear war disaster drills. I suspect that the present surge of Jewish renewal may owe less to the Me generation than the Yom Kippur War and the breakup of the Soviet state. It is highly probable that my generation could not begin its spiritual journey until the existence of Israel and our own were reasonably guaranteed.

My earliest thoughts about God may also be a legacy from my childhood synagogue. I have a friend who says there are five kinds of Judaism: Orthodox, Conservative, Reform, Reconstructionist, and Suburban. I was raised Suburban Conservative at a time when Brooklyn was a suburb and members took great pride in their new Danish modern synagogue building. My memories of it are airless and joyless; my memories of services are of angry sermonic outbursts wrapped in three hours of unexplained drone or interminable cantorial trill.

And yet there was light, however hidden. It was in the old synagogue that became the ghetto of the very old and the very young. I remember how good it felt to sit around the scarred old table, lit by mismatched *yizkor* (memorial) bulbs on walls of rusted plaques, strangely soothed by the pervasive smell of old books, old men, and morning schnapps.

Twenty years later, I learned Rabbi Mordecai Kaplan's concept of *sancta* (ritualized behaviors that strengthen one's ethnic loyalties). It's the only explanation for the effect of that old and shabby room on a thoroughly Americanized second-generation child. It certainly wasn't the efficacy of prayer. I had only one: "Please God. I'm sorry. I'll be good." And it wasn't any interest in study. By the time we graduated to that table, I was lost in alternative worlds of fantasy and fiction. Five years of rote memorization demanded by Old World tutors gave me no sense of the potential power of prayer.

Let me be fair: if my teachers mentioned a loving God, *I* didn't hear it. If there was anything more involved in being Jewish than living in a Jewish neighborhood, showing up at Hebrew school, and being a good Jewish daughter, I missed it completely. My bat mitzvah was on a Friday night in the middle of March, featuring a Haftarah I know now is usually read for Chanukah. It was memorable more for the dress—a cabbage-rose confection more suitable for slipcovers—than for any liturgical, emotional, or spiritual connection that I made.

But I was a good Jewish girl—or tried to be. I kept showing up at the two-night-a-week Hebrew high school at my synagogue. But the teachers might as well have saved their time; by then I was mentally AWOL. I emerged several years later with only the dates 586 and 70 stuck in my head and, inexplicably, a fairly comprehensive knowledge of the laws of *kashrut*. About that time, I also decided to stop going to services. I hadn't stopped believing in a vengeful God. I just figured he was going to get me sometime anyway, so why bother being nice?

By this point, Woodstock had hit. My college classmates were swilling Boone's Farm, dropping tabs of LSD, and calling their cats Siddhartha. The alcohol was fine, but Hesse's appeal escaped me. The only thing worse than having a spiritual quest was to read about one. And there were so many more interesting books to read.

Also by then, I was out and moving, literally, traveling and dancing, mostly second-generation Martha Graham. My teachers had been disciples of Martha and demanded absolute fealty. I was only too willing to turn my life and my will over and make them gods.

Dancing by itself is spiritual. Even standing still. A full second-position *plié* can hold the universe in its span. On the good days, the connection was there, more than the sum of the parts of music and movement. Modern dancers are grounded, and for a time, I was. But at night, when the studio lights went out, the light left me. And the doubts about talent, dreams, and drive would blanket my soul.

So I caromed over a few continents, always rebounding back to New York, chasing certainty through people, places, and things, escorted by the family demons, always thinking the next thing would be the fix. I'm glad for my adventures—you don't get to meet royalty filing your nails in Brooklyn. But it would have been a lot less wearing on me and others if I'd just known what I was looking for.

Thirty was fast approaching, the end of life as far as baby boomers knew it then. In a rare lapse, I became involved with someone Jewish, not my usual style. Jewish men were what you took to weddings, not what you took home. A friend with the same penchant suggested Saturday lunch, to which I agreed. She then suggested that I meet her at synagogue beforehand, to which I recoiled and reconsidered lunch. But staying home and watching Saturday cartoons suddenly seemed old. So I showed. She didn't. And I stayed. It was Mordecai Kaplan's mother church of the Reconstructionist movement, the Society for the Advancement of Judaism (SAJ).

It was the first step back—either the time was right, the place was right, or my planets finally aligned. I'd never before seen women or young people on the *bima* or heard the Torah read. I didn't know that you could *read* the Torah; I thought it was the province of speed-mumbling eighty-year-old men. And I didn't know Judaism was about philosophy. I heard Rabbi Alan Miller and remember thinking, "This is how I always imagined people would talk." Dangle an idea before an autodidact and they're hooked. I don't move slowly. I joined the congregation that very week.

I don't know why it had never occurred to me there was more than one form of Judaism or more than one kind of Jewish practice. I knew there was modern dance and ballet, I knew there was Alvin Ailey and the American Ballet Theater. My brother and I had actually heard about Reconstructionism from a second cousin at a party a few years before. He'd followed it up and joined a Reconstructionist congregation. At that time, I brandished my contempt and dismissed the notion of taking any form of Judaism seriously.

It was a fortuitous time to land at the SAJ. The institution had attracted an entire posse of people in their twenties and thirties, mostly single, mostly refugees from Orthodoxy or suburbia. And a community of Kaplanians delighted to succor the new brood in their midst. Rabbi Miller nurtured me and my male counterpart and exposed us to Julian Jaynes, *The Ordeal of Civility,* and huge lashings of Freud.

I was so ignorant of the liturgy. I didn't know that Mordecai Kaplan, the founder of Reconstructionism, had made changes in the prayer book to match his transnaturalist philosophy. But I was a very quick study. I had my first *aliyah* on my thirtieth birthday in cowboy boots. A few months later, I read my first *aliyah,* having taught myself trope (the musical notations attached to the Torah text).

Everything was strange; everything was wonderful. I was so underexposed I didn't know you had *shabbat* dinners, let alone that you sang. I was so delighted to have a community, to argue ideas, to be of service as usher or *shamash* (one who helps in a religious service), to have a place to center this restless energy and even more restless mind, that it drove the dark away for a significant period of time. I forgot that demons can be distracted but never depart. My body started to swell periodically, and I was diagnosed with an autoimmune disease. No sense of community could wipe out the terror that I felt. Though I was fortunate enough to recover after a year's worth of steroids, I couldn't shake the fear. As a natural whirling dervish, I frantically engaged in every possible activity as a way to distract me from the growing spiritual black hole in my soul.

Judaism that remains on an intellectual level is not a great force for healing an out-of-control life. I was a little more awake this time around, and the SAJ at this point wasn't talking much about God. I was present in body and in mind but not in heart. In all honesty, I am not sure how much I really was present, as I'd gotten romantically involved with an Episcopal priest. There's a certain dissonance between being *gabbai* (usher) on Saturday and holding the hymnal on Sunday. Then again, I wasn't exactly trying for clarity; the effects of my family's alcoholism was hitting me full-bore.

Alcoholism is bad enough for the alcoholic. Secondhand drinking is twice as deadly because you can't see it. It's like slow-leaking carbon monoxide over every aspect of your life. I looked fine. I had high-visibility jobs, first as a dancer and then doing public relations for a dance company. I had friends and serially monogamous relationships. I was the fixer of the community. But under the hoopla, I was living on an arid, barren plane. I not only had no trust in God, I had no faith that someone who left the room for a soda would ever come back again.

That's no way to live. And on my thirty-third birthday, I decided I didn't want to live it. I woke up in a hotel room in Atlanta with a free day on a media tour and spent the time plastered against the window, willing myself to jump. I'd been to that blackness before, but this was opportunity meeting intention. I'd never before had a high window available just at the right time to do the work that I'd been too afraid to do with pills or knives.

I have absolutely no idea how long I stood there, cursing my cowardice. I also have no idea what I would have done if the telephone hadn't rung.

The moment passed. The featured speaker on my media tour had collapsed; I would have to fill in. I was needed; I was wanted; there was something for me to do. But there was also a brief flash of sanity in which I realized that I needed help.

Any spiritual impetus that I have really began at that moment. I had lucked out again. The environment for transcending demons was a lot more conducive in the eighties for me than it had been earlier for my folks. Not only were people talking openly about addiction, there was an organization called JACS—Jewish Alcoholics, Chemically Dependent Persons, and Significant Others—to dispel the myth that Jews don't drink, do drugs, or marry people who do.

There's a saying in JACS that I learned at my first retreat: "Religion is for people who are afraid of hell. Spirituality is for those who have been there." I thought that I had chosen to do something about the family disease. It didn't take long for me to make the discovery that everyone else makes—recovery works only on a spiritual base. In Genesis, Jacob awakens from his dream and says, "God was in this place, and I didn't know it." That verse now took on special meaning for me.

You can't stay around recovering alcoholics, addicts, or family members long and remain an intellectual Jew. For one thing, recovery is just too bloody hard. You're not coming back home, you are creating a home built on the unconditional love of your peers and your Higher Power to replace the hell you knew. And for another, you witness just too many miracles to depend on randomness and felicity. Wrecked shells take shape; the maimed marry; the most damaged human being begins to bloom in an atmosphere of hope. This is not foxhole praying; this is life as prayer. You can't survive long being one person with those in recovery and another person back out in the world. Gradually, you learn that you will survive; gradually you learn to trust and to love. And by watching others make the spiritual transition, you begin to believe that you will too.

For a long time, I was in an odd space. I had a sense of spiritual connection, courtesy of those in recovery, but no Jewish outlet to practice it between JACS retreats. That's not to say that I wasn't in a synagogue; I had the concept of synagogue as community down fine, and I went each week. But I couldn't transfer the God I had met in recovery to the sanctuary. I got so frustrated that I stopped even trying, and once more, I walked away.

In February 1994, I took thirty-six members of JACS on a mission to Israel. By this point, I'd been the paid professional director of JACS for two years, a perfect position for a natural workaholic with an overdeveloped sense of responsibility. I'd been to Israel before on a Jewish National

Fund staff mission. Not only wasn't I looking forward to the trip, I was dreading two weeks on twenty-four-hour call with my notoriously fractious board.

We landed on Thursday. On Friday, we came back from Jericho in time to usher in *shabbat* at the *Kotel* (Western Wall). I was more concerned with keeping track of my wandering sheep than in joining them. But I had a note to be put in a crack from a friend dying of AIDS, so I had to go up to the Wall. I stepped forward into a column of time so intense that I started crying uncontrollably. I jumped back; it was gone. I stepped forward to put the paper in, and I was in it once again. And I found myself praying, "Please God, make me more Jewish." Over and over. I couldn't believe it. And I have no idea from where it came.

Two weeks after we got home, the day after Purim, the day of the Hebron massacre, I found myself at B'nai Jeshurun. I'd tried it two years before on my search but found the community closed and it didn't take. My guess at why it took this time was that we had all changed. The community had opened in the grief following Marshall Meyer's death two months earlier. And I had been opened by time and experience to meet it halfway.

I'd come for community. I'd been so enchanted with Israel on this trip that I was investigating making *aliyah*. I got community, but without intending it, I also got what I'd been looking for all along. It's hard to put it in words. I came for community, but I got a place to make a Jewish spiritual home. I came for connection, for ballast, and I got a place to put the points of light that had never quite burned out.

Kabbalat shabbat at BJ is pure magic, a release of the workweek in singing and dancing that culminates in pure joy. But it was in the quieter *davening* of my second Saturday morning that the connection was made. I was sitting by the wall, totally unfamiliar with this prayer book, baffled by different melodies, embarrassed by different customs that had me standing when I should sit and singing when I should have been still. And I felt the same warm glow that I'd felt in the old synagogue of my youth; the grounding I'd felt in a *plié,* and the living prayer that I had felt in JACS. It was as if someone had opened a door and I was willing to enter. One minute I thought that I knew everything, and the next minute there were possibilities that I never imagined would spread out for me to choose.

I came for community, enchanted by Israel, and became enchanted with the possibility of God. I don't know why I could suddenly hear it, but I realized that God was a god of creation as well as of destruction, that the angry God I knew was also a God of love. This time they were definitely talking about God, and this time I was present. Everything that had come before had brought me to the point where I could finally sit and be still enough to hear.

I have a lot of company. BJ's grown in size, relatively overnight, from a one-room schoolhouse to an inner-city high school. Perhaps because it is so galvanizing, perhaps because it is nonjudgmental, people come to watch, stay for the joy, and find themselves studying and putting *mitzvot* into their lives. If I had to put a term to it, I would say that it was service of the heart in all its meaning. My guess is that it is a combination of philosophy, personality, and practice. But I don't care. One of the gifts that I have gotten at BJ is that I deserve the chance for connection.

I'm in my second term of rabbinical school now as a direct result of what Marshall and Roly created with BJ. Actually, not having known Marshall, I'm in rabbinical school now because of Roly's love of God and love of what he does. I haven't a clue of how I will afford to stay in school, which isn't all negative. It makes each day I get to study a gift. And if I get to put enough days together and am deemed to be of service to some community, I hope to be a resource, to help others on their path from darkness to the light.

The darkness is still there; it's just been balanced by the half that I was missing. It's all about balance—work and worship, love and will, body and soul. It took a long time, but I found a place to sing and to identify with the song: "*Tov l'hodot l'Adonai u'lzamair l'simchah elyon,*" "It is good to praise God and to sing out my highest joy."

PART SIX

THE SPIRITUAL POSSIBILITIES OF THE AMERICAN SYNAGOGUE

16

AVIVA'S PATH

IS THAT REALLY ME on the crowded subway train? I am heading downtown to my data processing job on Wall Street, precariously holding on to my tote bag with one hand and to a page of Torah text on the other. I squeeze in thirty minutes of uninterrupted study on the number 2 train. Softly under my breath I am humming the *trope* (musical notation that accompanies the Torah text) in preparation for *shabbat,* when I will stand on the *bima* at Congregation B'nai Jeshurun and chant from the Torah.

I do this now two or three times a year. Each time, I am amazed that I *can* do it and that several decades after not having a bat mitzvah at age twelve, my life has turned in this unusual direction. Unusual? What is so unusual about a secular Israeli-born woman living in New York being active in and committed to Jewish life? And why, after ten years of active participation in synagogue life, does my journey still feel strange and new and remarkable?

Friends ask, "Are you religious now?" You can almost hear them adding "heaven forbid." But the question is a tough one to answer. To be religious has connotations that are still hard to own up to. Sometimes I avoid the issue by saying that I am "spiritually connected." The relevance of Judaism in my life is not grounded in definitions and in pat answers but rather in questions. There are questions about God and questions about the universe—and even more, questions about a God and a universe that permitted the Holocaust. But about my own life there are some answers. I feel

---

Aviva Malka Hay has been a writer, translator, publications editor, and desert farmer. For the past seventeen years, she has been a systems analyst at the Chase Manhattan Bank. She often collaborates with artists, writers, poets, and filmmakers to help promote their work. She enjoys exploring the quiet and majesty of nature and cherishes an extended network of family and friends.

a purpose and a sense that the answers to the bigger questions are in the asking. The quest is the essence.

As a member of Congregation B'nai Jeshurun in New York City, I find my life framed by a focus on religious, ethical, moral, political, social, and community issues that seem powerfully to connect three strong elements in my life: an unavoidable legacy as a child of Holocaust survivors, an Israeli childhood, and immigration to America. I find myself traveling between these three influences, with Judaism as the unexpected but powerful compass for the journey.

My parents, both from the Polish town of Lvov, married in Paris at the end of the war. So determined were they that their firstborn not enter the world on a continent soaked in the blood of generations of their families that they boarded a ship to Israel, leaving France a mere twenty-one days before my birth.

My childhood was spent amid the challenges of the early years of statehood. But without much warning, when I was eleven years old, my brother was nine, and my sister was two, our parents packed us up and took us to the United States to what they hoped would be an easier life for their family. And so I exchanged the blinding sunshine, fragrant air, Mediterranean sea, and sandals on my feet for tall buildings with dark facades, escalators, and heavy winter coats.

As a child, I wanted desperately to assimilate. I didn't want to speak Hebrew at home. I didn't want to be the kid with the accent. I wanted to belong, to be like the natives in my Brownsville neighborhood in Brooklyn. And after a while, I was. High school was followed by college and a summer study trip to France. I met students from many countries: Italians and English, Swedes and Danes, and lots of other Americans.

Somehow I was found out. It seems that in the directory posted in the university lobby, I was listed as a student from Israel; my place of birth had preempted my adopted nationality. After the first few days, townspeople would inexplicably come looking for me by name. Elizabeth, a young Hungarian student, sought me out too. "Are you Jewish?" she asked. "I am," I answered. "So am I," Elizabeth whispered, as if we were trading secrets. And thus began a deep friendship that continues to this day.

That summer of discovery was spent discussing antisemitism, the Holocaust, and Zionism, but not religion. The few local Jews, as well as Elizabeth, had sought me out because I was a Jew. They wanted to talk and spend time with me because Israel was the umbrella over my name. I didn't exactly understand. After all, I had come with the American group. During the day, I studied French literature and toured the magnificent castles of Normandy. But the nights, after the dinners and the socializing, inevitably ended in very serious conversations. I was trying to understand why my new friends, all of us born after the Holocaust, were speaking to me about antisemitism, about feelings of persecution that had no specific foundation in their day-to-day life in France or in Hungary.

My nighttime friends were speaking about mysterious places. They spoke of memories of the past, of lives inhabited alongside previous generations of souls. They were so connected to those who had perished before our lives had begun. I didn't understand. In Brooklyn I refused to speak Hebrew, but in the cafés of France I sat surrounded by friends who gave me a place of honor because I was an Israeli and a Jew.

The journey of that summer remains with me always. In the pursuant years, I returned to live for a number of years in Israel and my spirituality was expressed in a profound love for the city of Jerusalem, a city that permits souls to soar. Unlike most Israelis, who traverse the country at every spare moment, I hardly left Jerusalem, so excited was I by its magnificence. Looking back at those years, I realize that I never once attended synagogue services there. And the same was true when I returned to the States in the late 1970s. Formal religious participation had no relevance for me.

Yet the spirituality was there, on the periphery, always. The holidays were celebrated with family. And though I was not seen at synagogues, I was spending time in yoga ashrams, meditating and seeking to create a place of peace for myself in a turbulent and hectic world. Then I read Aryeh Kaplan's book *Jewish Meditation* and devoured his *Jewish Meditation in the Bible*. In these books, Kaplan details the skills, practices, and long tradition of Jewish meditation, which can be traced back to the days of the Jerusalem Temple. This was an exciting discovery. It was a realization that the space I longed to create for myself could be had within the context of Judaism. And then, as it often happens, I found the right teachers and a place that allowed for encounters.

A flyer left in the lobby of my apartment building extended an invitation to join for High Holydays with a new rabbi who had just returned from serving twenty-six years in Argentina. From the minute I walked into the sanctuary of Congregation B'nai Jeshurun, on New York's Upper West Side, the place felt different and also familiar. Giora Friedman, a superb clarinetist whose music I had first heard in Israel and who, coincidentally, frequented the same yoga retreats I was visiting, was there on the *bima* of B'nai Jeshurun. Music for *Kol Nidrei*? Yes, he was there, his voice expressed through the wails of his instrument. I felt that I was hearing the sound of the soul. I shivered to the music and fought with the inner voices that were protesting that this wasn't a real synagogue. But wasn't it?

How the music drew me in, and the Hebrew language used so elegantly, not in the rushed, indistinguishable mumble of many other synagogues. Here the prayers were spoken clearly, beautifully, and with intention. The singing was joyous and constant. Spoken words were often left behind as the melodies embraced and welcomed me into a place of tranquility and joy. I wasn't exactly comfortable with the idea that I was actually in synagogue. Even more confusing, I kept coming back. I soon gave up my Friday night ballet subscription, and week after week I found myself turning down other engagements and heading up to the Eighty-Eighth Street sanctuary of B'nai Jeshurun.

The encounter with B'nai Jeshurun and its dynamic rabbis, Marshall Meyer and his younger colleague, Rolando Matalon, did not remain confusing for long. As a teacher, Marshall was passionate about Judaism. In fact, he was passionate about almost everything: about music, about justice, about the environment, about the world. Here was a rabbi who taught about belonging, witnessing, and participating in our world with Judaism as the core, an embracing, inclusive Judaism. Both within the confines of the synagogue and in the practices of Jewish life cycles, I discovered a vibrant Judaism pertinent to a perplexing and complicated universe that counted all human beings as partners.

Here were rabbis who brought Native Americans, Christian ministers, Palestinians, scholars, artists, and politicians to the *bima*. And during services, a microphone traveled around the sanctuary as we dialogued about the issues of the day, partners in exploration. The world I found on the *bima* of B'nai Jeshurun was a world steeped in Torah, a world steeped in a Judaism made relevant, pertinent, and vital for me and soon for thousands of others who came flocking through its doors.

Marshall also spoke about choices in a powerful way, often in relation to death. When Marshall spoke about death, he was no less passionate than when he spoke about life. He dismissed death with a bold stroke when he said, "From the moment we are born we are heading toward death" and "Death is the only certainty in life." And then he challenged us to be careful with how we live our lives. "Choose *life!*" he implored us (invoking Deuteronomy 30:19) as he pounded his fist on the podium during what was to be his last Yom Kippur on this earth.

The Judaism I live is about choosing life. It is about participating in the creation of a vibrant, joyous, innovative, and challenging community. It is about a personal calendar that is framed by the Jewish holidays and their celebration. It is about a week that is crowned by *shabbat*. It is about creating a frame for time. It is about incorporating the sacred in a turbulent world.

We are thinking about paths of return in the testimonies of this book. I ask myself, "Have I returned? Did I ever leave? Was I ever anything or anywhere else?" Return is about coming back to a place where you've been before, about coming back to the familiar. None of this is familiar to me, even after ten years of participation. The Judaism I am exploring and have incorporated into my life feels new. Each *shabbat*, each Yom Kippur, each Passover *seder* feels new. But it is also indeed a return in the sense of a reunion with the past. Each week, I convene into my life many people I never knew—grandparents, aunts, cousins, and all the others that we lost.

What would my grandparents say about my place in the world if in the moment before their lives were taken they could have seen me as I am today? Would anything seem familiar to them? In that place where truth resides in one's soul, I say yes. The Judaism I am exploring would be familiar to past generations of my family, the Hays and the Wurms lost in the Holocaust. The Torah I chant from is the same one that generations of my grandfathers studied. The annual calendar that marks the days of my life also marked theirs. In my daydreams, I imagine that were we reunited, we would share many familiar words, melodies, customs, traditions, commandments.

But the ghosts of the past would note that many things are different. Seeing me on the *bima*, a *tallit* across my shoulders, would be a surprise. It still is to me. Each time I, as a Jewish woman, participate in this sacred manner, I feel the awe. And the muscles in my stomach tighten, the bones in my rib cage seem to rattle. Standing on the *bima*, as my shaking hands caress the ancient texts, as I chant in a trembling voice, the joy in my heart serves as the bridge across eternity.

CREATING THE
SYNAGOGUE-COMMUNITY

AVIVA'S STORY provides an appropriate bridge to our discussion of the spiritual possibilities of the American synagogue. Much of her early life was framed by the issues and concerns of a previous generation of Jews—Holocaust, Israel, survival. Her desire to assimilate was foiled on an overseas study program, as other Jews sought her out precisely because of her ethnic identity. Her return to the Israel of her birth marked the dawning of her ability to connect her spirituality with her Jewish legacy, even though she never attended synagogue while there. It was, however, her good fortune to "discover" B'nai Jeshurun on her return to the United States. It would be just the kind of place necessary for her to find the links between her family's Jewish legacy and her own spirituality.

○

The synagogues that we have profiled and the personal spiritual paths of the individuals who were touched by their respective congregations are unique, but they are not without parallels. Indeed, the congregations represent the cutting edge of an ever-growing number of synagogues that are coming to understand the particular tastes, inclinations, and values of the new American Jew, the Jews of the baby boom generation. As such they also represent synagogues that are beginning to break the mold of the synagogue-center, which developed during the postwar era and still dominate the landscape of American synagogues. They are beginning to chart the course of the fourth stage of the American synagogue, the synagogue-community.

It remains to be seen how quickly and to what extent this new model will be replicated in other communities across America. The success of this transformation will depend on the extent to which rabbis and the laypeople who lead synagogues listen to the voices of the new American Jew. It is therefore helpful to revisit the eight generational themes introduced in Chapter Two through the voices of the individuals who shared their respective paths of return in the preceding pages. It is worth remembering that for every one of the voices in this book who were fortunate to find their spiritual home, there are hundreds if not thousands of Jews who have not been as fortunate. These latter Jews are the lost souls for whom Judaism will forever be forsaken unless more synagogues become attuned to their spiritual longings.

The Paths

The eight generational themes outlined in Chapter Two emerged from the scores of interviews and personal testimonies gathered for this book. Though articulated in various ways, the themes recurred so regularly that they virtually define the new American Jew. As we revisit the paths that those individuals traveled and listen carefully to their voices, we will better understand the spiritual needs and religious interests of an entire generation.

The Turnoff of the Synagogue-Center

Tova Frank characterized her childhood synagogue first as "suburban" and only afterward as Conservative because those were the values that she took away from the experience. She remembers the pride of her parents and their friends at the beauty of the Danish modern design of their synagogue even as she remembers the place as "airless and joyless." She described the services as "angry sermonic outbursts wrapped in three hours of unexplained drone or interminable cantorial trill." Her bat mitzvah was remembered more for the fashion in evidence than for any deep emotional or spiritual connection experienced.

Mark Sameth is no kinder to the glitzy, upper-middle-class Reform temple of his childhood in New Rochelle. Not only does he deride the materialism of the place, but he remembers his religious school education as a farce, learning about ceremonies that no one observed and Bible stories that no one believed. While Nancy Hoffman remembers with admiration the courage of her Reform rabbi, Levi Olan, speaking out against the war in Vietnam, she also recalls that the message was ignored and even resented by most members. She is far less kind in remembering the Dallas temple itself—"its endless corridors of cold, gray stone . . . devoid of any hint of old world Jewry, of Brooklyn, of Jerusalem . . . as bare as the Reform Judaism of the time."

Phil Schneider's family were members of a cathedral-like Conservative synagogue in the Bronx, replete with choir and organ loft. His memory of being used by the rabbi as a prop at his bar mitzvah, feigning a personal familiarity that never existed, only added to his sense of alienation from Judaism. His family never attended synagogue despite their membership, although they did mark the High Holydays by coming to the synagogue in their finest clothes and greeting their Jewish friends before and after services. They themselves never went inside.

A Sense of Exclusion

Carole Oshinsky's family also spent the High Holydays loitering on the street in front of her neighborhood's Orthodox synagogue. In her case, it was less a rejection of any synagogue experience that she had than a sense that she just did not belong. Her father's negative experience with *cheder* (early childhood religious training) and his professed atheism made attending a synagogue out of the question. The secular tenor of the household was occasionally disrupted by flirtations with Passover and Christmas. Attendance at the local Workmen's Circle Secular/Yiddish school would be the only sanctioned exposure to Jewish culture. Synagogues were definitely off-limits.

Elaine Weiner had an early passion for Judaism, and she could see the Orthodox synagogue from her bathroom window. She soaked up everything that she learned in that synagogue—the Hebrew, the prayers, the holidays, and the religious intensity of the old men. And she found a strong connection to God. It was only upon attaining puberty that she discovered the glass *mechitzah* (partition separating men from women) that would keep her not just from becoming a rabbi but also from becoming a fully participating Jew. She became ashamed of being a woman and disillusioned with Judaism. It would take her decades to give Judaism a second chance and to enter a synagogue.

Alan Feldman (Nate Grad) and Phil Schneider continue to struggle with whether a synagogue is a proper venue for intellectuals who are inherently skeptics about matters of faith and belief. That they have found spiritual homes—one Reform and one Orthodox—is a testament to their respective rabbis, who demanded no surrender of their lingering questions and doubts.

Nor do the stories recounted here exhaust the tales of exclusion felt by this generation. Single, divorced, intermarried, disabled, gay, and elderly

Jews all tell stories of trying to find a place for themselves in one or more synagogues only to end up feeling isolated and alone. The fact that the American synagogue continues to focus almost exclusively on the healthy two-parent, heterosexual family with children is ironic in an age when that family configuration exists in fewer than half of all American households. Even when synagogues sponsor occasional outreach programs for one or more of these populations, the culture of the institution continues to send implicit signals that such "non-mainstream" Jews don't really fit in.

Religion Versus Spirituality

The yearning for spirituality is clearly evident in this generation, though most often the experience of spirituality is discovered in places other than conventional religious institutions. Phil Schneider found in the natural settings of his grandmother's country home and at summer camp a dimension of spirituality that he never experienced in the synagogue of his childhood. Even after he found a synagogue that he loved, he looks out the window on a spring *shabbat* morning from his pew in the sanctuary, wondering whether he might not get a deeper sense of spiritual satisfaction from a walk by the river. And as he moved his own family and children toward an Orthodox Jewish lifestyle, he continued to struggle with the seeming gap between surface ritual behavior and a spirituality that resided deeper in the core of his being.

Nancy Hoffman grew up in the Bible Belt and longed for the intensity of fundamentalist and evangelical Christianity that she saw around her. Not only did she not find that depth of faith in her Reform temple, but her later brushes with "gastro-Jews," intellectual Jews, and socialist Jews in the large Jewish communities of the Northeast, albeit far more ethnically rich than her childhood experience of Judaism, were no more spiritually compelling.

Debbie Chapel grew up with a deep faith in God and a personalized form of spirituality without any rootedness in the Jewish community or in the Jewish religion. Her awakening to Judaism came from her college boyfriend (later to be her husband) who, though receiving a rich Jewish education, informed her that he didn't believe in God and that such atheism wasn't any problem for most Jews. As long as you identified culturally as a Jew, you would fit in just fine.

Not all of the Jews raised in the synagogue-centers of the 1950s, '60s, and '70s were looking for God. But those who were would have to go elsewhere.

Alternative Spiritual Paths

Aviva Hay's path of return brought her to synagogue life only after she outgrew the assimilationist tendencies of her upbringing in America. Her journey of Jewish rediscovery took her to the Europe that her parents fled and to Israel, the land of her early childhood. Her time in Jerusalem filled her with a sense of awe and transcendence, though she never once entered a synagogue. Nor did synagogues seem to offer what she was seeking when she returned to the States. Instead her spiritual journey took her to yoga ashrams and to meditation. As with so many seekers who try to find a Jewish connection for their search, Aryeh Kaplan's *Jewish Meditation* and *Jewish Meditation in the Bible* showed her that there was, indeed, a deeply spiritual path in Judaism.

Though Elaine Weiner discovered the twelve-step program of Alcoholics Anonymous as a professional social worker and not as a recovering alcoholic, she, like thousands of others, found in the program a deeply spiritual approach to life and to understanding God. Her spiritual hunger was in no way satisfied by active membership in a local Reform temple, and she became increasingly disenchanted. Weiner's path of return included stops along the way at Sufism, Buddhism, Hinduism, Christian Metaphysics, the *I Ching*, tai chi, and rebirthing. As she understands her own path, each excursion into a different spiritual system provided a piece of a puzzle that finally led her back to Judaism. That this occurred after Elaine had become a grandmother indicates that the search for alternative spiritual paths is not exclusively a boomer phenomenon.

Inclusivity

Part of what helped Philip Schneider find his place in the Orthodox community was his realization that it did not have to include the ethnic chauvinism that he found so offensive. At the Hebrew Institute of Riverside, he was further motivated by finding Jews at many different points on their spiritual journeys. They were drawn, like Schneider, by an environment that accepted them rather than judged them.

Part of the attraction of B'nai Jeshurun for Mark Sameth was finding an eclectic assemblage of people in synagogue week after week—the Holocaust survivor in his suit and tie, twenty-somethings in jeans and sneakers, and gay couples holding hands. This was definitely not a scene that he could have imagined in his upscale New Rochelle Reform temple. So it was for Debbie Chapel, who was struck by seeing families, singles, elderly, gay couples, and even an African American couple at Beth El. And

Nancy Hoffman's integration at Adat Shalom was made immeasurably easier by recognizing how many other seekers, from every imaginable walk of life and background, had come to call this Reconstructionist synagogue home.

Social Justice

Mark Sameth and Aviva Hay were among the hundreds of Jews drawn to the revived B'nai Jeshurun in Manhattan under Marshall Meyer because it was a place that both talked about social justice and acted on its commitments. Many members were first attracted to projects like its work on behalf of the homeless or its commitment to gay and lesbian rights and only later discovered the more "religious" side of the institution.

Civil rights activism and protest against the war in Vietnam were important commitments in Philip Schneider's life. He found in Avi Weiss a rabbi no less committed to take risks to act for justice in the world. Indeed, a host of individuals first came to be aware of the Hebrew Institute through the work that Weiss promoted through an independent organization that he continues to lead called the Coalition for Jewish Concerns (AMCHA), which often garners Weiss publicity in the Jewish and secular press. In fact, some HIR members have accompanied Weiss to demonstrations all over the world and point to that work as among the most fulfilling they have ever undertaken as a Jew.

It is no coincidence that at Adat Shalom, the social justice committee is by far the most popular project engaging members on their own time. My own work heading up the Jewish Community Council of Greater Washington, D.C., the umbrella public policy arm of the Jewish community, and then the Washington Institute for Jewish Leadership and Values, an educational foundation that integrates Jewish learning with social and political activism, drew many people to our congregation for whom social justice was the core of their Jewish identity. Several citywide initiatives on social justice issues have been started at Adat Shalom or by Adat Shalom members. The message in the community has always been that there is no authentic Jewish spirituality without reaching beyond the self and making a commitment to act on behalf of those who are in need of our help.

Belonging and Communal Support

Carole Oshinsky was drawn to Orthodoxy in large measure because she experienced there an intensity of community that is otherwise hard, if not impossible, to find in America. The very demands of a traditional Jewish lifestyle are such that it requires community, from the need of a *minyan* for daily prayer to the communal support that gets generated around life-cycle events to the pursuit of teachers and partners for regular learning of classical Jewish texts. As so often happens, one's personal belief system and personal practice often follow the attachment to a community of believers.

Debbie Chapel tired of the lifestyle that she, like so many of her generation, spent a lifetime trying to achieve—a life filled with choices and alternatives. When she realized that "it was not such a good thing for life to be like a box of chocolates," she was psychologically ready to join a congregation. She surprised herself that the rules of Jewish life did not now strike her as constraints, nor did the commitment to the institution feel like a trap. As she became more comfortable bringing aspects of Jewish observance into her home and participating in worship as part of the Beth El community, she felt the fulfillment that comes from attachment to something larger than herself.

For both Tova Frank and Nancy Hoffman, their respective congregations became critical supports for difficult and challenging spiritual and personal journeys. For Frank, battling her own alcoholism, B'nai Jeshurun offered not only the comfort of Judaism but also the support of a community, something that she did not find in her previous synagogue affiliations. For Hoffman, the journey into the unfamiliar territory of Jewish practice and observance could not have taken place without Adat Shalom. Similarly, the community was as integral to the celebration of her daughter's bat mitzvah as it was to her as her marriage began to fail.

Empowerment

One person after another spoke of the importance of being invited to be part of a contemporary struggle with a three-thousand-year-old tradition. The thoroughly secular and skeptical Nate Grad was seduced into affiliation at Beth El because he found, in his first encounter with Larry Kushner, that he could argue with the rabbi! During a baby-naming ceremony, congregants were invited to call out their own blessings for the new child. Whether in a class or a service, it was clear that the rabbi was not the only one who controlled the airwaves. In the process of poring over the meaning of Jewish texts with his rabbi, every new thought became a message, filling Nate's previously dark universe with light. And he came to understand that he himself, a religious skeptic, was part of the message. He speculates that his life was always about writing his own Torah, but Beth El gave him the language to call it "Torah."

Nancy Hoffman learned that finding relevance in an ancient heritage does not come easily. At Adat Shalom, members were given a significant role in redefining and reinterpreting Jewish beliefs and practices in light of contemporary values and mores. But that role came with an expectation that members would study and consider, in the most careful and deliberate fashion, a significant amount of traditional texts and related materials. New to rigorous Jewish study and observance, Hoffman found this mandate frightening and exhilarating at the same time. It did have the effect, however, of making her, along with many others, feel part of the shaping of the tradition that she would then be prepared to live by.

Joan Kaye's spiritual journey was inspired by a community of Jews who seemed to be at the same place in wrestling with the tradition as she was. She became part of a *havurah* at Beth El that was seeking to grow in Jewish observance. As Reform Jews, however, they wanted to make their own decisions about issues of belief and practice. Supporting one another, they studied, discussed, and then experimented with a wide range of Jewish experiences in the process of shaping their personal Jewish practice. These same people were encouraged to play leadership roles in the congregation. When there wasn't a service for Passover morning, presumably because not many members of the congregation were committed to attendance on a weekday, the rabbi offered someone the opportunity of creating the service, and it happened. The best example of what could be accomplished when laypeople are empowered by the rabbi to take ownership of their own Judaism was the prayer book that was created by members of Beth El, *Vetaher Libanu,* a project that Joan herself cochaired. Ironically, as the congregation grew and attracted more people who were new to Judaism, it became increasingly difficult for Joan to find a community of fellow travelers to move to more advanced levels of study, deliberation, and grappling with the tradition. That development made it harder for Joan to sustain the level of Jewish intensity that she had become accustomed to and that she wanted to maintain.

The Congregations

The generational themes that weave as common threads through the personal stories in this book are the same ones that characterize the congregations profiled, notwithstanding the fact that they represent four different movements in American Jewish life. It needs to be noted that the congregations are far from typical of their movements. Indeed, each of the synagogues represents a significant, if not daring, departure from the practices that characterize most other congregations in their respective movements. It is what puts them at the vanguard of the transition from the third-stage synagogue-center to the new paradigm synagogue-community. It is this latter model that holds so much promise to attract the group that I have called the new American Jew.

As a group, the four congregations attract an uncommonly high percentage of the people that Wade Clark Roof categorized as "dropouts." To a large extent, this drawing power is attributable to the fact that each congregation, in its own way, has rejected certain conventions of synagogues in which most of the baby boom generation has been raised. Some of these changes are cosmetic insofar as they are changes that immediately meet the eye of the casual observer: entering a synagogue and seeing the clergy positioned close to the worshipers as opposed to on a raised *bima;* experiencing a service where members are singing together in full voice, sometimes accompanied by instruments, clapping, or movement; seeing members of the congregation have an opportunity to stand on the *bima* and give a talk or make a comment as part of a Torah discussion. These are stylistic changes from the "high-church" practices of the synagogue-center to the "low-church" style of the synagogue-community. For boomers who sat through sermons from rabbis in robes and a series of operatic solos from cantors performing the liturgy, the low-church style is infinitely more inviting. It involves the worshiper, valuing each individual's participation in singing, speaking, and responding to elements of the service.

The conscious and deliberate attempt of the rabbis in each of the four congregations to speak about matters of God and spirituality has resulted in the ability of these congregations to attract a significant number Jews who have themselves explored alternative spiritual paths. We found many Jews in these congregations who once despaired of ever finding a mystical or transcendent experience of God within a Jewish context. Their joining of these particular congregations was often driven by an enthusiasm about the fact that a synagogue might offer them a place to continue their spiritual journey. The three liberal synagogues in our study seem to have significantly more Jews whose paths took them to alternative forms of religious and spiritual experience. Yet even Orthodox Rabbi Avi Weiss took a trip to the Siddha Yoga ashram in the Catskill Mountains to seek a better understanding of the attraction that its guru, Baba Muktananda, had for so many Jewish followers.

We have seen that many younger Jews cannot cross the bridge from spirituality, which they seek, to religion, which typifies the offerings of most American synagogues. It is a phenomenon that keeps many Jews away from synagogue affiliation. In many cases, the missing ingredient is the personalization of religious teaching and texts.

Judaism represents a historical religion with a mind-numbing body of rabbinic texts and teachings. In many cases, the tradition is taught in a way that gives Jews the sense that they are listening in, as outsiders, to a centuries-old conversation between learned rabbis. No authentic Judaism can be transmitted without significant exposure to these sources. At the same time, synagogues and rabbis who make conscious attempts to empower Jews to enter this historical conversation will be uniquely able to provide the bridge into Judaism that so many are looking for. This was the effect on members of Beth El writing their own religious services and, eventually, a series of prayer books. This was also the effect on members of Adat Shalom wrestling to write contemporary guidelines on the observance of *shabbat* or the way they should engage in the *mitzvah* of *tzedakah*. Essentially, these Jews were being invited to become insiders, participants in Judaism's historical conversation.

Members of the boomer generation desperately want to have a hand in shaping their religious life. They have been trained to think that they are too ignorant to do that with Judaism. Eastern religions, which put a much greater emphasis on personal experience, give almost immediate validation to the spiritual power of one's own journey. No prior knowledge necessary. That is rarely the experience in synagogues. But when Larry Kushner allows a member to talk about her relationship with her mother on the first anniversary of her mother's death in the context of a *d'var torah,* or when Fred Dobb of Adat Shalom invites a mother whose child died a few days after birth to share that experience in the context of a talk about the biblical story of Hannah on Rosh Hashanah, the moment carries power not only for the presenter of the story but also for all who hear it and realize that the sacred texts of the Jewish tradition can provide a valuable prism through which we can better understand our own lives.

Money, Status, and the Synagogue-Community

New American Jews, particularly those who have grown disenchanted with Jewish life, include at the top of their list of dislikes the "country club" aspects of most synagogues. Several things are meant by that broad-brushed indictment. First is the pervasive institutional stress on materialism, status, and wealth. Second is the suffocating homogeneity of so many suburban synagogue-centers. Third is the fact that most of these synagogues do little to reach out or to make welcome the increasingly diverse population of Jews in the community.

It is noteworthy that all four congregations lack many of the status markers typical of most synagogue-centers. A Jewish family looking for a synagogue in which to have the most elegant bar or bat mitzvah affair would not likely choose to join any of the four. Each of the congregations has facilities that, although adequate, are modest. It is not a coincidence that common to all four congregations are deliberate policies that prevent prominent naming plaques on the major rooms and articles in the synagogue. Quite independently, each congregation came to recognize that the overt honoring of people of wealth for their generosity to the congregation was anathema to the spirit of the community that they were trying to create. The leaders acknowledge that such a policy has probably limited the amount of money the synagogue could have raised. It certainly kept away many Jews of wealth who might relish just such an honor. At Adat Shalom, the two most coveted honors conveyed each year are for voluntarism and service to the community and for completing our Ben/Bat Torah program of Jewish study and growth. At Beth El, the most elitist designation is that of *gabbai,* which goes to a handful of members because of their knowledge and ritual literacy. They in turn bear significant responsibilities for the weekly Torah service.

One phrase that we heard over and over again in our interviews was some form of "the beautiful people don't join here." Several things were meant by this comment. One was that people were generally aware of which synagogues the "beautiful people" did join, and they were in no way envious. In fact, those synagogues represented the Judaism that they were determined to avoid. Another differentiation was the pronounced informality of dress in the synagogue-community. Some people may come in suits, dresses, jackets, and ties, but no one would feel out of place in casual attire. One conclusion to be drawn is that appearance and status counts less in the synagogue-community than in the synagogue-center. One member of Beth El couldn't answer a question about the demographic makeup of the congregation and remarked, "Despite how close I feel to many of the members here, I realize that I don't even know what most of them do for a living!"

Both Beth El and B'nai Jeshurun have sliding-scale dues structures, meaning that dues are relatively inexpensive for lower-income households and fairly steep for higher earners. The Hebrew Institute of Riverdale and Adat Shalom have extremely liberal dues-forgiveness policies; people pay what they can afford, with no questions asked and no income verification required. All of this sends a strong message that the synagogue is not an upper-middle-class entitlement out of the reach of those at a lower socioeconomic level.

All four of our congregations make pronounced efforts to include a wider cross section of the Jewish community than the two-parent, heterosexual family unit with children. The HIR has made outreach one of its primary missions. On any *shabbat,* one can find there elderly Jews, new immigrant Jews, Jews with physical and mental disabilities, single Jews, and poor Jews. The fact that singles represent more than half of B'nai Jeshurun's membership is partly a function of its urban location, but it remains remarkable even compared to other big-city congregations. One of the points of contention between BJ and the Conservative movement is the former's insistence on allowing homosexual couples to have joint *aliyot* to the Torah and the rabbis' willingness to perform commitment ceremonies sanctifying such unions in a Jewish context. As a result, BJ boasts a significant percentage of gay members who rarely find comfortable homes in other congregations where their sexual identities are given no sanction. Thus as the Jewish community profile becomes increasingly diverse in terms of lifestyles beyond the nuclear family, the eclectic composition of the synagogue-community signals a welcome that is hard to find in many synagogue-centers.

Social Justice and the Synagogue-Community

High on the list of what draws so many disaffected Jews to the congregations that we have profiled is their respective commitment to social justice and activism. In surveys of American Jews through the 1970s and 1980s, "commitment to social justice" and "support for the state of Israel" were the two statements that garnered the highest percentage of popular approval. A decade later, support for Israel started to lag significantly, but commitment to social justice remained just as strong as ever. Jews have pursued their passion for causes, from civil liberties to human rights to working with the poor and underprivileged, through a variety of secular agencies. Whereas most synagogues have some committee that sponsors one or more social action projects each year, large numbers of Jews pursue some form of social or political activism outside of the rubric of the organized Jewish community.

Marshall Meyer's rebuilding of Congregation B'nai Jeshurun placed social action at the very center of the Judaism that was preached and acted out through such activities as forums on the Israeli-Palestinian conflict, lunch programs for the homeless, a shelter, monthly brunches for AIDS patients, and the adoption of a public school in a low-income neighborhood where members tutor and provide technical support. Jews came to BJ to live out their understanding of Judaism's prophetic mission. Similarly, Jews came to Adat Shalom after meeting members on projects like Sukkot in April, which is a Jewish version of Habitat for Humanity, volunteering monthly at a women's homeless shelter, or sorting foodstuffs monthly at an area food bank. Avi Weiss attracted loyal followers when he demonstrated for Soviet Jews and against bigots like David Duke and Louis Farrakhan, protested the erection of crosses at Auschwitz, and threw himself into many other such political actions. But he inspired just as many Jews to greater involvement in Judaism from less publicized activities, including regular visits to elderly shut-ins, programs for the mentally handicapped, clothing drives for the homeless, and fighting to prevent the building of a local incinerator. Beth El's community was galvanized by the adoption of a family of Vietnamese "boat people."

All of these activities represented a living out of values that most American Jews hold dear. New American Jews, especially, can be very harsh in pointing out the hypocrisy of institutions that profess high ideals but fail to act on them. They are no less rigorous in evaluating people. So often the most powerful sermon comes in the imitation of the small act. When Marshall Meyer insisted that the custodian at BJ be given a raise so as to ensure him a livable wage, the act was done in the privacy of a small meeting room, but the message was heard loudly through the entire community. Similarly, when the Hebrew Institute sacrificed precious (and income-producing) seating to build a ramp for the disabled to ascend the *bima,* the living out of principle was taken to a higher level.

"Hello. I Love You. Please Tell Me Your Name"

Above all, the synagogue-community is about providing people with a sense of acceptance, love, warmth, and belonging. Each of the congregations finds ways to do so in large and small settings. At B'nai Jeshurun, ushers are specially trained to provide a friendly welcome along with each prayer book. Beth El has congregants introduce themselves to each other during the service. Adat Shalom invites newcomers to stand and introduce themselves before the close of the *shabbat* morning service, which breaks the ice for conversation at the luncheon following the service. The fact that members wear name badges also helps reduce anonymity as the congregation grows larger. A visitor to the Hebrew Institute is unlikely to leave a *shabbat* morning service without an invitation to lunch at the home of a member or a hug from Rabbi Weiss as he wanders around the *shul.*

Most synagogues have committees that support members through times when they might lose a loved one. But this is hardly the only time that people need support. Harold Schulweis, rabbi of Conservative congregation Valley Beth Shalom in Encino, California, has pioneered two programs that deserve wide replication in synagogue-communities. He institutionalized a program of synagogue-based *havurot* so that member households living in a certain area and with similar interests and family status might come together on a regular basis for the celebration of a holiday, for study, or for socializing. The ten or so families thus become a support group within a large congregation in which one might otherwise feel lost. They are also likely to be the ones who will provide mutual support in times of need.

The other program Schulweis pioneered is a para-rabbinic program in which members of the synagogue are trained by mental health professionals to provide counsel and support to other members who find themselves in need of help at a time of crisis. The program was devised in part because in a congregation of more than one thousand families, it became impossible for the two rabbis to meet the demand for counseling and support. But just as important, the program created strong bonds between members of the congregation who might otherwise have never met. Given our increasingly technological and mobile society, congregations must be catalysts for just these kinds of connections.

Each of the four congregations has implemented aspects of these two programs in various forms. The Hebrew Institute has *havurot* of five to seven couples that meet regularly in homes studying rabbinic text materials provided by the rabbis. B'nai Jeshurun has its *havurot* organized around Saturday evening gatherings in homes for twelve to fifteen people for *havdalah* and study. This is in addition to occasional larger gatherings, called *Shabbat B'yachad,* at which over one hundred people gather for a potluck *shabbat* dinner. Beth El has approximately a dozen *havurot* meeting on their own in addition to a men's spirituality group and a meditation group that meets weekly. Adat Shalom has interest-based groups that meet regularly, including an interfaith couples group, a women's spirituality group, a Jewish book club, and the Ben/Bat Torah group. Furthermore, once a month on a Friday night, there might be as many as seven homes sponsoring *shabbat* potluck dinners with attendant ritual for members.

The message of caring transmitted by a synagogue-community starts from a person's first contact with the institution. At Adat Shalom, membership recruitment and integration were taken very seriously. Regular "meet the rabbi" sessions would take place after *shabbat* morning services. Prospective members would have already experienced the service and the phenomenon of more than two hundred people eating a lunch catered by a dozen families on a rotating basis. I would start the session, which might have ten to twenty prospective members, by telling a little about myself and what motivated the founders of Adat Shalom. I would then invite people to share their Jewish story, asking, "What was the nature of your experience, both positive and negative, with Judaism and with the Jewish community when you were growing up?" An existing member would always be the first respondent so as to model the sharing format. It was a modest form of spiritual autobiography, lasting a mere three to five minutes, yet it was powerful. Before one word was spoken about the synagogue's program, a mood had been created in which people could share intimate details of their lives with others. In not a few cases, acquaintances made at that "meet the rabbi" session became lasting friendships. It modeled the kind of deep, spiritual conversation that people so rarely have a chance to engage in. And the principle of spiritual connection continued after a person joined, as every new member was paired up with a veteran member who would host them for dinner and accompany the newcomer to programs and services.

Of course, each of the congregations maintains extensive adult education offerings, which reinforce this attempt to get members to connect. Various committees and subgroups carry out para-rabbinic functions, providing member-to-member support in times of illness, death, or other life crisis. What is unique about the organizational principle that characterizes all four congregations is the recognition that the cohesiveness of the congregation is only as strong as the relationships between the members. Community doesn't come from sponsoring marquee events attended by hundreds of people. It comes from members spending time in one another's homes, getting to know each other personally, and forging bonds of friendship. It gives people a sense of belonging and of being in a caring network of relationships.

The Future

Chapter Three introduced the four distinctive characteristics of the synagogue-community: organizational culture, spiritual leadership, articulation of mission, and framing of serious Judaism. Let us now revisit those characteristics in light of the profiled synagogues, both to see how those characteristics manifested themselves in real communities and to see more clearly how the synagogue-community model can be replicated.

Organizational Culture

Organizational culture refers to the atmosphere, feel, and mode of human interactions in any particular setting. You know it better by example than by definition. You sense a difference between the environment in a bank and that in a tennis shop. You expect your children to behave differently at school than they might at the swim club. The organizational culture at a start-up software company in the Silicon Valley is very different from the one at, say, General Motors or the Bank of America.

Similarly, there is a dramatic difference between the organizational culture in a synagogue-community and that in a synagogue-center. This difference goes well beyond the style of worship, although all four featured synagogues adopted a conscious and deliberate plan to create a "low-church" style of worship, with much singing and lay participation and a minimum of performance by professional clergy. All four congregations provide ways for members to participate in a Torah discussion, offer a short talk, lead some part of the *davening*, or speak during celebrations of life-cycle events. Congregants at these synagogues are not passive, solemn observers but actively engaged participants in the service in a variety of ways. The effect is a sense that worship is inclusive and spontaneous.

There are other measures of a unique organizational culture as well. Because each of the synagogues puts a strong emphasis on connecting people, one to the other, a guest at a service is in no danger of being ignored. I have visited dozens of synagogues in my life, and it continues to amaze me that after two to three hours at a service and attending an *oneg* (refreshments) for another twenty minutes, I could still leave the building without a single person having said hello or reaching out to me in any way. Not so in a synagogue-community. A couple of our profiled congregations have official greeters, but the culture in each of the four places is such that no guest will go unnoticed or ungreeted for long.

The spirit of egalitarianism is also central to the organizational culture. In most synagogue contexts, egalitarianism refers to the inclusion of women in ritual roles. This is certainly the case with our profiled synagogues, including the Hebrew Institute's pioneering efforts in the Orthodox world. But egalitarianism goes beyond mere inclusivity. It signifies that ownership of the community is broadly shared by all the members. This manifests itself in several ways. First, even peripheral members of the community seem to have an intense loyalty to the synagogue. I have marveled at hearing that members of Adat Shalom who are not particularly active will talk to their friends about nothing but the synagogue at outside social functions. I found a similar phenomenon at other synagogue-communities when I deliberately sought out people whose involvement had diminished over time for a variety of reasons. Second is in the area governance. The old Jewish adage that "everybody has an opinion" may never have been more true. Significantly, well-run synagogue-communities find ways to channel dissatisfaction and dissent into the deliberations of their governing structures. This has the effect of limiting negative under-currents, which can do enormous harm to communities, even as it presents a mighty challenge to leaders of the synagogue who can never be sanguine that a consensus of the board of trustees is sufficient to set policy. Third, the egalitarian spirit of synagogue-communities will often provide new and uninitiated members with significant responsibility. The message is clear: "Don't join us if you want things done for you. Be prepared to roll up your sleeves and make a contribution of your time and talent."

A word about size. We live in a society in which bigger has always been perceived as better. The development of the synagogue-center was very much influenced by this ethic. If the suburban synagogue was going to be a status marker and provide the array of services that Jews demanded, economics drove these synagogues to become as big as possible. Professional staff grew to include executive directors, maintenance crews, secretaries, and bookkeepers. As membership grew, a second and sometimes even a third rabbi was hired, along with youth directors, educational directors, cantors, choir directors, and other employees. In such an institution, it is sometimes hard to feel a sense of warmth and intimacy, two qualities that new American Jews value. Personal contact with the rabbi is infrequent, if it takes place at all. One revolution in the emergence of the synagogue-community and the organizational culture that it tries to manifest is that big is not necessarily better. Almost every quality that we have spoken of is done more easily in a smaller synagogue than in a large one. And yet the explosive growth of B'nai Jeshurun to over one thousand households in just a few short years challenges the assumption that synagogue-communities cannot function and maintain the same organizational culture beyond a certain size. Both rabbis and long-term congregants at BJ will admit, however, that size does challenge many of the modes of operation that the community cherishes.

The organizational culture of the synagogue-community also extends to a certain casualness of style. Some of this is about dress. At a *shabbat* service, it is not unusual to see men without ties and jackets or women in pants (though the latter will not happen at HIR due to religious restrictions). Many congregants are comfortable calling their rabbis by their first names. The lack of formality in the service also lends itself to many moments of laughter and unscripted comments from the attendees. Sometimes it is a response to a statement made by the rabbi. Sometimes it is a response to a special moment on the *bima*. Finally, there is a strong sense in each of the institutions that people are happy to be there. People are smiling and joyful. They seem fulfilled. And that feeling is contagious.

Spiritual Leadership

Can it be that what makes a handful of congregations stand out is just a matter of a skilled, powerful, or charismatic rabbi? The answer is more complex than it might appear.

On the one hand, it is undeniable that all four profiled synagogues were led by extraordinary rabbis. Many of the personal stories and interviews spoke of being drawn back to Judaism at least in part by the teaching and role model of the rabbi. On the other hand, there are numerous rabbis in America who equal the profiled rabbis in speaking ability, charisma, skill, and intellect. In fact, I conducted interviews in several other synagogues with just such rabbis, and I concluded that despite their impressive accomplishments, their institutions did not fully represent the synagogue-community paradigm. What was the difference?

Unique to our set of four synagogues was the fact that in each case, the rabbi was present at the congregation's founding in one way or another. This was not a criterion in choosing the synagogues originally, but it turned out to be essential to the rabbi's achieving what he set out to do. Marshall Meyer came to a synagogue that had all but died, with only a handful of elderly members remaining. Larry Kushner was Beth El's first full-time rabbi, as was Avi Weiss after the Hebrew Institute relocated to Riverdale. I founded Adat Shalom with a handful of close friends.

What this meant in each case was that the rabbi played a much more central role in shaping not only the worship service but also the organizational culture. As noted, that culture was distinctly different from the organizational culture of most other synagogues. When the rabbi is permitted to pursue a particular vision as the spiritual leader of a community, it can powerfully motivate and inspire synagogue members. The people who seek out such congregations will be drawn to the community because that vision pervades the organizational culture and every facet of congregational life. People drawn to such a community become not only loyal followers of the rabbi and his or her vision but advocates and missionaries for that vision as well.

Perhaps the most vital role played by the rabbis is in recruiting lay leaders and inviting members to share their particular gifts with the community. Rabbis are seen as the guardians of the Jewish tradition; they are in a unique position to empower their congregants to become active shapers of that tradition instead of passive recipients of it. I know that I gave a lot of thought to who should serve on the board, who might offer some teaching or music in a service, and who might chair a new initiative that I wanted to launch. I was acutely conscious of reaching out to relatively

new members on the periphery of the congregation and bringing them
into positions of leadership. Beth El accomplishes much the same objective by having term limits for board members. In this way, a closed community maximizes the feeling of ownership among a large percentage of
its membership.

In most communities, leadership is inbred to an unhealthy extent. Even
well-intentioned nominating committees are acquainted with a limited
circle of people; as a result a small percentage of members tend to cycle
through leadership positions again and again. The majority of members
resign themselves to the existence and leadership of this small coterie of
machers (important people). Nor are there many opportunities for members to share their talents or gifts in a public forum, since services tend to
be led exclusively by the clergy. It is a recipe for peripheral membership
that will invariably have a short life span.

Unfortunately, the corporate organizational structure of most synagogues is inhospitable, if not antagonistic, to the kind of singular rabbinical leadership that characterizes our four featured synagogues.
Boards hire rabbis, who are given a job description that rarely goes beyond the conventional areas of clerical functioning. The rabbi may have
some success in changing the tone of religious services and will have relative freedom to speak and teach as they wish, but changing the organizational culture is next to impossible. Larry Kushner observed that if he
were to become the rabbi of an established Reform congregation, even
with his clarity about what he wants a congregation to be and his unparalleled ability to articulate that message, he would need a good five to
seven years to change its organizational culture. Part of that culture is allowing the rabbi to function as a spiritual leader with considerable pre-
rogative to determine how the community functions. Most rabbis go to
congregations with a lot less skill and experience than a Larry Kushner.
To say that they face a formidable challenge to change the way a congregation understands itself and functions is a vast understatement. Most
consider themselves lucky to get a good performance rating and have
their contracts renewed.

Obviously, it is impossible to raze all the synagogues in America and
re-create them from the ground up, although there is evidence that it is
much easier to create a synagogue-community from scratch than to transform a synagogue-center into a synagogue-community. It is important,
however, to recast the roles and responsibilities of rabbi and board in
American synagogues in order to move away from a corporate structure
and more toward a spiritualized model of religious fellowship. This
speaks to the need to raise the issue of spiritual leadership at a level be-

yond the congregation, although eventually the congregation has to transform itself as well.

Most rabbis are not hired to be spiritual leaders, even though that is often the nomenclature that attaches itself to their office. They are hired instead to be religious functionaries, orchestrating religious services, performing life-cyle events, and teaching the tradition. A generation that is starving for spiritual direction will not be drawn to religious functionaries. And while many younger rabbis are inclined themselves to move in the direction of becoming spiritual mentors to Jews searching for meaning, there is a serious question as to whether the congregations that hire them understand and support such a change in the way that a rabbi might interact with the community. To move in this direction, the seminaries that train rabbis will have to cultivate these skills in the next generation of rabbis. In turn, the umbrella synagogue bodies of each denomination will need to work to transform the governance structure of their member synagogues to enable rabbis to emerge as true spiritual leaders. This represents a formidable undertaking.

Moving toward a spiritual leadership model calls for more than a change in the way synagogue boards function. It requires a different mind-set on the part of the rabbi as well. One of the ways that rabbinical schools and associations have responded to the corporate structure of the synagogue-center is to give more attention to training rabbis how to function in such an environment. It has had the effect of making the rabbinate much more of a profession. Rabbis are now instructed how to set limits on the time they are available to congregants. Days off are sacrosanct. Rabbis hire lawyers to negotiate their contracts with the other lawyers on the board. Congregants get the sense that the rabbi spends more time thinking about the perquisites of the office than about his or her "calling." Rabbis may, as a result, be a tad wealthier than the generation of rabbis that preceded them, but they are not happier. I know of rabbis who spent five or six years in rabbinical school and were never once pushed to think about their rabbinate as a spiritual vocation. It is a disaster.

Can synagogues burn out their rabbis? Sure. Can congregants be insensitive to a rabbi's need for time alone or with family? Sure. But a true spiritual leader never runs an hourly clock on the time spent helping an individual with a problem, leading a crusade for social justice, or teaching Torah. Rabbis who understand what it means to be a true leader of communities and of people are also prepared to shoulder the responsibilities that come with that role. They will, in turn, be rewarded with congregants who are devotees and not employers. I believe that there are communities hungry for spiritual leaders and rabbis who would give anything to serve in such a capacity. The tragedy is that the institutional design of the synagogue-center does not allow such a relationship to emerge. The synagogue-community has the potential to be different, and the evidence of our four congregations proves it.

It is instructive to compare the prerogatives enjoyed by the rabbis in our profiled congregations with the more typical relationship of rabbis to their lay leadership. Avi Weiss's invitation to women's prayer at the HIR as well as his outreach to non-Orthodox Jews would have created major institutional discord at most Orthodox synagogues. No such controversy occurred at the HIR. Similarly, Marshall Meyer's singular role in hiring Roly Matalon as his associate would be unheard of in most congregations.

Compare these leadership models to the one profiled in Paul Wilkes's book *And They Shall Be My People: An American Rabbi and His Congregation*.[1] This portrait of Rabbi Jay Rosenbaum, rabbi of Congregation Beth Israel in Worcester, Massachusetts, observed by the author over the course of a year, would be considered sorrowful if it were not so typical of the experience in most American synagogues. Rabbi Rosenbaum, a rabbi of significant intelligence, commitment, and caring, was continually frustrated in his attempt to get his congregants to take Judaism more seriously. With his board leadership continually raising the specter of an institutional financial crisis, Rabbi Rosenbaum was reduced to a defensive posture as he sought to retain his job. Ultimately, he agreed to take on more responsibility for no increase in pay. The power relationships that got played out in this exchange were such that it was almost impossible for the rabbi to exert any level of spiritual leadership. Unfortunately, it is a pattern that is fairly typical in the American synagogue, and American Jewry is considerably weaker for it.

Spiritual leadership is only partly about the leader. It is more about the context. I have seen people of modest ability invested with trust, love, and loyalty, and I have seen their leadership ability blossom. One would be making a terrible mistake to dismiss our four congregations as being "just about exceptional rabbis." Notwithstanding the powerful and dynamic presence of Marshall Meyer at B'nai Jeshurun and the devastation to the community upon his sudden death, the organizational culture that he created helped his successor, Roly Matalon, emerge as a remarkable spiritual leader. The fact that the personalities of the two were as different as night and day suggests that the spiritual leadership of the synagogue-community is not just about personality. I have seen a similar transition in the three years since I stepped down as the rabbi of Adat Shalom. In fact, part of what motivated my decision to step down was my recognition of how deeply ingrained many of the principles and modes of operation were within the community. When I heard the voices of so many members insist on inclusivity, spirituality, social justice, and creating a sense of belonging in every facet of congregational life, I knew that the organizational culture that I promoted had taken deep root and that whoever succeeded me would be given the mantle of spiritual leadership because the model required it.

Articulation of Mission

Corporate America has long practiced the art of the mission statement as a way for top management to achieve some clarity about why the business exists, what need it fills, and how the products or activities of the business are consonant with the "why" and the "what." Religious functionaries fall into the trap of thinking that all adherents of their religion are as clear about the mission or purpose of their religious heritage as they might be. Tremendous amounts of time and attention are devoted to conveying the "how to" of the religion: "What do we believe?" "How do we practice?" "What prayers get said when?" "What are our holidays and how do we celebrate them?" The problem with this approach is that fewer and fewer boomers start off with a deep commitment to their birth religion. Surveys tell us that they are more than willing to shop around and to explore alternative religious and spiritual groups. In such an environment, religious leaders must directly address the "why" of their religious tradition or accept increasing numbers of dropouts from the tradition.

In the Jewish community, this trend is abundantly clear. In the 1990 National Jewish Population Survey, 35 percent of born Jews no longer identified with Judaism.[2] They either identified as Jews in totally secular ways (16 percent) or were currently adherents of some other religion (19 percent). Of the remaining 65 percent, a large number would be hard pressed to answer the question "Why be Jewish?" The fact that only 40 to 50 percent of the Jewish population is affiliated with a synagogue at any one time, and much of that affiliation is tepid at best, speaks volumes about the importance of making the case of why Jews should remain a people apart in a country with little antisemitism and where the host culture has been so welcoming.

Most synagogues function as if the answer to the question "Why be Jewish?" is implicit in a person's decision to join. "I was raised as a Jew and my parents belonged to a synagogue; therefore, I will follow in their footsteps as I raise my children." However, fewer and fewer Jews are prepared to make that simple statement and act accordingly.

Few synagogues spend much time trying to articulate their mission. Yet all four of the featured synagogues did so in one way or another. B'nai

Jeshurun's rabbis issued three different documents that set forth core principles for the congregation. Avi Weiss made the mission statement for the
Hebrew Institute simple—"Torah, Outreach, Activism, Israel"—and the
four principles are prominently displayed on all congregational materials
including the letterhead. His extensive writing on each of these issues in
books and columns and his articulation of the principles of "open Orthodoxy" provided a clarity of mission that is rare in most congregations.
The same can be said about Larry Kushner and Beth El. Few rabbis in
America have been as deliberate about creating an alternative form of
congregation and setting down those principles in writing. His core principles were empowerment (never do for the congregation what members
can do for themselves) and focusing all congregational activities on "primary Jewish acts"—holy study, communal prayer, and good deeds.

Adat Shalom's statement of principles was central to its self-perception
and in turn helped the community explain to a public that often had not
heard of Reconstructionism just what we were about. The work on the
statement was the first communal undertaking upon the formation of the
group. It evolved, however, much more from the bottom up than was the
case in the other congregations. I had experimented with a statement of
principles in my first congregation, with very positive results. Although it
is true that I presented the model to the founding members of Adat
Shalom, it was for them to write. On some levels, the task was made easier in that Reconstructionism is the most distinctive ideology of the four
movements in American Jewish life, with extensive development of its key
points in books by Mordecai Kaplan and his followers. At the same time,
the founding members who drafted the initial statement and those who
followed a few years later with an updated version truly made the statement their own. The commitment to democracy in the community led to
the second statement of principles being revised several times before being ratified by congregational vote. In addition, the sections on *shabbat,
tzedakah,* Israel and the Jewish people, and *gemilut chasadim* were
modified using the guidelines developed through our program of retreats
and communal decision making on those issues. It led to a much higher
level of ownership by the congregation and continues to be used to measure ongoing programs and community direction.

Framing of Serious Judaism

The fourth characteristic of our model congregations has to do with the
promotion of serious Judaism. When one compares the program of the
four congregations to most other synagogues in America, one sees an em-

phasis on prayer, study, and acts of lovingkindness. No sisterhoods. No men's clubs. No theme nights to swell attendance at a service.

One walks away from our four model congregations impressed with the percentage of members attending services, engaging in study, and participating in social action projects. A dizzying array of programs are being spearheaded by members and not by professionals. People are wrestling with big questions: "What does this text say to me about my life?" "Should I incorporate higher levels of Jewish observance into my home?" "Does being Jewish make me a better person?" "How far beyond the boundaries of the Jewish community does my obligation for compassion and action extend?"

The do-it-yourself spirit of *The Jewish Catalog* generation is reinforced by rabbis and communities that say in a thousand different ways, "You cannot live your Jewish lives vicariously through the synagogue or through the rabbi. We are here to teach you, inspire you, and to facilitate your Jewish growth." The result is scores of formerly marginal Jews having *shabbat* dinners, learning Hebrew, studying classical texts, and engaging in meaningful social action projects with fellow members.

This is one of the most promising and least understood phenomena of the new American Jew. What motivated membership in the synagogues in the 1950s and beyond was the desire to mark the entrance of Jews into middle-class suburban America. Synagogue-centers provided just such status markers to that generation of American Jews and, by many measures, thrived. The desire to "fit in" on the new suburban frontier resulted in Jews' supporting their synagogues just as their Christian neighbors supported their churches. But in personal behavior, Jews avoided, as much as possible, practices that would set them apart. Norman Podhoretz's 1967 book *Making It* well described the aspirations of the generation; they were not spiritual aspirations.

New American Jews are far more confident and comfortable in the American setting than their parents were. It is a generation that has "made it" in every sense of the word. Their aspirations are very much spiritual. And they have no qualms about being different provided that it offers them some form of personal fulfillment. It is what explains the explosive growth of day school attendance in the liberal Jewish community. In the Orthodox community, parochial schooling has long been standard, but a generation ago it would have been rare for a non-Orthodox family to send its children to a Jewish day school; it was tantamount to turning one's back on the blessings of America and its embrace of its Jewish population. Today, community-based Jewish day schools are springing up around the country, and most have waiting lists.

Another indicator of the willingness of this generation to "differentiate" and to pursue once ignored Jewish practice is what I call the *sukkah* quotient. During the fall harvest festival of Sukkot, the festival of booths, Jewish tradition calls for Jews to build and dwell in temporary huts at their homes. A generation ago, each synagogue would build a communal *sukkah,* and the members would fulfill this *mitzvah* when (and if) they frequented the synagogue by taking a meal in the *sukkah* or saying a blessing in it. It would be rare for a family to build its own *sukkah.* Today it is not uncommon for a synagogue to have dozens of member families build *sukkot* in their backyards, on their porches, or on their decks. There is hardly a more striking metaphor for the willingness of new American Jews to stand apart from their Gentile neighbors than the presence of a ramshackle hut in their backyard for one week every fall in celebration of a Jewish holiday.

The point is that this generation is extremely open to the kind of serious Judaism that we saw being promoted at our four model synagogues. The same people who dropped out of synagogues because of the perceived superficiality, pretense, and obsession with materialism are willing to come back to synagogues that offer an authentic encounter with a heritage rich with custom and filled with wisdom. Congregational leadership must recognize that this is a generation that is embarrassed by its Judaic ignorance and Hebraic illiteracy. Most will blame the synagogues of their childhood, however fair or unfair that accusation may be. They will enter the portals of synagogues only if they do not feel judged, are not made to feel ashamed, and are given the tools to achieve the competency that they long for.

Key to the success of synagogues that want to capture this generation of seekers is that they be welcoming of the most uninitiated. But this is not the same thing as catering to the lowest common denominator. A generation that expects excellence from their children's schools, from the businesses they frequent, and from the arts and cultural performances that they attend have little patience for synagogues that strike them as mediocre. It is also true that there is a difference between the way liberal congregations and Orthodox congregations understand and practice the primary Jewish acts of study, prayer, and good deeds. Still, as savvy consumers, new American Jews will have high expectations of synagogue programming and will rise to the challenge if the programming demands of them serious engagement with the Jewish tradition.

18

THE CHALLENGE OF
TRANSFORMATION

EXAMINING THE HANDFUL OF CONGREGATIONS on the cutting edge
of a new paradigm of synagogue life reveals the challenges of replicating
these institutions and the success that they have had. These synagogues
are hardly typical of the American Jewish community. The paths of return
traced in these pages could just as easily have led to places outside the
orbit of Jewish life had the seekers not found welcoming synagogue-
communities. They were Jewish dropouts who became returnees only because their particular paths of return happened to intersect with
congregations that recognized the legitimacy of their search and had an
organizational culture and program that spoke directly to their needs as
new American Jews. A great many others on the same journey encounter
nonreceptive congregations and rabbis. Most of these seekers remain outside the tent of organized Jewish life.

Synagogue Affiliation, American-Style

Synagogue affiliation in America today is very different from what I have
portrayed in Chapters Four through Fifteen. Typically, a family will join
a synagogue at the time that the oldest child is between the second and
fourth grade so that the kids can be enrolled in the Hebrew school and be
placed on track for a bar or bat mitzvah at age thirteen. Because the parents' memories of Hebrew school and synagogue are generally negative,
they have few expectations that the experience will be much different for
their children. Unless the synagogue requires parent participation in programs or religious services as a condition of the child's successful completion of the requirements for bar or bat mitzvah, the parents will likely

keep their involvement with the synagogue to a minimum, much like their parents before them.

With the exception of the High Holydays and when invited to a bar or bat mitzvah, most families are strangers to the inside of the sanctuary. When they do attend, their own lack of familiarity with the service adds to their sense of alienation. Jews who are well educated and professionally successful come to feel uneasy when they are put into a setting that makes them feel incompetent. That is precisely the experience of most Jews on their occasional visits to services. If they once learned to read Hebrew, it is frustrating to try to follow prayers that they haven't seen for years. The translations of the prayers leave them cold. The few melodies that they may remember from childhood have been changed. If someone is thinking, "I should give this Jewish thing another chance," a casual encounter with most synagogues will leave them alienated. The welcoming entry points for lapsed Jews are simply not there.

It is therefore little surprise that within a year or two of the youngest child's bar or bat mitzvah, the family allows their membership in the synagogue to lapse. Rabbis may bemoan the phenomenon, but from the perspective of the family, it is a logical step. Synagogue membership is expensive. It was worth paying for while they were receiving a desired service in exchange—preparation for bar or bat mitzvah. Once the synagogue renders the service and the event passes, there is no longer any sense of obligation to the institution. During the five to ten years of membership, most adult Jews do not receive any personal sense of meaning from their synagogue affiliation. To the extent that they would like to attend on the High Holydays, most synagogues will sell them seats for those few days at a much lower cost than annual dues.

As much as lay and clerical leaders may bemoan this state of affairs, most are clueless about how to change it. Part of this reflects a failure to recognize the changing needs of a generation. Part of it is a failure to identify and emulate successful synagogue models. The largest part is being unwilling to tackle the organizational culture of their synagogues and engage in some institutional transformation.

Outreach

While many in the Jewish community talk about the need to engage in "outreach" so as to attract the growing percentage of Jews who are unaffiliated, the reality is that what passes for outreach in most synagogues is really just a form of marketing an existing program. Most synagogues are made up of two groups: families who are in it for the short term, as just described, and the loyalists. The loyalists make up the leadership of the congregation because they are in it for the long haul. They are Jews whose experience of synagogue growing up was mostly positive. Roof identifies them as the sector of the boomer generation that was least influenced by many of the values of the generation (gender revolution, political protests, spiritual explorations, and so on).[1] It is therefore no surprise that the leadership of the congregation loves the synagogue's program. They feel connected to the other loyalists in the congregation, whom they see on a regular basis. The rabbi is hired by this group, and he or she is in turn is eager to please the loyalists who attend services, take adult education classes, and serve on the board.

If the leadership of synagogues were to really engage in a serious examination of who the unaffiliated are and what they want, it would suggest changes in practice and style that would be threatening to the status quo. Some number of members in any congregation would probably welcome an infusion of Jews with attitudes and expectations different from their own. But few synagogues will risk alienating their existing, loyalist constituency in exchange for the long-shot chance of attracting some number of dropouts who, if they joined, probably couldn't even articulate what they wanted and what changes would be required to allow the synagogue to meet their needs.

It would be foolish and wrong to cast synagogue loyalists and rabbis as the villains in the crisis that currently challenges the American synagogue. A little perspective is helpful to avoid this trap. Religions are highly resistant to change. Religions pass down ideas, traditions, rituals, sacred ceremonies, and texts from one generation to the next. The attraction of most religions for their adherents is that they represent ties to a cherished past. The followers of a given religion or denomination form a community of memory that connects people to a transcendent history. Peter Berger, in his classic work *The Sacred Canopy*, observes that as churches seek to keep pace with changes in the cultural context in which they find themselves, they put at risk the "plausibility" that gains them legitimacy in the eyes of adherents. That plausibility is tied to the ability of a religious system to embody an ancient tradition.[2] It is thus no easy task to set about creating wholesale change in synagogues, which are the "retail outlets" through which most Jews experience Judaism. This explains why leaders of American synagogues may indeed be resistant to change what is familiar and comfortable in their congregations. But many could probably be convinced to support innovations if they were persuaded that such innovations might be successful in attracting unaffiliated Jews.

Make no mistake about it. It will take a great deal of dedicated effort on the part of existing synagogue leadership to engage unaffiliated Jews in a meaningful conversation about what they would want in a synagogue.

Most would probably say something like "my life is already full and, while I wish you no harm and respect the fact that you are providing a needed service to many, I just don't have the time, the inclination, or the resources to pursue synagogue involvement right now."

Someone once described a leader as a person who can convince others that they have needs that they themselves are unaware of. The institution that is currently called "synagogue" is associated with a range of services and a mode of operation that has little attraction to increasing numbers of new American Jews. Ironically, these same people are spending a good deal of time and money looking for places where they can find a sense of belonging, a context of meaning, and a taste of spirituality. It may be that many new American Jews are not all that savvy about the way that the Jewish community works and what it provides. But it is certainly fair to ask, how can synagogues become the addresses that such Jews turn to for their spiritual needs?

New Options

At present, many unaffiliated Jews are being drawn to Jewish options that have been recently created and are outside of the orbit of American synagogues. One of the most interesting phenomena of the past decade in American Jewish life has been the appearance of *Tikkun* magazine. Self-described as "a progressive voice on spirituality, American politics and culture, religion, psychology and Jewish issues," the magazine and its founder and editor, Michael Lerner, have tapped into a constituency of new American Jews who are seeking much of what the synagogue-community is offering. But because there are so few synagogue-communities around, the vast majority are unaffiliated with any synagogue. The thousands who have attended *Tikkun*-sponsored conferences in New York, San Francisco, and Washington are hungering for real synagogue-communities that care about spirituality, social justice, and creating nurturing social networks. Many don't believe that such institutions exist.

Even when such congregations do exist nearby, it takes much to overcome the suspicion that anything of value and relevance could actually be taking place in a synagogue. David Shneyer, a gifted teacher and musician in the Washington, D.C., area, has been attracting thousands of Jews for the past twenty years in a host of Jewish groups of his creation sponsoring study, worship, the arts, and social justice. Many of these groups are now organized under the rubric of an organization that he heads called Am Kolel. The participants are classic new American Jews. They are quite serious about their Jewish pursuits, excited about exploring spiritual alternatives, and seemingly allergic to anything the least bit reminiscent of a synagogue. It is clear that the boomer generation is hungry for a Jewish connection and that it represents a significant pool of Jews who prefer to stand at arm's length from organized Jewish life.

Many other young and unaffiliated Jews have been drawn to seminars and workshops sponsored by several new Jewish Renewal retreat centers: Metivta: A School for Jewish Wisdom, founded in 1991 by Jonathan Omer-Man in Los Angeles; Elat Chayim, founded by Rabbis Jeff Roth and Joanna Katz in 1992 in upstate New York; and Chochmat ha-Lev, founded in 1995 by Avram Davis in the San Francisco Bay Area. Each of these retreat centers sponsors courses and *shabbatonim* (weekend retreats), and each has sponsored major conferences on meditation and Jewish life in recent years, drawing on hundreds of primarily young Jews hungering for a more spiritual experience of Judaism.

Most of these new groups identify themselves as part of the Jewish Renewal movement and are organized loosely under the umbrella of Aleph, the Alliance for Jewish Renewal. Aleph includes many new prayer and study groups, often meeting in homes or rented facilities, which experiment liberally with meditation and Eastern spiritual practices. The movement is influenced heavily by Rabbi Zalman Schachter-Shalomi, known affectionately as "Zalman." A European-born rabbi ordained by the Lubavitcher Hasidim, Zalman's personal odyssey has traversed the entire gamut of contemporary spiritual practice, both inside and outside of Judaism. His cutting-edge experimentation with "prayer technology" pushes the envelope beyond what will be found in most American synagogues. Alternating between playful and profound (often both simultaneously), the prayer style that Zalman has innovated has a particular appeal to Jewish seekers who would find the prayer services in most American synagogues boring if not impenetrable.[3]

In many ways, Jewish Renewal serves as an important laboratory for new ways to experience a spiritually inspired Jewish practice. Though the groups affiliated with Jewish Renewal span the spectrum with regard to observance levels, it is fair to say that most Jews walking into a Renewal service who are used to the conventional services of the American synagogue would find little that is familiar. Every movement in American Jewish life has its own orthodoxies, and Renewal boasts that it has created a new paradigm. Renewal tends to be more committed to the spiritual transformation of the individual than to the preservation of Jewish practice and observance. Much of what happens in Renewal settings breaks Peter Berger's "plausibility" test necessary to convince the faithful that the new form of religious practice bears any connection to the historical antecedents that are valued. To be fair, much of the "plausibility" framework for today's synagogue leadership is based more on the suburban synagogue-center than what happened at Mount Sinai. Fans of Renewal can make a fair case that theirs is a more authentic expression of Judaism than what takes place in synagogues. But it does explain why so little of what is happening in Renewal circles makes its way into most synagogue settings.

Jewish Renewal is still organizationally undeveloped. It has nothing close to the institutional infrastructure of the major synagogue denominations. It has not succeeded in generating significant financial support. Many of the rabbis in the Renewal network have private ordination from Zalman, a practice common in Europe but not widely accepted by the major rabbinical professional organizations in America. And the total number of people Renewal has personally reached may not number more than several thousand.

Yet American synagogues have a lot to learn from Jewish Renewal. If Renewal might be faulted for giving insufficient attention to the continuities with the past, most American synagogues can be faulted for failing to ask themselves questions about the personal spiritual transformation of its members. Spending time in Renewal gatherings, one begins to understand the deep interest in a spiritual form of Judaism felt by the new American Jew. The spiritual practice in these Renewal settings evidences a passion that is all but impossible to find in American synagogues. In many ways, Jewish Renewal is to the 1990s what the *havurah* movement was to the 1970s. Much of it will be dismissed by leaders of the Jewish community as too far out, too flaky, or too New Age. But those who ignore it and assume that it will go away do so at the peril of overlooking a significant generational phenomenon. Just as many elements of *havurah* Judaism made their way slowly into the practice of the American synagogue, so too is it likely that in twenty years, one will be able to trace new modalities of prayer in the synagogue-community to the Jewish Renewal movement of the 1990s.

Changes . . . "Blowin' in the Wind"

Indeed, many of the similarities in style between *havurah* Judaism and Renewal Judaism are among the elements that are accelerating the transition of the American synagogue to the synagogue-community paradigm. The veritable explosion of "library *minyans*" in American synagogues (which can assemble in any room in the building) signals a desire on the part of laypeople for leading their own services in a distinctly "low-church" style.

These services are the impetus for many Jews to develop the synagogue skills and literacy necessary to lead all parts of the service, including a talk about the assigned Torah reading for the week. The popularity of these lay-led services is not lost on the rabbis and leaders of synagogues who themselves are eager to capture the energy and enthusiasm of these Jews.

A new generation of American Jewish songwriters has begun writing music that draws worshipers into a spiritual mood. The late Rabbi Shlomo Carlebach, a hip, guitar-playing Orthodox rabbi, created a genre of prayers set to catchy, upbeat melodies. His concerts turned into the closest thing that the Jewish community has ever seen to revivals, with people swept up into frenzied and spirited singing and dancing. His melodies have been popular in Jewish circles for years. The younger generation of singer-songwriters include Debbie Friedman, Hannah Tiferet Siegel, and Shefa Gold, and their music ranges from pieces of liturgy, rendered alternately in Hebrew and English in the same song, to rhythmic chanting, which allows for a more meditative tone to be set during a part of a service. This music, along with wordless *niggunim,* are gradually replacing the operatic cantorial music or choral selections that were so long the staple of synagogue music and is making it more possible for worshipers to feel some spiritual energy in a service through music and song.

American synagogues are starting to sponsor healing services. These are services of readings and song that allow an individual experiencing some physical ailment or some deep psychological or spiritual pain, perhaps when a loved one is sick, to feel supported in a Jewish context. These are often settings in which Jews can tell their own stories of alienation and return to the Jewish community, not unlike the stories in this book. Most important, such services allow Jews to personalize their experience of Judaism. It is no coincidence that the last decade of the twentieth century has seen several dozen books and scores of articles on the theme of Jewish spiritual journeys. These stories are not only finding a receptive audience in the marketplace but also sowing the seeds for significant changes in the way that Judaism is taught and experienced.

Synagogue 2000 is a project, sponsored by the Nathan Cummings Foundation and the Righteous Persons Foundation, whose goal is to transform the American synagogue into an institution better prepared to function in the next century. Led by Ron Wolfson of the University of Judaism in Los Angeles and Rabbi Larry Hoffman of the Hebrew Union College in New York, many of its objectives are similar to the synagogue-community model outlined in this book. Its greatest contribution may be in its ability to shepherd synagogue-centers through the difficult adjustment of organizational culture to become synagogue-communities.

A final trend is toward greater adult Jewish learning among new American Jews. Thousands of boomers have turned to classes and study programs that introduce them to a mature presentation of Judaism. Scarred by inadequate and juvenile presentations in the Hebrew schools of their youth, an impressive number of Jews are giving the tradition a second chance. They figure, a religion that has survived for three thousand years must have something to it. Indeed it does. Our model synagogues were noteworthy in that none of them built their program around Judaism for the kids, even though that is what drives most Jews to join synagogues in America today. Each institution was built on presenting a serious form of Judaism geared to adults. The belief, which turns out to be true, is that when the adults are taking Judaism seriously, it is far easier to transmit the tradition to the children.

Evolution, Not Revolution

The transition of the American Jewish community from the synagogue-center to the synagogue-community model will happen in evolutionary and not revolutionary ways. It is possible that the shocking statistics about Jewish dropouts that were revealed in the 1990 survey of the American Jewish community will be reinforced by the 2000 survey, and pressure will build to look at the institutions of Jewish life, asking why they are not connecting with the generation that now constitutes the majority of the target population.

It is also possible that Jewish communal leaders will find some compelling trends in the larger society among churches, which are somewhat further along in identifying major shifts in attitudes and tastes of the baby boom generation and adjusting church structures and programs accordingly. A recent book published by the Alban Institute, which works with Protestant congregations, families, and communities, noted important changes taking place in American churches that parallel much of what we saw happening in our model Jewish congregations.[4] Among these changes were the growing phenomenon of empowerment of the laity, the emergence of "gifted leadership" in the form of members contributing significantly to the spiritual life of the church through their particular talents and spiritual journeys, and a new sense of mission. The mission, in particular, was for churches to reach beyond their traditional memberships to reach out to parts of the community that have largely been overlooked by congregations—precisely the challenge that we are putting forth for American synagogues.

To bridge the current gap between American synagogues and the new American Jew, two things must happen. First, there must be serious outreach on the part of synagogue leadership. Not public relations or membership drives. Serious outreach. This means discovering the many pockets of Jews interested in engaging in Jewish study, worship, and spiritual exploration who are currently synagogue-averse. Synagogues should open their facilities to these Jews at no charge. Rabbis, cantors, and educators should spend time with these groups. Reach out to independent *havurot,* Jewish Renewal groups, Jewish meditation groups, Jewish study groups. They are all over the place. Jewish professionals should offer to teach whatever is within their field of expertise. And more important, they should engage in some active listening. The professional leadership of the Jewish community will be pleasantly surprised with how hungry these Jews are for what they were trained to impart.

Second, when American synagogue leaders come to know new American Jews as real people, not as the "unaffiliated," not as "dropouts," and not as some misguided group that poses a threat to the future of Judaism as we currently know it, they might be motivated to take a hard look at the institutions for which they are responsible. Those with the courage and ability to lead will consider how their synagogues can begin to incorporate some of the characteristics of synagogue-communities that we have talked about in this book. It is critically important that the existing lay leadership of synagogues be part of the interaction with these new constituencies. These loyalists might surprise their rabbis with their receptivity toward making changes. But even the most hard-nosed, conservatively inclined loyalist can be affected by encounters with new American Jews who want to take part in shaping twenty-first-century Judaism. These Jews are their children. They are the future. If there is no place for them in the synagogues that the loyalists have built, what good has been the older generation's lifetime of commitment?

Denominationalism

A word has to be said here about denominationalism. Much is made of the existence of four movements in American Jewish life and the differences between them. Recent conflicts over the definition of who is a Jew and which rabbis may perform life cycle ceremonies that will be recognized by other movements have accentuated the divisions between the streams. It is notable that despite some obvious differences in practice and observance patterns, the four profiled synagogues are much more alike than different. In terms of style, energy, approach, and organizational principles, the four synagogues are remarkably similar. I would have a more difficult time being a member of the typical synagogue-center of my childhood, so many of which still exist, than being a member of any of the four synagogue communities profiled in this book.

Some would make a case here for a postdenominational form of Judaism. Certainly there is evidence that at least three of the four of the profiled synagogues (Adat Shalom being the exception) are testing the limits of their respective movements' standards and conventions. Significant percentages of members in these congregations do not identify with the national denominations of which the congregations are a part. Simultaneously, there is a growth of congregations that choose not to affiliate with any of the major national denominations. Many of the newer congregations being formed today align themselves with the Jewish Renewal movement or with the loose confederation of *havurot* under the aegis of the National Havurah Coordinating Committee.

I see the future slightly differently. The organizational infrastructure of the national movements, including schools, camps, publications, institutes, policy arms, and rabbinical and cantorial seminaries, are not so easily waved aside. Any renaissance of Jewish life will need to include this array of well-established institutions. They would be hard to replicate. At the same time, it would be foolish to ignore the indications of a growing disenchantment with the national movements and the slowness with which they are able to grasp and respond to the signs of the times. There is no question that American synagogues are headed into the synagogue-community model described in this book. There *is* a question about the pace of that transition. To the extent that the loyalists who support the synagogues and the national movements of which they are part are interested in meeting the needs of a generation that has become increasingly alienated from conventional Judaism, the transition will occur more rapidly. But such a transition will require a level of openness to new constituencies and a deep commitment to institutional transformation that has not been in great evidence in the American Jewish community to date.

The Challenge

For every one of the people whose spiritual journeys we have chronicled in this book, there are thousands of Jews whose journeys do not end up in a synagogue. This is not because they do not find synagogues on their journeys; they do. But most synagogues are deaf to the needs of this generation. Synagogues want the new American Jew to join their membership rolls on the synagogues' terms. Increasing numbers are not interested.

The tragedy is that the unaffiliated, whom the sociologists might dismiss as "dropouts," are in fact seekers. They are asking ultimate questions about life, meaning, God, morality, transcendence, justice, suffering, conscience, and purpose. Judaism addresses all of these issues and more. These are theological questions, religious questions, spiritual questions. Synagogues should be places where Jewish seekers can enter into this conversation with their own heritage, wrestle with it, and learn to love it, despite whatever questions remain unresolved. Most synagogues have failed to engage these Jews.

The Jewish community has lost some of the most sensitive spiritual souls of this generation. They are Jews who were looking for God and found spiritual homes outside of Judaism. Their journeys traversed the Jewish community, but nothing there beckoned them. The creation of synagogue-communities in which the voices of seekers can be heard and their questions can be asked will challenge many loyalist Jews. It will upset and enrage them. But it would also enrich them. And synagogues would find themselves to be places where people argued about how one can find God—all in all, not a bad place to be.

EPILOGUE

IF YOU CAN'T FIND IT, CREATE IT: TEN STRATEGIES TO TRANSFORM YOUR CONGREGATION

IT NEVER FAILS. I prepare a talk. I slave over its preparation. I assemble data to support my analysis of the problem. I propose solutions. I give reasons why the solutions may actually work. And then I end with a really inspiring closing.

I savor the satisfaction of a job well done. Then I am approached by an attentive listener. "Tell me, Rabbi," this person says politely. "What exactly is it that I am supposed to do now?" This final chapter is directed to that attentive audience member.

You have certainly by now been able to identify yourself as a falling into one or more of the categories described in this book: loyalists, who are members of synagogues and who often participate in the leadership of those institutions; returnees, whose membership in synagogues may be marginal but who are at least reachable for a period of time while the congregation meets their individual or family needs; and dropouts or seekers, who by and large stand outside the orbit of synagogue life. Do you feel that you fall into more than one category? You've got lots of company! The more you can identify with each of these categories, the more effective you can be as a change agent in a synagogue, bringing it more in line with the synagogue-community model that I advocate in this book.

To attempt these strategies requires a commitment to contribute your time, energy, and talents to the challenging but rewarding task of institutional transformation. It also requires assessing the best approach to the existing professionals and lay leadership in the congregation. Some people will be more open and supportive than others. Your strategy needs to be adjusted accordingly.

A former member of my congregation relocated to another community because of a job opportunity that became available to her husband. She was upset and despairing over the prospect of finding another congregation like Adat Shalom. After checking out a good many congregations in her new community, she joined the one that seemed to hold out the promise of being most like our synagogue-community. But it wasn't quite what she'd hoped it would be. As she pondered her options, she realized that she could (1) join the religious committee to help modify the service, (2) start her own *minyan* in the congregation, or (3) become a rabbi and start her own congregation.

This well describes the range of possibilities depending on the situation, from working within the existing structures of your congregation to starting something totally new. What follows are ten strategies to try within your congregation or to use as a guide for starting a new *minyan, havurah,* or synagogue. In every case, the success of the strategy will require your willingness to be the chief advocate and worker for the idea.

1. Create a Mission Statement

See if a group of members would be interested in thinking through the primary purpose of the synagogue. Remember, a list of programs is not a statement of objectives. First try to articulate the why: Why does our synagogue exist? What are its objectives? What is the purpose of Judaism?

As you try to commit your ideas to writing, circulate it to ever wider circles of members, and invite their input. See if what begins to take shape makes you proud. If it does, you are on the right track. Only then begin to examine the program of the synagogue to see if it is successfully advancing the objectives set forth in the mission statement.

2. Bring Singable Music into the Worship Service

As you sit in a service, take note of how many people are singing how many songs. If most people are sitting passively, listening to a cantor or a choir, you need some serious music therapy.

Talk to your cantor about whether he or she is willing to introduce new melodies that lend themselves to congregational singing. Track down tapes of Jewish music to find suitable melodies. The simpler the song, in terms of words and melody, the better. A *niggun* requires no words at all and is generally repeated often enough so that even the most musically challenged can join in. Even easier is to encourage the cantor to take a few of the peppier melodies and to sing them with "la la la" a couple of times after the words have been sung. Especially if some people find the Hebrew intimidating, this is an excellent way to draw worshipers into some singing.

See if you can identify one or more members who are musically talented, and see if they can introduce a melody on occasion. If the religious standards permit it, introduce instruments or drums. If not, clapping serves a similar purpose.

3. Create *Havurot*

Any way that you can break down the congregation into smaller, more intimate units will strengthen the bonds of community. The *havurot* might be organized around study, *shabbat,* social action, holidays, or any other topic. They may be based on geography (who lives near whom) or life stage (singles, young couples, families with small children, and so on). The more Jewish content the better.

What is most important is that members get into each other's homes and get to know one another. If your objective is to strengthen your synagogue, make sure that the *havurah* is committed to attendance at synagoguewide events on a regular basis; otherwise, it will become an impetus for pulling energy out of the congregation instead of putting energy into it. Ideally, the *havurah* should, on occasion, sponsor a program for the rest of the congregation.

4. Create Systems for Personal Support

Nothing invalidates the synagogue enterprise more than if a member experiences a life trauma and there is no congregational response. This is the Jewish *mitzvah* of *gemilut chasadim,* acts of lovingkindness. A visit or call from the rabbi is nice, but it is not enough. *Havurot* are natural response teams during such times because of the familiarity of the members with one another.

Often the biggest barrier to congregations functioning as support networks for each other is the reticence of members to share their pain, sickness, or personal crisis with a wider group of people. The synagogue-community is challenged to come up with ways to overcome this American predilection for privacy. Healing services are one vehicle that gives permission for people to share pain publicly. Committees that respond to sickness or death in the congregation are very important, but the response must go beyond a small group of people.

5. Create a Social Justice Agenda

A minister friend of mine once made a quintessentially Jewish observation when he said, "Sometimes the heaviest burden is having no one to carry." It is easy to get wrapped up in one's own world of professional and personal concerns. A true synagogue-community provides motivation to look around, see the pain and suffering in the world, and begin the work of repair, known in Hebrew as *tikkun olam*.

Many congregations sponsor occasional social action projects. Yet if a congregation were to undertake the mission statement initiative, it is likely that it would find that one of the main purposes of Judaism is to bring aid and comfort to those less fortunate than oneself. A justice agenda will move a community to the high ground of noble purpose. It will strengthen relationships between people doing important *mitzvah* work with each other. It will also result in attracting Jews to the congregation with deep commitments to working for peace and justice in the world.

6. Experiment with the Prayer Experience

All of the greatest rabbinic teachers who addressed the issue of prayer insisted that it must be a service of the heart and not a rote recitation of the lips. And yet the latter is the form of prayer that is offered in most American synagogues. Since officiation at worship is one of the duties assigned to rabbis, you will need a cooperative rabbinic figure who is open to experimentation with prayer. Explore whether there is an openness to trying different forms of prayer at the main service in your synagogue. If not, see if you can create another setting for this.

Among the ways that Jews are experimenting with prayer today are the writing and sharing of personal prayers; use of alternative liturgies such as Marcia Falk's *Book of Blessings;*[1] use of movement, dance, and yoga as part of a prayer experience; extended periods of silent meditation; breathing exercises; spontaneous prayer elicited from those gathered for worship; and sharing of poetry from other traditions and cultures that parallel themes in the Jewish liturgy. Even if these experiments happen outside of the main service, there will likely be some constituency drawn to them whenever they are scheduled. There is always the possibility that some of the experiments might recommend themselves for integration into the main service on occasion.

7. Create a Lay-Led Service

Even if you love your rabbi and enjoy the service, good things will happen at a lay-led service that will never happen at the main service. Members will become more proficient at leading the prayers. Members will learn how to read Torah and Haftarah. Members will study the Torah reading of the week to give a talk or lead a discussion. The service does not have to happen weekly. Start modestly. Be consistent in terms of when and where it meets. You will draw a constituency.

Most important, participants will get a feeling of owning their own Judaism in a way that can never happen in a service when professional clergy run the show.

8. Get the Actors at Life-Cycle Events to Speak to the Moment

Part of what contributes to the rote nature of Jewish prayer in American synagogues is that much of the service is so highly scripted. Creating moments when people can give expression to their emotions is one way to heighten the sense of spirituality in a service.

Most synagogues have a heavy schedule of life-cycle functions at their primary services. Most often these are bar and bat mitzvah celebrations, but they might also include baby namings, and *aufrufs* (a wedding couple's honor on the *shabbat* before their marriage). All too often these occasions are so highly tailored to the celebrants and their guests that regular worshipers might as well leave the sanctuary for a walk around the block. But these are moments pregnant with tremendous emotional power.

Consider the possibilities. A parent shares a short, personal message to a son or daughter who is to become bar or bat mitzvah. A new father or mother says a few words about a deceased relative as their baby is given that relative's name. These give everyone in attendance a palpable sense of the passing of the generations and the timeless emotions related to the creation of legacies for ourselves and our families.

9. Share Personal Stories

Without question, the most spiritual moments that I have ever experienced in a synagogue setting have been when someone shares something about his or her own life journey and connects it to Judaism. I have created a service where there is ample opportunity for such sharing—during Torah dialogue, in talks by members about a given prayer, in a *d'var torah* given by a member. But such opportunities can be created in other settings as well.

Congregations committed to orienting new members to their organizational culture and their programs might host new member coffees that begin with people talking about their spiritual journeys. This exercise shouldn't be restricted to new members. New American Jews must know that their journeys, however far they may have taken them from the Jewish community, are important and are valued. The attitude should *not* be "wherever you have been, we don't care, as long as you are now with us in this synagogue." Rather it should be "your journey represents a struggle that many of us have had around our faith. What can we learn from your journey that will make our synagogue a better community and that will make us better Jews?"

10. Reach Out to New Constituencies

Never let your synagogue be satisfied with its existing constituency. For every person who is a member, at least two are not. And of the actual members on the roster, think of those who never come around. Look around the room the next time you are in the synagogue and ask who is not there. Singles? Older people? Poor Jews? Disabled? Gays? Teenagers? Seekers? For each of these constituencies, there is a strategy for outreach and inclusion. Ask, "How can we reach these people? How might they be made to feel more comfortable here?"

How will you know when you have succeeded? When any Jew, anywhere in the community, can walk into your synagogue and call it home.

———— o ————

A final story. For several years, an elderly couple used to walk into our *oneg* luncheon and help themselves to the food. They were never at services, but judging from their dress, they had gone to one of the several other services around the Jewish Community Center where we hold services. Not only did they take lunch, but they also filled shopping bags with enough food for several meals. For a long time I resented them. They were not members of our congregation. They were not coming to our services. They ate alone in the corner, speaking to no one, and then left. They were mooching off our lunch. Period.

Finally, after a weekday holiday service when the food exceeded the appetites in attendance, I approached the couple. They seemed embarrassed, as if I had caught them in the act. I wished them a *chag sameach* (happy holiday greeting) and offered to help pack the extra food in their bags. They were most grateful and said, "Even though we go to services at the Conservative synagogue across the street, we always come here to eat and feel at home. Thank you."

I finally understood my own book.

DISCUSSION GUIDE

Book clubs, *havurot,* or adult education classes might find it helpful to discuss some of the themes in *Finding a Spiritual Home.* The following questions would serve as a useful guide for that conversation. Tailor the questions based on the makeup of your group.

1. Of the ten essays in this book that recount people's personal spiritual journeys and their return to active involvement with Judaism, are there any you identify with? Which ones? How are they similar to your own story? Do you know Jews whose spiritual journey has led them away from the Jewish community? What are they looking for that they cannot find in the Jewish community?

2. Discuss the characteristics of the "new American Jew" described in Chapter Two. Do they ring true? Do they describe you?

3. Think of some of your most profound spiritual experiences. How many of these experiences happened within the context of a synagogue or temple? How can congregations create environments where deep spiritual experiences may occur? What would such an environment look like?

4. Think about synagogues that you have visited as a guest. Were there practices or ways that those synagogues functioned that you found appealing? If so, what appealed to you?

5. Chapter Seventeen sketches four characteristics of the synagogue-community: an organizational culture that promotes a high level of participation and engagement of large numbers of members, strong spiritual leadership, an ability to articulate the mission of the institution, and the willingness to promote a serious and challenging version of Judaism. If you are a member of a congregation, discuss the degree to which these characteristics are present in your synagogue. Which of these features could use some work?

6. The book talks about how the Jewish community breaks down into synagogue loyalists, returnees, and dropouts. Which category best

describes you? Discuss how each of these distinct constituencies regards the other two. Can a synagogue successfully program for and satisfy more than one of these groups?

7. The Epilogue offers ten strategies to transform a congregation. For those not currently in a congregation, the same strategies represent an agenda for creating a new synagogue-community. Who would your allies be in trying to implement some of these suggestions? What would the obstacles be? List the obstacles and brainstorm strategies to overcome them.

NOTES

CHAPTER 2: SYNAGOGUES AND THE NEW AMERICAN JEW

1. For an excellent in-depth treatment of these themes, see part two of Jack Wertheimer, *A People Divided: Judaism in Contemporary America,* New York: Basic Books, 1993.

2. Jonathan Woocher, *Sacred Survival: The Civil Religion of American Jews,* Bloomington: Indiana University Press, 1986; see especially chapter five.

3. The National Jewish Population Study conducted by the Council of Jewish Federations in 1990 found that the younger the age cohort, the lower was the commitment to "public Judaism." Similar results were confirmed almost ten years later on a range of Jewish ethnic loyalties such as Israel attachment, commitment to Jewish peoplehood, and support for Jewish institutions. See Steven M. Cohen, *Religious Stability and Ethnic Decline: Emerging Patterns of Jewish Identity in the United States,* New York: Jewish Community Center Association Research Center, 1998.

4. On the changing nature of ethnic identification in America, see Richard Alba, *Ethnic Identity: The Transformation of White America,* New Haven: Yale University Press, 1990. On baby boomers and civic commitment, see Robert Bellah, Richard Madsen, William Sullivan, Ann Swidler, Steven Tipton, *Habits of the Heart: Individualism and Commitment in American Life,* Berkeley: University of California Press, 1985.

5. Abraham Maslow, *Motivation and Personality,* New York: HarperCollins, 1954. This analysis is more fully developed in Wade Clark Roof, *A Generation of Seekers: The Spiritual Journeys of the Baby Boom Generation,* New York: HarperCollins, 1993, chapter two.

6. Charles Liebman, *The Ambivalent American Jew,* Philadelphia: Jewish Publication Society, 1973, chapter three.

7. Roof (1993), p. 57.

8. Dean Hoge and David Roozen, "Some Sociological Conclusions About Church Trends," in Hoge and Roozen (eds.), *Understanding Church*

Growth and Decline, 1950–1978, Cleveland: Pilgrim Press, 1979, pp. 320–330.

9. Roof (1993), pp. 154–156.

10. Ronald Inglehart, *Cultural Shift in Advanced Industrial Society,* Princeton: Princeton University Press, 1990.

11. Roof (1993), pp. 255–261.

12. For a sampling of voices that helped raise the consciousness of the Jewish community about feminism, see Elizabeth Koltun (ed.), *The Jewish Woman: New Perspectives,* New York: Schocken, 1976, and Susannah Heschel (ed.), *On Being a Jewish Feminist: A Reader,* New York: Schocken, 1983.

13. On the need for the Jewish community to be more open to the intermarried and to converts, see Lena Romanoff, *Your People, My People: Finding Acceptance and Fulfillment as a Jew by Choice,* Philadelphia: Jewish Publication Society, 1990, and Gary Tobin, *Opening the Gates: How Proactive Conversion Can Revitalize the Jewish Community,* San Francisco: Jossey-Bass, 1999. On the experience of gays and lesbians in the Jewish community, see Christie Balka and Andy Rose (eds.), *Twice Blessed: On Being Lesbian or Gay and Jewish,* Boston: Beacon Press, 1989.

14. Two accounts of Jews on spiritual odysseys, who in turn encounter numerous other Jews as teachers and students are Tony Schwartz, *What Really Matters: Searching for Wisdom in America,* New York: Bantam, 1995, and Sylvia Boorstein, *That's Funny, You Don't Look Buddhist: On Being a Faithful Jew and a Passionate Buddhist,* San Francisco: HarperSanFrancisco, 1997.

15. Michael Lerner speaks extensively about this phenomenon in *Jewish Renewal: A Path to Healing and Transformation,* New York: Putnam, 1994; see the prologue, "Why Jews Left Judaism."

16. Bellah, Madsen, Sullivan, Swidler, and Tipton (1985), especially chapters nine and eleven.

17. Robert Wuthnow, *Sharing the Journey: Support Groups and America's New Quest for Community,* New York: Free Press, 1994, chapters two and twelve.

CHAPTER 3: THE EMERGING SYNAGOGUE-COMMUNITY

1. The relationship between the social integration of American Jews, their changing areas of settlement over time, and the kinds of synagogues that arose in each area is suggested in Marshall Sklare, *Conservative Judaism:*

An American Religious Movement, New York: Schocken, 1972, especially the first three chapters. For a more elaborate treatment of the stages of development of the American synagogue, see Abraham Karp's essay "The Synagogue in America: A Historical Typology," in Jack Wertheimer, *The American Synagogue: A Sanctuary Transformed*, Hanover, N.H.: University Press of New England, 1987. An excellent survey of the earlier period is Leon Jick, *The Americanization of the Synagogue, 1820–1870*, Hanover, N.H.: University Press of New England, 1976. A more recent treatment that links generational change to synagogue change is Lawrence Hoffman, "From Ethnic to Spiritual: A Tale of Four Generations" (pamphlet), New York: Synagogue 2000 Library, 1996.

2. Will Herberg, *Protestant, Catholic, Jew*, New York: Doubleday, 1955.

3. The synagogue-center idea was advanced by Mordecai Kaplan, one of the leading Jewish intellectuals of the twentieth century and the founder of Reconstructionist Judaism. Kaplan maintained that since Judaism was a religious civilization, encompassing culture, the arts, history, and literature, synagogues had to house more than just places of worship. He conceived of synagogue-centers as meeting places for Jews who could enrich their knowledge and appreciation of all that Jewish civilization had to offer. Although the YMHA and, later, the Jewish Center movement would expand on this idea, building institutions that had everything but worship space, many rabbis and synagogues came to adopt the terminology and pieces of Kaplan's programmatic conception.

4. Summaries of these surveys of American Jewry accompanied by analysis can be found in B. Lazerwitz, J. A. Winter, A. Dashefsky, and E. Tabory, *Jewish Choices: American Jewish Denominationalism*, Albany: SUNY Press, 1998.

5. Leonard Fein, R. Chin, J. Dauber, and B. Reisman, "Reform Is a Verb" (commission report), New York: Union of American Hebrew Congregations, 1972.

6. Lawrence Hoffman, "From Uncommon Cold to Uncommon Healing," *CCAR Journal: A Reform Jewish Quarterly*, Spring 1994.

7. See analysis by Daniel Elazar, "The Development of the American Synagogue," in Alexandra Korros and Jonathan Sarna (eds.), *American Synagogue History: A Bibliography and State of the Field Survey*, New York: Marcus Wiener, 1988. Also N. Linzer, D. Schnall, and J. Chanes (eds.), *A Portrait of the American Jewish Community*, New York: Praeger, 1998, chapter six.

8. Two major studies of *havurot* are Bernard Reisman, *The Havurah: A Contemporary Jewish Experience*, New York: Union of American Hebrew

Congregations, 1977, and Riv Ellen Prell, *Prayer and Community: The Havurah in American Judaism,* Detroit: Wayne State University Press, 1989.

9. Rabbi Edward Gershfield, speech to the Rabbinical Assembly convention in 1970, quoted in Sklare (1972), p. 280.

10. The pioneer in this regard is Rabbi Harold Schulweis, who brought an elaborate program of *havurot* to his congregation of more than one thousand, Valley Beth Shalom in Encino, California. See his "Restructuring the Synagogue," *Conservative Judaism,* Summer 1973.

11. For an overview of the range of alternative Jewish groups emerging over the past twenty years, see Judy Petsonk, *Taking Judaism Personally: Creating a Meaningful Spiritual Life,* New York: Free Press, 1996.

12. Although this term has since turned up in some other contexts, I first coined its meaning in the way that it is used throughout this book, in a piece that I wrote in the late 1970s: "The Synagogue as Community," *Shefa Quarterly,* 1980, 2(3).

13. See Dean Kelley, *Why Conservative Churches Are Growing: A Study in the Sociology of Religion,* Cleveland: Pilgrim Press, 1979.

14. See Dean Hoge, Benton Johnson, and Donald Luidens, *Vanishing Boundaries: The Religion of Mainline Protestant Baby Boomers,* Louisville, Ky.: Westminster/John Knox Press, 1994.

15. See Donald Miller, *Reinventing American Protestantism: Christianity in the New Millennium,* Berkeley: University of California Press, 1997.

16. See Seymour Sarason, *The Creation of Settings and the Future Societies,* San Francisco: Jossey-Bass, 1972, a work on this topic that exerted a tremendous influence on me.

CHAPTER 5: CONGREGATION BETH EL,
SUDBURY, MASSACHUSETTS

1. Background for this profile was gleaned from congregational records and publications and interviews with Rabbi Larry Kushner, Anita Diamant, Peter and Nancy Gossels, and Lorel Zar-Kessler. Personal essays by Shoshi Kahn-Woods, Nancy Lee Gossels, Janet Strassman Perlmutter, and Rosie Rosensweig added immeasurably to my understanding of the community.

2. Lawrence Kushner, *The Book of Letters: A Mystical Alef-Bait,* New York: HarperCollins, 1975, p. 17.

CHAPTER 8: THE HEBREW INSTITUTE OF RIVERDALE,
BRONX, NEW YORK

1. Background for this profile was gleaned from congregational records and
   publications and interviews with Rabbi Avi Weiss, Rabbi Barry Gelman,
   Rabbi Aaron Frank, Hillel Jaffe, David Mann, and Karen Rotter. Personal
   essays by Eliot Arons, Howard Bromberg, Ruth Bromberg, David Eise-
   man, Sharon Godlewicz, Larry Greenfield, Glenn Jasper, Tzipora Jung,
   and Pamela Madsen added immeasurably to my understanding of the
   community.

CHAPTER 11: ADAT SHALOM RECONSTRUCTIONIST
CONGREGATION, BETHESDA, MARYLAND

1. I am indebted to the following members of the Adat Shalom community
   for their insightful essays about their own journeys that helped them find
   their place in the community: Jayme Epstein, Betty Hilton, Susana Issacson,
   Sheila Feldman, Joel Kaufman, Mitchell Max, Minna Morse, Sarah Rosen-
   son, Pauline Schmookler, and Marjorie Silverton.

CHAPTER 12: NANCY'S PATH

1. Edmond Fleg, "I Am a Jew" (appears in *Siddur Sim Shalom,* ed. Jules Har-
   low, New York: Rabbinical Assembly and United Synagogue of America,
   1985, p. 814).
2. Elizabeth Barrett Browning, "Aurora Leigh," Chicago: Cassandra Editions,
   1979, Book 7, line 820.

CHAPTER 14: CONGREGATION B'NAI JESHURUN,
NEW YORK

1. Background for this profile was gleaned from congregational records and
   publications and interviews with Rabbi Rolando Matalon, Merril Feinstein
   Feit, Fred Goldstein, and Judith Stern Peck. Personal essays by Anita Alt-
   man, Todd Chanko, Penelope Dannenberg, Stu Feit, Tony Fisher, Bruce
   Gitlin, Mark Horn, Warren Kozak, Madeline Lee, Robert Pollack, Martin
   Radburd, and Phyllis Schatsky added immeasurably to my understanding
   of the community.

CHAPTER 17: CREATING THE SYNAGOGUE-COMMUNITY

1. Paul Wilkes, *And They Shall Be My People: An American Rabbi and His Congregation*, New York: Grove/Atlantic, 1994.

2. Barry Kosmin, *Highlights of the CJF 1990 National Jewish Population Survey*, New York: Council of Jewish Federations, 1991.

CHAPTER 18: THE CHALLENGE OF TRANSFORMATION

1. Wade Clark Roof, *A Generation of Seekers: The Spiritual Journeys of the Baby Boom Generation*, New York: HarperCollins, 1993, pp. 188–203.

2. Peter Berger, *The Sacred Canopy: Elements of a Sociological Theory of Religion*, New York: Doubleday, 1967.

3. For a fascinating treatment of the personalities behind the Jewish Renewal movement and how they are reaching unaffiliated Jews, see Rodger Kamenetz, *Stalking Elijah: Adventures with Today's Jewish Mystical Masters*, San Francisco: HarperSanFrancisco, 1997.

4. C. Jeff Woods, *Congregational Megatrends*, Bethesda, Md.: Alban Institute, 1996.

EPILOGUE. IF YOU CAN'T FIND IT, CREATE IT: TEN STRATEGIES TO TRANSFORM YOUR CONGREGATION

1. Marcia Falk, *The Book of Blessings: New Jewish Prayers for Daily Life, the Sabbath, and the New Moon Festival*, San Francisco: HarperSanFrancisco, 1996.

GLOSSARY

Note: where two forms of a word are given (for example, *chag, chaggim*), the first is singular and the second plural.

ahavat Yisrael	love for the Jewish people
aliyah	a higher place: often used with reference to (1) being called up the *bima* to read a prayer or (2) moving to Israel
am Yisrael	the people of Israel
Amidah	standing prayer
aufruf	blessing of a couple on the sabbath before their wedding
avodah	classically, service of God; in Temple times, through animal sacrifice; post-Temple, through prayer; in contemporary usage, it relates to service to the community
baal tefillah	prayer leader
baalei teshuvah	those who return; Jews from a non-Orthodox background who return to religious practice
bayit	house or home
bikkur cholim	visiting the sick
bima	ritual center stage in a sanctuary; raised platform from which Jewish worship is conducted
brit milah	ritual circumcision
bubba meisas	old wives' tales (literally, "grandmother stories")
chag; chaggim	Jewish festivals
chag sameach	happy holiday (greeting)
challah	traditional sabbath bread
chametz	leavened bread, prohibited on Passover
chametzdik	containing leavening (and therefore not kosher for Passover)

chasidishe rebbe	Hasidic master
chazan	cantor
cheder	Jewish elementary school
chesed	kindness
chumash	Bible
chuppah	wedding canopy
daven; davening	to pray
drash; drashim	textually based presentation
d'var chinuch	words of teaching
d'var torah; divrei torah	presentation on the biblical portion of the week
gabbai; gabbaim	person who organizes and assists in the Torah service; usher
gemilut chasadim	acts of lovingkindness
get	divorce decree
goy; goyim	non-Jew
halacha	Jewish law
halachic	legal, from a Jewish perspective
hashkafa	worldview, perspective
havdalah	ritual marking the end of the sabbath
havurah; havurot	small fellowship group, usually for prayer and/or study
hevrah kaddisha	burial society
hevruta	one-on-one (diad) text study
kabbalat shabbat	the Friday evening prayers welcoming the sabbath
Kaddish	the prayer for the dead
kashrut	dietary laws
kavanah	prayer intentionality
kedushah	central prayer in the Amidah (standing prayer)
kehillah	congregation, community
kibbutz	collective farm in Israel
kibbutznik	resident of a collective farm in Israel
kiddush	ritual blessing of wine; also refers to refreshments after a religious service
kippa; kippot	head covering; skullcap
kiruv	bringing Jews closer to Judaism

klal Yisrael	the community of Israel; all Jews; communal solidarity
kollel	program for training Orthodox rabbis
leil shabbat	Friday evening, the start of the sabbath
leyn	to chant from the Torah
maariv	evening worship service
machzor	High Holyday prayer book
matzah; matzot	unleavened bread eaten on Passover
mechitzah	barrier separating the women from the men in an Orthodox synagogue
menschlikeit	a person of good moral character
midrash	legend or story expanding on a biblical or rabbinic text
mikvah	ritual bath for cleansing
mincha	afternoon service
minyan; minyanim	quorum required for prayer; prayer group
Misheberach	prayer for blessing or healing
mishnah	postbiblical compilation of laws and wisdom redacted by Rabbi Judah the Prince at the end of the second century CE
mitzvah; mitzvot	good deed; biblically based commandment
makom tefillah	place of prayer
mohel	circumciser
neshima	breath; soul or life force
niggun; niggunim	wordless melodies
oneg	after-service refreshments
otiyot	letters of the Hebrew alphabet
parashat hashavua	weekly Bible reading
parsha	section of the Bible
parve	containing neither milk nor meat (and hence able to be eaten with either without violating the dietary laws); also, bland or neutral
pidyon haben	redemption of the firstborn
psukai de'zimrah	early part of the morning service
rebbe's tisch	a celebratory meal at which a Hasidic master offers a talk to his followers
ruach	joyful spirit
schlep	to drag or haul

seder; seders	ritual Passover meal
seudat shlishit	late afternoon meal on the sabbath
shabbat; shabbatot	sabbath
shabbos tisch	festive meal for the sabbath
shacharit	morning worship service
shaliach tzibbur	leader of prayer
shamash	ritual helper or usher
shiva	mourning period
Sh'ma	prayer proclaiming that there is but one God
shomer shabbat	observing all laws governing the sabbath
shteibel	small neighborhood synagogue
shtetl	Jewish village in Eastern Europe
shul; shuls	synagogue
shulchan	table
shule	Yiddish school
siddur	prayer book
sukkah	makeshift booth with a roof of branches erected on the holiday of Sukkot, Feast of Tabernacles
tallit; tallitot	prayer shawl worn during worship
talmud torah	Hebrew school
tefillin	phylacteries
teshuvah	repentance; also used to connote a return to Judaism
tikkun olam	social justice (literally, "repair of the world")
tsimtsum	voluntary self-contraction
tzedakah	righteousness; charitable giving; the uses and sharing of wealth
tzedek	justice
tzelem Elohim	image of God
ulpan	an intensive Hebrew course
yeshiva	Jewish parochial school
yiddishkeit	Jewishness
yizkor	memorial service for deceased
zemirot ameinu	songs of our people

BIBLIOGRAPHY

Alba, Richard. *Ethnic Identity: The Transformation of White America.* New Haven, Conn.: Yale University Press, 1990.

Balka, Christie, and Rose, Andy (eds.). *Twice Blessed: On Being Lesbian or Gay and Jewish.* Boston: Beacon Press, 1989.

Bayme, Steven. *Outreach to the Unaffiliated Communal Context and Policy Directions.* New York: American Jewish Committee, 1992.

Bellah, Robert, and others. *Habits of the Heart: Individualism and Commitment in American Life.* Berkeley: University of California Press, 1985.

Berger, Peter. *The Sacred Canopy: Elements of a Sociological Theory of Religion.* New York: Doubleday, 1967.

Boorstein, Sylvia. *That's Funny, You Don't Look Buddhist: On Being a Faithful Jew and a Passionate Buddhist.* San Francisco: HarperSanFrancisco, 1997.

Bubis, Gerry, Wasserman, Harry, and Lert, Alan. *Synagogue Havurot.* Lanham, Md.: University Press of America, 1983.

Carroll, Jackson. "Leadership and the Study of the Congregation." In Nancy Ammerman, Jackson Carroll, Carl S. Dudley, and William McKinney (eds.), *Studying Congregations: A New Handbook.* Nashville, Tenn.: Abingdon Press, 1998.

Cohen, Steven M. *American Modernity and Jewish Identity.* New York: Routledge, 1983.

Cohen, Steven M. *American Assimilation or Jewish Revival?* Bloomington: Indiana University Press, 1988.

Cohen, Steven M. *Religious Stability and Ethnic Decline: Emerging Patterns of Jewish Identity in the United States.* New York: Jewish Community Center Association Research Center, 1998.

Cohen, Steven M., and Eisen, Arnold. *The Jew Within: Self, Community, and Commitment Among the Variety of Moderately Affiliated.* Los Angeles and Boston: Susan and David Wilstein Institute of Jewish Policy Studies, 1998.

Dashefsky, Arnold. *Jewish Choices: American Jewish Denominationalism.* Albany: State University of New York Press, 1998.

Danziger, M. Herbert. *Returning to Tradition: The Contemporary Revival of Orthodox Judaism.* New Haven, Conn.: Yale University Press, 1989.

Eisen, Arnold. *Rethinking Modern Judaism: Ritual, Commandment, Community.* Chicago: University of Chicago Press, 1998.

Elazar, Daniel. *Community and Polity: The Organizational Dynamics of American Jewry.* Philadelphia: Jewish Publication Society, 1976.

Elazar, Daniel. "The Development of the American Synagogue." In A. S. Korros and J. Sarna (eds.), *American Synagogue History: A Bibliography and State of the Field Survey.* New York: Wiener, 1988.

Elkins, Dov Peretz. *Humanizing Jewish Life: Judaism and the Human Potential Movement.* Lanham, Md.: Barnes & Noble Books, 1976.

Fein, Leonard. *Where Are We? The Inner Life of America's Jews.* New York: HarperCollins, 1988.

Fein, Leonard, and others. *Reform Is a Verb.* New York: Union of American Hebrew Congregations, 1972.

Feldman, Alan. "The Changing Functions of the Synagogue and Rabbi." In Jacob Neusner (ed.), *Understanding American Judaism.* Hoboken, N.J.: Ktav, 1975.

Fishbane, Simcha, and others. *Ritual and Ethnic Identity: A Comparative Study of the Social Meaning of Liturgical Ritual in Synagogues.* Groton, N.Y.: Wilfried Laurier University Press, 1995.

Fowler, James. *Stages of Faith: The Psychology of Human Development and the Quest for Meaning.* San Francisco: HarperSanFrancisco, 1981.

Friedman, Edwin. *Generation to Generation: Family Process in Church and Synagogue.* New York: Guilford Press, 1985.

Friedman, Peter, and Zober, Mark. *Factors Infuencing Synagogue Affiliation: A Multicommunity Analysis.* Occasional Papers, no. 3. New York: North American Jewish Data Bank, United Jewish Communities, 1987.

Furman, Frieda Kerner. *Beyond Yiddishkeit: The Struggle for Jewish Identity in a Reform Synagogue.* Albany: State University of New York Press, 1987.

Geertz, Clifford. *The Interpretation of Cultures.* New York: Basic Books, 1973.

Gelber, S. Michael. *The Failure of the American Rabbi.* Old Tappan, N.J.: Twayne, 1961.

Gilman, Neil. *Conservative Judaism: The New Century.* West Orange, N.J.: Behrman House, 1993.

Goldscheider, Calvin. *Jewish Continuity and Change: Emerging Patterns in America.* Bloomington: Indiana University Press, 1986.

Green, Arthur. *Seek My Face, Speak My Name: A Contemporary Jewish Theology.* Northvale, N.J.: Aronson, 1992.

Green, Arthur. *Restoring the Aleph: Judaism for the Contemporary Seeker.* New York: Council for Initiatives in Jewish Education, 1996.

Heilman, Samuel. *Synagogue Life: A Study in Symbolic Interaction.* Chicago: University of Chicago Press, 1976.

Herberg, Will. *Protestant, Catholic, Jew.* New York: Doubleday, 1955.

Heschel, Susannah (ed.). *On Being a Jewish Feminist: A Reader.* New York: Schocken, 1983.

Hoffman, Lawrence. *The Art of Public Prayer.* Laurel, Md.: Pastoral Press, 1988.

Hoffman, Lawrence. "From Uncommon Cold to Uncommon Healing." *CCAR Journal: A Reform Jewish Quarterly,* Spring 1994, pp. 1–30.

Hoffman, Lawrence. *From Ethnic to Spiritual: A Tale of Four Generations.* New York: Synagogue 2000 Library, 1996.

Hoge, Dean, Johnson, Berta, and Luidens, Donald. *Vanishing Boundaries: The Religion of Mainline Protestant Baby Boomers.* Louisville, Ky.: Westminster/John Knox, 1994.

Hoge, Dean, and Roozen, David. "Some Sociological Conclusions About Church Trends." In Dean Hoge and David Roozen (eds.), *Understanding Church Growth and Decline, 1950–1978.* Cleveland, Ohio: Pilgrim Press, 1979.

Inglehart, Ronald. *Cultural Shift in Advanced Industrial Society.* Princeton, N.J.: Princeton University Press, 1990.

Jick, Leon. *The Americanization of the Synagogue, 1820–1870.* Waltham, Mass.: Brandeis University Press, 1976.

Kamenetz, Rodger. *The Jew in the Lotus.* San Francisco: HarperSanFrancisco, 1994.

Kamenetz, Rodger. *Stalking Elijah: Adventures with Today's Jewish Mystical Masters.* New York: HarperCollins, 1997.

Karp, Abraham. "A Century of Conservative Judaism." In *American Jewish Yearbook.* Philadelphia: American Jewish Committee, 1986.

Karp, Abraham. "The Synagogue in America: A Historical Typology." In Jack Wertheimer (ed.), *The American Synagogue: A Sanctuary Transformed.* Hanover, N.H.: University Press of New England, 1987.

Kaufman, David. *Shul with a Pool: The Synagogue-Center in American Jewish Life.* Hanover, N.H.: University Press of New England, 1999.

Kelley, Dean. *Why Conservative Churches Are Growing: A Study in the Sociology of Religion.* Cleveland, Ohio: Pilgrim Press, 1979.

Klaas, Alan C. *In Search of the Unchurched: Why People Don't Join Your Congregation.* Bethesda, Md.: Alban Institute, 1996.

Koltun, Elizabeth (ed.). *The Jewish Woman: New Perspectives.* New York: Schocken, 1976.

Korros, Alexandra S., and Sarna, Jonathan (eds.). *American Synagogue History: A Bibliography and State of the Field Survey.* New York: Marcus Wiener, 1988.

Kosmin, Barry, and Lachman, Seymour. *One Nation Under God: Religion in Contemporary American Society.* New York: Harmony Books, 1993.

Kurshan, Neil. "The Rabbi as Spiritual Mentor: Reimagining the Role of the Rabbi." *Conservative Judaism,* Fall 1997, pp. 19–27.

Kushner, Lawrence. *Honey from the Rock: Visions of Jewish Mystical Renewal.* New York: HarperCollins, 1977.

Kushner, Lawrence. *The River of Light: Spirituality, Judaism, Consciousness.* New York: HarperCollins, 1981.

Kushner, Lawrence. "The Tent Peg Business: Some Truths About Congregations." *New Traditions,* Spring 1984, pp. 87–92.

Kushner, Lawrence. *God Was in This Place and I, I Did Not Know: Finding Self, Spirituality, and Ultimate Meaning.* Woodstock, Vt.: Jewish Lights, 1991.

Lazerwitz, Bernard, Winter, J. Alan, Dashefsky, Arnold, and Tabory, Ephraim. *Jewish Choices: American Jewish Denominationalism.* Albany: State University of New York Press, 1998.

Lenn, Theodore, and others. *Rabbi and Synagogue in Reform Judaism.* New York: Central Conference of American Rabbis, 1972.

Lerner, Michael. *Jewish Renewal: A Path to Healing and Transformation.* New York: Putnam, 1994.

Liebman, Charles. *The Ambivalent American Jew.* Philadelphia: Jewish Publication Society, 1973.

Liebman, Charles. *Deceptive Images: Toward a Redefinition of American Judaism.* New Brunswick, N.J.: Transaction, 1988.

Linzer, Judith. *Torah and Dharma: Jewish Seekers in Eastern Religions.* Northvale, N.J.: Aronson, 1996.

Linzer, Norman, Schnall, David, and Chanes, Jerome (eds.). *A Portrait of the American Jewish Community.* Westport, Conn.: Praeger/Greenwood Press, 1998.

Martin, Bernard (ed.). *Movements and Issues in American Judaism.* Westport, Conn.: Greenwood Press, 1978.

Mayer, Egon. *Love and Tradition: Marriage Between Jews and Christians.* New York: Plenum, 1985.

Mead, Loren B. *Five Challenges for the Once and Future Church.* Bethesda, Md.: Alban Institute, 1996.

Miller, Donald. *Reinventing American Protestantism: Christianity in the New Millennium.* Berkeley: University of California Press, 1997.

Moore, Deborah Dash. *At Home in America: Second Generation Jews in New York.* New York: Columbia University Press, 1981.

Neusner, Jacob. *American Judaism.* Hoboken, N.J.: Ktav, 1972.

Neusner, Jacob. *Contemporary Judaic Fellowship in Theory and Practice.* Hoboken, N.J.: Ktav, 1972.

Neusner, Jacob. *Conserving Conservative Judaism: Reconstructionist Judaism.* New York: Garland, 1993.

Neusner, Jacob. *The Rabbinate in America: Reshaping an Ancient Calling.* New York: Garland, 1993.

Ochs, Carol, Olitsky, Kerry M., and Saltzman, Joshua (eds.). *Paths of Faithfulness: Personal Essays on Jewish Spirituality.* Hoboken, N.J.: Ktav, 1997.

Olsen, Charles E. *Transforming Church Boards into Communities of Spiritual Leaders.* Bethesda, Md.: Alban Institute, 1995.

Peck, M. Scott. *The Different Drum: Community-Making and Peace.* New York: Simon & Schuster, 1987.

Petsonk, Judy. *Taking Judaism Personally: Creating a Meaningful Spiritual Life.* New York: Free Press, 1996.

Pirsig, Robert H. *Zen and the Art of Motorcycle Maintenance: An Inquiry into Values.* New York: Morrow, 1974.

Podhoretz, Norman. *Making It.* New York: Random House, 1967.

Pogrebin, Letty Cottin. *Deborah, Golda, and Me: Being Female and Jewish in America.* New York: Anchor Books, 1991.

Polner, Murray. *The American Experience.* Austin, Tex.: Holt, Rinehart and Winston, 1977.

Prell, Riv-Ellen. *Prayer and Community: The Havurah in American Judaism.* Detroit, Mich.: Wayne State University Press, 1989.

Raab, Earl, and Lipset, Seymour Martin. *Jews and the New American Scene.* Cambridge, Mass.: Harvard University Press, 1995.

Raphael, Marc Lee. *Profiles in American Judaism: The Reform, Conservative, Orthodox, and Reconstructionist Traditions in Historical Perspective.* San Francisco: HarperSanFrancisco, 1984.

Reisman, Bernard. *The Havurah: A Contemporary Jewish Experience.* New York: Union of American Hebrew Congregations, 1977

Romanoff, Lena. *Your People, My People: Finding Acceptance and Fulfillment as a Jew by Choice.* Philadelphia: Jewish Publication Society, 1990.

Roof, Wade Clark. *A Generation of Seekers: The Spiritual Journeys of the Baby Boom Generation.* San Francisco: HarperSanFrancisco, 1993.

Roof, Wade Clark, and McKinney, William. *American Mainline Religion: Its Changing Shape and Future.* New Brunswick, N.J.: Rutgers University Press, 1987.

Rosenthal, Gilbert. *Four Paths to One God.* New York: Bloch, 1973.

Rubenstein, Richard. *Power Struggle.* New York: Scribner, 1974.

Sarason, Seymour. *The Creation of Settings and the Future Societies.* San Francisco: Jossey-Bass, 1972.

Schachter-Shalomi, Zalman. *Paradigm Shift.* Northvale, N.J.: Aronson, 1993.

Schiffman, Lisa. *Generation J.* San Francisco: HarperSanFrancisco, 1999.

Schulweis, Harold. "Restructuring the Synagogue." *Conservative Judaism,* 1973, 27(4), 13–23.

Schulweis, Harold. *For Those Who Can't Believe: Overcoming the Obstacles to Faith*. New York: HarperCollins, 1994.

Schwartz, Tony. *What Really Matters: Searching for Wisdom in America*. New York: Bantam Books, 1995.

Schwarz, Sidney. "The Synagogue as Community." *Shefa Quarterly*, 1980, 2(3), 77–80.

Schwarz, Sidney. "Beyond Responsive Readings." *Reconstructionist*, May 1982.

Schwarz, Sidney. "Law and Legitimacy: An Intellectual History of Conservative Judaism, 1902–1973." Unpublished doctoral dissertation, Temple University, 1982.

Schwarz, Sidney. "A Synagogue with Principles." *Reconstructionist*, June 1985, 50(7), 21–25.

Schwarz, Sidney. "Operating Principles for Reconstructionist Synagogues." *Reconstructionist*, 1988, 53(4), 28–31.

Schwarz, Sidney. "Some Call It God." *Reconstructionist*, 1994, 59(1), 5–11.

Silberman, Charles. *A Certain People: American Jews and Their Lives Today*. New York: Summit Books, 1985.

Simons, Howard. *Jewish Times: Voices of the American Jewish Experience*. Boston: Houghton Mifflin, 1988.

Sklare, Marshall. *America's Jews*. New York: Random House, 1971.

Sklare, Marshall. *Conservative Judaism: An American Religious Movement*. New York: Schocken Books, 1972.

Sklare, Marshall. *Observing America's Jews*. Hanover, N.H.: University Press of New England, 1993.

Sklare, Marshall, and Greenblum, Joseph. *Jewish Identity on the Suburban Frontier*. Chicago: University of Chicago Press, 1967.

Stark, Rodney, and Glock, Charles Y. *American Piety: The Nature of Religious Commitment*. Berkeley: University of California Press, 1968.

Stevens, Elliot (ed.). *Rabbinic Authority*. New York: Central Conference of American Rabbis, 1982.

Strassfeld, Michael, Strassfeld, Sharon, and Siegel, Richard. *The Jewish Catalog: A Do-It-Yourself Kit*. Philadelphia: Jewish Publication Society of America, 1973.

Tobin, Gary. *Opening the Gates: How Proactive Conversion Can Revitalize the Jewish Community*. San Francisco: Jossey-Bass, 1999.

Tobin, Gary, and Berger, Gabriel. *Synagogue Affiliation: Implications for the 1990s*. Waltham, Mass.: Cohen Center for Modern Jewish Studies, 1993.

Weiss, Avi. *Women at Prayer*. Hoboken, N.J.: Ktav, 1990.

Wertheimer, Jack (ed.). *The American Synagogue: A Sanctuary Transformed*. Hanover, N.H.: University Press of New England, 1987.

Wertheimer, Jack. *A People Divided: Judaism in Contemporary America.* New York: Basic Books, 1993.

Whyte, William H., Jr. *The Organization Man.* New York: Simon & Schuster, 1972.

Wiesel, Elie. *The Jews of Silence.* New York: NAL/Dutton, 1972.

Wilkes, Paul. *And They Shall Be My People: An American Rabbi and His Congregation.* New York: Atlantic Monthly Press, 1994.

Woocher, Jonathan. *Sacred Survival: The Civil Religion of American Jews.* Bloomington: Indiana University Press, 1986.

Woods, C. Jeff. *Congregational Megatrends.* Bethesda, Md.: Alban Institute, 1996.

Wuthnow, Robert. *Experimentation in American Religion.* Berkeley: University of California Press, 1978.

Wuthnow, Robert. *The Restructuring of American Religion.* Princeton, N.J.: Princeton University Press, 1988.

Wuthnow, Robert. *Sharing the Journey: Support Groups and America's New Quest for Community.* New York: Free Press, 1994.

THE AUTHOR

SIDNEY SCHWARZ is the founder and president of the Washington Institute for Jewish Leadership and Values, an educational foundation dedicated to the renewal of American Jewish life through Judaic study, social justice, and civic activism. Holder of a Ph.D. degree in Jewish history, Schwarz has been on the faculties of the University of Maryland, Temple University, and the Reconstructionist Rabbinical College. He has served as faculty for the Wexner Summer Institute and the Whizin Family Education Institute.

Raised in a traditional Jewish home including an Orthodox *yeshiva* and growing up in the Conservative movement, Schwarz graduated from the Reconstructionist Rabbinical College in Wyncote, Pennsylvania. His first pulpit was Congregation Beth Israel in Media, Pennsylvania. He helped launch and served as the first editor of *Raayonot,* the journal of the Reconstructionist Rabbinical Association. As an adjunct professor at the Reconstructionist College, Schwarz developed a course on alternative spiritual communities, a subject that finds full expression in this book.

Schwarz moved to Washington, D.C., in 1984 to serve as the executive director of the Jewish Community Council of Greater Washington, D.C., the umbrella public policy arm of the Jewish community. In 1988, he left the council and founded the Washington Institute for Jewish Leadership and Values. At that time, he also helped found Adat Shalom Reconstructionist Congregation in Bethesda, Maryland. He served as rabbi of Adat Shalom for eight years and now, as its emeritus rabbi, continues to teach and lead services upon occasion.

Schwarz is the coauthor of *Jewish Civics: A* Tikkun Olam/*World Repair Manual* (1994) and *Jews, Judaism, and Civic Responsibility* (1998). He has contributed more than seventy articles to journals such as *Judaism, Sh'ma, Moment,* and the *Reconstructionist,* and is a frequent lecturer on Judaism, the American Jewish community, and contemporary Jewish affairs.

Under the aegis of the Washington Institute, Schwarz has created several nationally acclaimed programs. *Panim el Panim* High School in

Washington is a four-day leadership seminar, run regularly throughout the school year, combining study of Judaism, public policy issues, and political activism. It serves more than one hundred communities around the country. The Jewish Civics Initiative is a program that promotes Judaically inspired community service and social change projects for high school students through synagogues and day schools. The *E Pluribus Unum* Project is an interfaith program on religion, social justice, and the common good supported by grants from the Lilly Endowment, the Righteous Persons Foundation, and the Ford Foundation. Institute programs have reached over ten thousand people in the twelve years since its founding.

Schwarz is an avid tennis and basketball player. He lives with his wife, Sandy Perlstein, and their children, Danny, Joel, and Jennifer, in Rockville, Maryland. He can be contacted at SidSchwarz@aol.com.

INDEX

Temple Israel
Minneapolis, Minnesota

A SPEEDY RECOVERY TO
SOLLY TARSHISH
FROM
GEORGIA & IVAN KALMAN